OPTIMIZING LEARNING

The Integrative Education Model in the Classroom

Barbara Clark
California State University

Merrill Publishing Company
A Bell & Howell Company
Columbus   Toronto   London   Sydney

Cover photo © Royce Bair
Photo on page 45 by Charles J. Quinlan

Published by Merrill Publishing Company
A Bell & Howell Company
Columbus, Ohio 43216

This book was set in Garamond

Administrative Editor: Vicki Knight
Production Coordinator: Rebecca Bobb
Cover Designer: Cathy Watterson
Text Designer: Susan King

The quotes on pages 219 and 220 are reprinted from *The Prophet,* by Kahlil Gibran by permission of Alfred A. Knopf, Inc. Copyright 1923 by Kahlil Gibran and renewed 1951 by Administrators C.T.A. of Kahlil Gibran Estate, and Mary G. Gibran.

Library of Congress Catalog Card Number: 85–52366
International Standard Book Number: 0–675–20482–8
Printed in the United States of America
3 4 5 6 7 8 9—91 90 89

To all the teachers from whom I have learned and from whom I am still learning, most especially those with whom I have shared the New Age School

FOREWORD

Optimizing Learning: The Integrative Education Model in the Classroom is not just an education model, but *the* model for educational reform.

Dr. Barbara Clark has picked up the fife, drum, and American flag to lead us to the new Revolution, and we must all follow. We must oppose the tyranny of measuring learning only by graduation requirements and test scores. We must cry out against the unrecognized child abuse that occurs in homes and in public schools when children are not accepted as fellow human beings.

Rarely indeed can an author present technical, scientific information in a way that is as straightforward as a recipe in a cookbook. Dr. Clark has done just that. Her skill in providing the necessary theoretical base for practical application is unsurpassed.

If Professor Clark's book does not become the most discussed item in education circles since *The Nation at Risk Report,* we will have to assume that true reform in American schools is no longer a high priority.

—George Sheperd
University of Oregon

PREFACE

As you read this book, bring to it your thoughts, your feelings, your senses, and your best intuition, for that is the intention with which it was written. You are invited to take from these pages whatever your professional judgment tells you would work best for you and your children, and to change it in any way you feel is needed.

Allow yourself to entertain and to view as possibilities the ideas that are new to you. Allow those you already know to validate you and strengthen your commitment. And share what is exciting to you, for potential is always in need of support.

You and your students are the only ones who can truly develop your experience with Integrative Education.

ACKNOWLEDGMENTS

Ideas are like shooting stars: You never know for sure from whom they came, who has seen them already, or who has contributed to their existence. The Integrative Education Model is such an idea. I would like to acknowledge all of the people who have contributed to it, but I truly don't know all of you. Some I do know and to whom I want to express my gratitude most are Christine Cenci, Tobias Manzanares, Saundra Sparling, Peggy Shackelton, and Beverly Galyean, all of whom have been and continue to be my strongest guides. Others have been important too, including the CEEGHAL group, especially Alice, Cindy, Robin, Kaz, Barbara, Lorrie, Michael, and Steve; the teachers who have studied at the New Age School and have left so much of themselves with us; the NAS students who showed all of us what unlimited minds could do and the difference trust and choice and love could make in learning; and people all over this country, indeed the world, like George Betts, Patricia and Martin Beyer, Kay Bruch, Marian Diamond, Gillian Erickson, Sara Lampe, Bob Ristow, George and Bernadette Robb, Zoa Rockenstein, Susan Ryan, Jim Webb, and Ruben Zacarias. They and so many others believe in these ideas and make them a part of their lives, and have a special place in mine. My thanks also go to my colleagues who reviewed the manuscript and shared their suggestions: George Sheperd, University of Oregon; Thomassine E. Sellers, San Francisco State University; Emily Stewart, University of Arkansas at Little Rock; and Richard B. Voorneveld, College of Charleston.

CONTENTS

PART II
USING INTEGRATIVE EDUCATION

PART III
DEVELOPING CURRICULUM

OPTIMIZING LEARNING

PART I
Understanding Integrative Education

Changing to Optimal Learning

At this moment in the history of education there is a unique opportunity for all who wish to develop optimal learning in the classroom. Ideas and information from many disciplines are leading to a better understanding of how humans learn and how educators can support and encourage the learning process, placing the development of high levels of intelligence within our grasp. We now may be looking at the beginning of true education, as in the root of the word, *educare:* to bring forth. The world is in need of truly educated human beings who know and share their uniqueness, and who can more fully use their complex brain/mind.

Fields such as psychology, child development (especially fetal research and early learning inquiry), sociology, linguistics, neurobiology, and physics are reporting valuable data and yielding information that will allow better organization and use of the classroom and other areas of the environment, the establishment of more efficient learning processes, and the empowerment of each student. By attending to how the brain best functions and to the amazing possibilities of what might enhance that functioning, every student can become a more successful, effective learner.

One of the most obvious conclusions from the data being collected is the need for an integrative use of brain functions. It is clear that each function is intricately *inter*dependent on each other function; any methodology that focuses only a part of the brain process on the learning task is inefficient at best and, at worst, wasteful of human talent and ability. The vast resources of the brain/mind complex are best developed when opportunities are made available for that interdependence. The Integrative Education Model, which is the subject of this book, and its organizations and strategies create such opportunities.

Our current education system is built on solutions to problems that existed in the early 1900s. Its goal was to educate the masses since a strong democracy could exist only if the electorate was an educated one. The very core of our chosen cultural system, even our approach to civilization, rested on how well we could educate our citizens. In the early 1900s Horace Mann, a New Englander, reacted to the problem of mass education by devising the grade level curriculum, an orderly and progressive approach he believed would assure students basic information and skills. All children age six would cover the first grade curriculum, all seven-year-olds the second grade curriculum, eight-year-olds the third grade and so on through a twelve year progressive sequence. Mann's solution to one simple problem, however, has been allowed to become educational dogma, and for nearly a century educators have attempted to adjust children to this inadequate system.

Children of like ages are always different both in their abilities and their background experiences; further, their unique experiences—not age—are what develop much of their learning abilities. Experience in combination with genetic programs dictating process and use of that experience give all individuals unique and personal learning needs. No grade-level curriculum designed for all seven-year-olds can hope to meet these individual needs or expect to create effective learning; yet, Mann's system can be found in place in every district throughout the country, and is still expected to produce results. There are many far more effective organizational patterns available now that will not result in the mediocre classroom achievements too often seen today, but in continuous progress, challenge, and optimal learning. In this book such patterns of organization will be explored.

It is important to carefully examine our own educational procedures and expectations. We tend to teach and organize as we were taught and have experienced organization, but because change is now essential, our old beliefs and attitudes must be altered, even discarded. Change is never easy, but the problem can be better understood by examining a single long-held belief and how it has limited our ability to best educate the student.

When the process of how learning occurred was first investigated psychologists began to ask meaningful and important questions. Certainly no professional, regardless of how important the question, would risk a human life to gain the answer, so psychologists turned to lower life forms to obtain information on learning. The result was a vast and impressive body of data that provided the basis for learning theory which in turn became the rationale for educational methodology and classroom organization. Belief systems grew from these philosophies of education, and attitudes became established dogma. Much of what now occurs in classrooms throughout the country can be traced directly to these experiments and the resulting theories.

One such belief system involves the development and accepted limitations of intelligence. For years it was believed that each person was born with a finite amount of intelligence built into the genetic program. This limitation could not be changed; restricted testing procedures prevented an accurate assessment of the exact dimension of a person's intelligence. One was born gifted, average, or retarded, thus removing intelligence from the sphere of educability.

Intelligence, it was believed, continued its gradual, predictable growth only until about age eighteen, when cells of the brain ceased their growth and began a pattern of maintenance that was to last until age 45. Then brain cells began an inevitable deterioration that eventually resulted in senility. Major tests of intelligence were developed and standardized from that belief system and still retain this bias today.

Learning can be fascinating.

Research now indicates that little of this progression pattern, which was assumed to show the growth of intelligence, is correct. With improved instrumentation and research methods, neurobiologists now look directly at the learning process as it occurs in humans. Those old theories developed from the observation of how rats learn now seem partial, often inaccurate and, when valid, only generalizable at the cellular level. Learning is, we have found, far more complex, far more exciting, and far less limited.

Intelligence is neither established immutably at birth, nor is it the total responsibility of the genetic endowment. Long before birth (some researchers believe during the months prior to conception), the mother's health and well-being can have much to do with the future intellect of the unborn child. In addition, the growing fetus is highly influenced by the environment surrounding the mother's pregnancy. Data indicate influencing factors ranging from the nutritional to the psychological (Verny, 1981). The birth process itself will affect the intellectual processes that later are available to the child.

From the moment of birth each human infant has over 100 billion neural cells in the brain ready for use, and is capable of creating trillions of connections for learning, memory storage and retrieval, problem solving, rational and abstract thinking, sophisticated motoric involvement, emotional expression, and intuitive and creative production: in short, the use of intelligence. It is believed that most humans use only a small percentage of this vast potential, and of this potential far more is lost than is actualized in a lifetime. Since it is the degree of use that determines our level of intelligence, the loss becomes an important concern for educators, who can affect that loss.

Infants use experience to set up more pathways, more connectors within the brain; the more stimulating the experiences and the more responsive the environment, the more the brain becomes capable of handling increasing amounts of complex learning. While genetic patterns do carry limits to some types of responses and dictate much of the uniqueness of the individual, the environment does, in fact, actualize or inhibit the use of these patterns and unique abilities. As some brain researchers report, either you must use what you have or you lose it (Diamond, 1980). There is no maintenance, no apparent plateauing, only progression or regression in the growth of intelligence.

Many believe the period from birth to age three is the most crucial to the child's intellectual development (Bloom, 1964; White, 1975). Others, while acknowledging this period as essential, believe that at approximately two year intervals through at least age eighteen the brain again shows growth spurts that can be utilized to enhance the learning process (Epstein, 1978). However future growth of the individual is viewed, the early period must be seen as critical for the development of intelligence.

Our intellectual progression or regression may be understood as the brain interacting with the experiences of the environment to either strengthen or deny the genetic endowment. The possibility of growth even in old age still exists, as researchers have indicated evidence of continued brain development well into the eightieth year of life (Buell & Coleman, 1981). The belief system held by so many that intelligence is limited at birth must be reconsidered. Intelligence may well rest on the effectiveness of opportunities and experiences provided by the child's home and school. The possibilities for enhancing an already vast potential are exciting.

From these two examples—grade level curriculum and the notion of fixed intelligence—direct implications for change in the educational approach can be found. New organizations for curriculum presentation must be devised if a more personalized approach is to be given each learner, and learning opportunities must be restructured for the limitless possibilities of the brain/mind system. The need for many other changes will be shown as we explore Integrative Education, the brain-based approach.

Chapter 2 presents the synthesis of ideas and data from physicists, psychologists, neurobiologists and educators to form the basis for the Integrative Education Model. In Chapter 3 all four major functions of the brain—thinking, feeling, physical sensing, and intuition—are discussed as part of the definition of the Model. These functions form the structure for a total brain approach to learning and for the development of curriculum. The organization, conditions, attitudes and strategies necessary to implement the Model in the classroom can be developed through the seven key components also outlined in this chapter.

Section two discusses the use of the seven keys as guides to help Integrative Education become a classroom reality. Each key is important and can be tried alone or in concert with any of the others. The eventual goal, regardless of the order in which they are tried, is to have all seven key components functioning. The timing and order of introduction must be left to the judgement of the teacher.

Key I, The Responsive Learning Environment, is explored in Chapter 4. This chapter seeks to help with the creation of an environment, a climate for integrative learning. The elements of a responsive learning environment and examples of existing environments presented in this book will help teachers bring the necessary supportive atmosphere their classrooms need.

Learning techniques derived from and responsive to current brain/mind theory begin in Chapter 5 with Key II, Relaxation and Tension Reduction. Using relaxation and tension reduction techniques is an important step toward creating the optimal learning environment and allows the learner to utilize the support of the physical functions of the brain. Chapter 5 also introduces Key III, Movement and Physical Encoding, which gives examples of strategies that use the physical body to enhance learning.

Key IV, Empowering Language and Behavior, helps incorporate the emotional functioning of the brain, as we will see in Chapter 6. This key presents language and behavior that can empower a student to be a more successful and responsible learner. Key V, Choice and Perceived Control, further develops the teacher's skill to aid students in becoming responsible for their own learning.

Chapter 7 offers a discussion of the importance of Key VI, Complex and Challenging Activities, to cognitive function. This key provides opportunities for total cognition, including linear and analytic as well as spatial, holistic processes, thus increasing the effectiveness and motivation of the learner.

Intuition and Integration, Key VII and the last of the Model's components, is presented in Chapter 8. Much remains to be known about the intuitive process, the most powerful and uniquely human brain function, but the work of others in this area can provide important clues.

Chapter 9 includes examples of curriculum strategies and integrative lessons that have been field-tested with children from a wide range of grade and ability levels. The examples used can become a good starting place for the classroom teacher, giving a structure with which to develop and adapt the suggested strategies to the unique needs and developmental levels of any particular group.

Chapter 10 explores ideas for future use and possible outcomes of the Model. The unlimited nature of what is being learned about the human brain and its learning potential make such future visions rich indeed.

Once the need for the Model is understood, and the willingness to use it is shown, just how will the average classroom change? Each classroom will differ with each teacher's skill and interpretation of the material and each student's response. There are, however, some basic starting points. It is the intent of this book to give these basic guidelines, and to give examples of organizations and strategies that have succeeded. Because the teachers who devised these strategies had not themselves experienced integrative learning, the suggestions presented here have been their inventions, the results of several years of research and development in their own classrooms. Readers are invited to change and modify these ideas as they see fit. This is not a book about *the* way to optimize education. It is rather *one* way of interpreting new data, and of bringing that data into the classroom to better meet the needs of learners. As the data continue to expand so must our beliefs and ideas; as new information points to inadequacies in our approaches, new approaches must be devised. Only if educators are willing to create, explore, grow, and learn will they succeed in bringing the opportunity for excellence into the classroom and into the lives of all children.

2

Implications from Brain/Mind Research for Optimizing Learning

The Integrative Education Model is based upon recent findings which show that intelligence can no longer be defined as only a rational, analytic process. For over thirty years intelligence has been known to be interactive (Hunt, 1961); now it has been found to be integrative. Intelligence requires not just the use of the rational, analytic thinking function, but also the spatial, holistical processes of the brain, and the integration of the emotional, physical sensing, and intuitive thinking functions as well. While these functions can be regarded separately, it is their integration that creates high levels of intelligence and the optimal development of human potential.

Current thought regarding physical reality and brain organization validate this emphasis on function integration. Many important thinkers are engaged in a reconceptualization of reality structures, leading us from notions of fragmentation, separable and discreet entities, hierarchies, and dichotomies toward the concepts of connectedness, oneness, and indivisible wholeness. Such views are being expressed by physicists, neurobiologists, physiologists, as well as by philosophers, systems theorists, psychologists, and educators. By examining a few of these ideas we can see the importance of understanding the development of intelligence and the concepts of learning and teaching.

ENERGY AND WHOLENESS FROM THE PHYSICIST

Early in the 1900s Albert Einstein attempted to communicate two very amazing ideas. In his first paper, published in 1905, he outlined his special theory of relativity, proposing that time and space were not two separate and absolute realities, but were joined in a single entity, time-space, which was the creation of the human mind. In his second paper, published the same year, he discussed electromagnetic radiation and subatomic particles called *quanta,* and in the discussion suggested that we are not composed of nor surrounded by solid matter, but rather are all basically a form of energy. The universe was no longer a fixed entity to understand, but had become a construct of the human mind and changed according to the nature and situation of the human observer. Mind and matter had become one (Einstein & Infeld, 1961).

David Bohm (1980), an English physicist and mathematician and a protégé of Einstein, and Karl Pribram (1977), a neurophysiologist and respected researcher from Stanford University, ask that reality cease to be thought of as made up of independent fragments, but be viewed as holographic. A major attribute of a hologram is its ability to capture in each segment of the system the complete information of the entire system. For example, each cell of the human body has within its chromosome structure all of the genetic information for the entire body. In a photographic hologram each area of the holographic negative, if given a coherent light source, can reproduce the entire image. In the case of the cell, a chemical referent is needed and for the image a coherent light source is necessary. The notion of a holographic universe expresses a belief in oneness and in total integration.

> The notion that all these fragments are separately existent is evidently an illusion, and this illusion cannot do other than lead to endless conflict and confusion. Indeed, the attempt to live according to the notion that the fragments

are really separate is, in essence, what has led to the growing series of extremely urgent crises that is confronting us today. (Bohm, 1980, pp. 1–2)

Among the crises Bohm mentions are the widespread and pervasive distinctions made
between races, national or family origins, professions, socio-economic statuses, etc.
His ideas require that the self and the universe be seen as deeply and totally connected.

One of the complex systems affected by this theory is the human brain. Bohm and
Pribram conclude that the brain itself operates as a hologram and that it interprets in
a holographic manner the larger hologram of the universe. The brain is far more
complex, they believe, than is now imagined, and that it operates in unknown dimensions.

The holographic theory assumes that harmonious, coherent states of consciousness are more the intended and optimal functions of the brain. Ferguson (1980)
suggests that such harmony is disrupted by anger, anxiety, and fear and eased by love
and empathy, a suggestion validated later in this chapter by information from the field
of neurobiology. Such a notion has important implications for teaching and learning.
Better education will require attention to what produces harmony, and to what mini-
mizes disruption.

Itzak Bentov (1977) illustrated how the action of microreality affects our view of
the world. He saw the action of atoms as being empty space filled with oscillating
fields of energy. The smallest disturbance in one field carries into other fields so that
while we are separate entities, we are also interconnected. This interrelationship
allows positive effects to quickly influence an entire group or system. A strong harmo-
nizing force applied to this web of interconnecting fields will influence all parts of the
group or system. One positive action can give orderliness to the entire system. As
Bentov points out, "Whether that energy is electric, magnetic, gravitational, or acous-
tic, it will always interact and affect us somehow, whether it is applied from a distance
or directly to our skin" (p. 48). He further comments, "Our physical bodies and all
matter is {*sic*} made up of interacting electromagnetic fields vibrating at tremendous
frequencies" (p. 57).

While it may seem enough to consider all matter as being composed of energy,
Bentov asks us to go a step further when he suggests that "A thought is energy that
causes the neurons in the brain to fire in a certain pattern" (p. 122). The connections
and firing of neurons have long been considered the biological basis for thought;
however, Bentov believes that our brain is not just the source of thought but rather a
thought amplifier. Where then is the source of thought? Such an idea allows the most
intriguing possibilities.

Gary Zukav (1979), in a book that allows laypersons to become familiar with the
exciting ideas now extant in physics, asks us to examine another assumption about
reality. In the past we have assumed that reality was a fixed entity out there some-
where. Einstein suggested it is what each one of us believes it to be and, therefore,
changes as we change. It is, in a very real sense, created by us. Zukav comments,
"Quantum mechanics is based upon the idea of minimal knowledge of future phenomena (we are limited to knowing probabilities) but it leads to the possibility that
our reality is what we choose to make it" (p. 54).

He, too, sees the interconnectedness of all things. Throughout his book Zukav expresses the concept of unity:

> . . . the philosophical implication of quantum mechanics is that all of the things in our universe (including us) that appear to exist independently are actually parts of one all-encompassing organic pattern, and that no parts of that pattern are ever really separate from it or from each other (p. 73).
>
> . . . what we experience is not external reality, but our *interaction* with it (p. 115).
>
> "This" and "that" no longer are separate entities. They are different *forms* of the same thing (p. 297).

One of the ideas to be challenged by these notions of interconnectedness is the belief in objectivity. As Zukav sees it, "according to quantum mechanics there is no such thing as objectivity. We cannot eliminate ourselves from the picture. We are a part of nature, and when we study nature there is no way around the fact that nature is studying itself" (p. 56). Though we have an effect on measuring or evaluating processes, we do not have to disregard them. Rather, we must carefully view the data, and subsequent decisions made, within the limitations of those processes.

Through the quantum view reality has lost its "either-or" perspective. While the question was raised as to whether energy is expressed in waves or particles, investigators proved it to be both. At the most basic level, reality is "and-also"; dualities, it seems, are also interconnected.

Fritjof Capra (1982), a physicist at the Lawrence Berkeley Radiation Laboratory, expands on these ideas. In his exploration of the atomic and subatomic world, he finds that the universe is interdependent and involved in cyclical change. Seemingly separate objects thought to exist in the world are in reality patterns in an inseparable cosmic process, patterns which are intrinsically dynamic, continually changing into one another, holistic, and ecological. His views focus again on the human being as part of the universal hologram. Humans, by interpreting what they experience, create their reality. The organization of the universe is holistic, inclusive of the human as a living paradox: totally unique and individual, we are at the same time an intricate, inseparable part of the total energy that is the universe.

> The crucial feature of quantum theory is that the observer is not only necessary to observe the properties of an atomic phenomenon, but is necessary even to bring about these properties. My conscious decision about how to observe, say, an electron will determine the electron's properties to some extent. . . . We can never speak about nature without, at the same time, speaking about ourselves. (pp. 86–87)
>
> The conception of the universe as an interconnected web of relations is one of two major themes that recur throughout modern physics. The other theme is the realization that the cosmic web is intrinsically dynamic. (p. 87)

Capra sees this view of reality as affecting all forms of social organizations and institutions, and introduces Systems Theory as a field of study that "looks at the world in terms of the interrelatedness and independence of all phenomena, and in this framework an integrated whole whose properties cannot be reduced to those of its parts. . ." (p. 43). Here again a dynamic balance is required, an integration of connectedness and self-assertion. Intelligence as interactive, dynamic, and integrative follows naturally from this view of reality.

Ferguson (1980) reminds us that

> All wholes transcend their parts by virtue of internal coherence, cooperation, openness to input. The higher on the evolutionary scale, the more freedom to reorganize. An ant lives out a destiny; a human being shapes one. . . . If we try to live as closed systems, we are doomed to regress. If we enlarge our awareness, admit new information, and take advantage of the brain's brilliant capacity to integrate and reconcile, we can leap forward. (pp. 169–170)

Understanding such theories will lead educators to teaching methods that reduce anxiety and fragmentation, and to activities that create harmony, coherence, and connectedness.

BRAIN/MIND DATA FROM THE PSYCHOLOGIST

As we change our understanding of the physical world we must also rethink our beliefs about learning. The principles of behavioral psychology as derived from laboratory research have been most responsible for theories and practices regarding learning. Hunt (1982) points out that these theories did not work as well in the classroom as in the laboratory. "The principles of behaviorism are not wrong," he states, "but describe elementary processes that are only a small part of the psychology of higher vertebrates and only a minuscule part of the psychology of the human being" (p. 73).

Psychology has always attempted to parallel the scientific method as closely as possible; as other areas of science change basic paradigms, the field of psychology must reconsider its paradigms as well. When physics assumed the universe was a closed system wherein matter was constant and reducible to one basic element, psychologists decided that intelligent action could be explained as pieces of matter in motion, as behavior with no need for a mind, human intent, or internal motivation. Scientific materialism entered psychology as a movement called Behaviorism. Objective science dictated that any study of the human would be limited to overt observable behavior and denied the importance of mental events. The concept of consciousness was as unneeded in behavioral psychology as it was in chemistry and physics. But then physicists claimed that "it was not possible to formulate the laws of quantum theory in a fully consistent way without reference to consciousness" (Wigner, 1970). How then did this view affect the behaviorist?

Newtonian physics conceptualized the universe as being matter composed of elementary parts. These parts, all identical in nature, could be assembled into a variety of forms. Consequently complex phenomena could always be understood by reducing them to their basic parts and by looking for the mechanism through which they interacted.

Based on the Newtonian ideas of reality the behaviorist view held that humans were complex machines that reacted to external stimuli with predictable responses. Thinking, learning, and emotions were not seen as subjective experiences but as behaviors in response to external stimuli. As control of behavior and dominance of nature became valued, the notion of behavioral engineering of human beings became the goal.

Behavioral psychologists have begun to incorporate new data from other disciplines to change the rigidity of their view. Though the behavioral model still remains based on concepts limited to mechanistic paradigms, the brain *and* the mind, as well as behavior *and* consciousness, must now be included in our definition of ourselves.

Psychologists are now investigating recent brain research from several points of interest. There are psychophysiologists and neuropsychologists who study attention, emotional and motivational controls, neural structures, delineations of brain systems, and the neurochemical mechanisms of the brain; cognitive psychologists who research cognitive functions, visual perception, memory, individual differences, and hemispheric processes; psycholinguists who delve into language and its relationship to the structure of the brain; developmental psychologists who relate child development, individual differences, and environmental intervention to the brain's mediating structures; and educational psychologists who place new emphasis on the generative and cognitive brain processes that can lead to new models of teaching and learning. This review will sample only a few of the findings to have created a significant change in established belief systems.

It was mentioned in Chapter 1 that age has limited usefulness in defining the learning experience. Age is also not an adequate index of neurological and physical maturation, as both are substantially influenced by the child's environment and genetic program. However, neurological maturation, which is highly individual, affects the impact the environment has on the child (Jeffrey, 1980). The interaction between child and environment can now be seen as far more complex and meaningful than was before suspected.

A large number of studies have found that people organize, encode, and store information in at least two different ways, a fact that shows learning is more than a rational, analytic process; it also involves spatial, gestalt processing (Bogen, 1977; Gazzaniga & LeDoux, 1978; Luria, 1973; Pribram, 1978). Utilization of both these processes seems far more important to effective learning than does any attempt to favor one or the other. Wittrock (1980) contends that these kinds of studies make it clear that teachers "should attend to each learner's information processing systems and to the process-oriented individual differences among learners at least as much as we attend to the characteristics of the external stimuli presented to learners during instruction" (p. 394). Many educational psychologists have used the new knowledge of brain function to understand learning and performance problems, allowing the development of predictive tests that permit early intervention (Heilman, 1978).

Centered more on the brain as the mediating system, the theory proposed by William Gray (Ferguson, 1982a), a Massachusetts psychiatrist, has important implications for human learning. "Feelings," he states, "may be the organizers of the mind and personality. Finely tuned emotions may form the basis of all we know" (p. 1). According to this new theory, feelings form the underlying structure of thought, with emotion serving as the key to memory, recognition, and the generation of new ideas. Humans, Gray believes, are more intelligent than other species because they have a richer supply of emotional nuances available to them. This results from the larger human forebrain and the more extensive connections between the frontal lobe and the limbic system. Gray states,

> I had important confirmation in Einstein's repeated statement that ideas come
> to him first in the form of vague and diffuse bodily sensations that gradually
> refined themselves into exact and reproducible feeling-tones. Only when this
> process was completed could Einstein mathematically define the new concept.
> (p. 4)

Paul LaViolette (Ferguson, 1982a), a systems theorist, combined many of the
current theories to explain how the brain physically processes new ideas. "Mental
events—sensation, perceptions, feelings, emotions—are encoded and processed by
the brain as if they were AM/FM neuroelectric waveforms" (p. 1). The encoded waveforms are then amplified into thoughts moving between the limbic and cortical systems. A higher degree of intelligence then means a higher degree of emotional involvement.

According to both Gray and LaViolette, the brain uses feelings to structure information. Even though abstract information may be difficult to recall because it is cut off
from feelings, often the rational cognitive learning mode is most highly valued. Ironi-
cally the efficiency of learning is prevented by ignoring feelings. Learning is much
easier and more efficient, Gray contends, if emotion and cognition are integrated.

Jerre Levy (1980), a University of Chicago psychologist, finds that the brain operates at its best only when the emotional as well as cognitive systems are challenged,
thus allowing physical and intuitive involvement. Motivation is a result of highly integrated brain action.

Whether used for the purposes of remediation or for optimization of learning,
new understanding of the human brain has moved the field of psychology far from the
old, narrow limits. The old paradigms will shift and, like the physicist, the future
psychologist will behold an unrestricted view of the universe and of the humans
within it.

BRAIN RESEARCH FROM THE NEUROBIOLOGIST

The physical structure, organization, and function of the brain also reveals the need
for the integration of brain functions.

Early in the 1960s Rosensweig (1966) and Krech (1969, 1970), a brain research
team from the University of California at Berkeley, found that environment had a
significant effect on the physiology of the brain. Since then the Berkeley team and
other researchers throughout the world have investigated the extent of that impact.
Some physiological changes resulting from environmental stimulation include an increase in dendritic growth, indicating higher levels of intelligence and more complex
patterns of thought; a more powerful exchange of neural impulses resulting in accelerated thought processing; and an increase in the production of neuroglial cells which
provide nutrients and support the functioning of the brain.

The process of learning can be changed by increasing the strength and the speed
of transmission within the brain. Changes in teaching and learning procedures can
promote growth of dendritic branching and an increase in glial cells, brain activities
that indicate advanced and accelerated development. Enhancing the environment provided brings about changes in children at the cellular level, not just in their behavior.
As children become more intelligent they also become biologically different from

average learners as a result of using and developing the wondrous, complex structure with which they were born.

The human brain is organized into three systems with radically different structures and chemistry. This hierarchy of three-brains-in-one may be called the triune brain (MacLean, 1978). This organization presents, however, some important considerations: two of the three brains have no system for verbal communication; since the integration of total brain functions results in human intelligence, a test that measures primarily verbal communication as its sampling of intelligence may be seen as limited.

The three systems are

1. The reptilian brain. The simplest and oldest brain system, this provides autonomic function, the neural pathway for many higher brain centers, motor control, and communication links between the rest of the brain and the cerebellum. It houses the reticular formation that is the physical basis for consciousness, and plays a major role in the state of being awake and alert.
2. The old mammalian brain or limbic system. This houses the biochemical centers activated by the emotions of the learner and enhances or inhibits memory, affects such diverse emotions as pleasure, joy, anxiety, rage, and sentimentality, and alters the attention span.
3. The new mammalian brain. Also known as the neocortex or cerebrum, this is where sensory data are processed, decisions are made, and action is initiated. The neocortex includes the functions of language and speech and provides for reception, storage, and retrieval of information. The most recently evolved area of the neocortex, the prefrontal cortex, provides for behaviors associated with planning, insight, empathy, introspection, and other bases for intuitive thought (MacLean, 1978). The prefrontal is engaged in firming up intention, deciding on action, and regulating a human being's most complex behaviors (Restak, 1979). It is, in fact, the area that energizes and regulates all other parts; it houses purpose.

The reptilian brain comprises the brain stem; surrounding it is the larger, newer limbic system; above and around the mammalian brain is the cerebrum or neocortex, the largest brain, made up of the newest, most sophisticated structures. Under stress this largest, most complex system begins shutting down, turning over more and more functions to the limbic system brain. While rote learning can be continued, higher and more complex learning is inhibited (Hart, 1981). The Integrative Education Model was created to provide a program model and curricular approach for the development of these total brain processes.

In order to better understand learning and the development of intelligence, we also need to look at the asymmetry of the brain hemispheres, and examine the idea that each hemisphere of the brain specializes in a particular type of function. This specialized functioning points to the necessity for different types of educational experience if the potential each person possesses is to be realized. Schools have concentrated on cognitive, left brain processes while ignoring and, in some cases, actually suppressing any use of the more holistic right brain processes.

Although it seems that the entire brain is capable of performing all the activities exhibited by any of its divisions, each hemisphere does, under normal conditions, assume specific duties (Pribram, 1977). The left hemisphere is most responsible for linear, sequential, analytic, rational thinking; the right for thought of a metamorphic, spatial, holistic nature. Rather than viewing a person as right-brained or left-brained, we would be more accurate to speak of one hemisphere leading the other during certain tasks. The goal would be to have the appropriate hemisphere lead in a given situation, as the ability to use the strategies from both hemispheres is ideal.

The separate functions of the hemispheres, therefore, must not be overemphasized. The obvious need for integration is apparent even in the structure of the brain itself. According to brain research, mammalian sensory systems must be used in environments that are facilitating for normal development to occur (Blakemore, 1974). Haggard (1957) found that early focus on rational cognitive (left-brain) performance can give children more competitive, hostile attitudes toward their peers as well as disdain for adults. The human requires both hemispheres to function in close integration, allowing us to understand both the computation and the conceptualization of mathematics, the structure and melody of music, and the syntax and poetry of language. "The existence of so complex a cabling system as the corpus callosum must mean, it is important to stress again, that the interaction of the hemispheres is a vital human function" (Sagan, 1977, p. 175). There are more neural connectors between the hemispheres of the brain through the corpus callosum than between the brain and any other part of the body. The human being is biologically structured to integrate functions.

For years it was assumed that information was processed only from the external senses (sight, touch, smell, taste, hearing) to the associative areas of the brain for interpretation and action. Current data (Pribram, Spinelli, & Reitz, 1969) show that this simple one-way flow of stimulus to response is not an adequate view of the process. The mind actively shapes what is picked up by the senses almost from the beginning rather than by simply recording and processing information from the environment.

New brain research technology has allowed researchers to map the brain more accurately than ever before. Once limited to collecting data only from the behavior of persons with brain damage or pathology, neurobiologists can now measure brain activity by injecting harmless radioisotopes into the bloodstream, then recording the varying levels of radioactivity throughout the brain (Lassen, Ingvar, & Skinhoj, 1978). These data clearly show that the processes of the brain are complex, highly organized and interdependent to a degree that had not been considered. So much of the human brain, unlike brains of other animals, is uncommitted to specific sensory and motor functions and, therefore, is available for higher mental processes.

As with the physicist and the psychologist, paradigms for the neurobiologists are shifting. New and exciting possibilities for learning and teaching are suggested by the critical nature of environment, the complexity of structure and function, and evidence of integration and wholeness within the brain. The basic biological processes of the human learner are now being revealed.

THE SYNTHESIS: THE INTEGRATIVE EDUCATION MODEL

In the late 1960s my attention was drawn to the brain research of the Berkeley team and their inquiry into environmental impact on the brain. This research provided me with an explanation of how giftedness occurs as well as the appropriate use of human potential. At this point I began to research early learning, and attempted to turn laboratory brain study into educational practice. Much of the information I gathered during that period showed me the importance of early sensitive and critical periods and supported the idea of a dynamic intelligence (Dunn, 1969).

When in the early 1970s brain/mind research suggested significant differences between old learning theories and new findings, I was intrigued. As a result of techno- logical advances in laboratory equipment the human brain now could be studied without disrupting function; lower animals were no longer the only source of data.

The complexity of the human brain, that new research found, required different conditions for learning than were indicated by the older, more limited data collection techniques.

The first condition that drew my interest was the claim that the human brain functions more effectively and at a higher level when stress is reduced. Indeed, anxi- ety created biochemistry in the limbic area that, in fact, shut down higher centers of the brain (Krech, 1969; Lozanov, 1977; Martindale, 1975; Restak, 1979).

This finding led me to a new perspective of my teaching and my classroom environment. I sought to discover what created tension and anxiety in the classroom and what I could change to help my students. I found that the environment played a far more significant role in supporting the learning process than I had previously imagined. As Diamond (1976) was experimenting with color in her brain research laboratory at Berkeley, I experimented with the environment of my university class- room. As Lozanov (1977) used tension reduction techniques to optimize learning in his clinic in Bulgaria, I taught tension reduction to my graduate students. Motivation in my students improved, interaction increased, and the quality and quantity of the prod- ucts of learning grew impressively.

What most held my interest was investigating the controversy between those who held that brain functions occurred in specific areas and those who believed those functions were referred and non-specific in nature. Both sides seemed to be right, paralleling the debate regarding the nature of creativity where at least four points of view were amassing data separately. The answer to these and similar questions pro- ducing contradictory results seemed to lie in viewing the issues as connected, holistic, and more broadly unified. This had been true for Carl Jung (1933) as he sought the explanation for the differing expressions of human function. Just as Jung had theo- rized, the new brain/mind data revealed that the human function was organized into thinking, feeling, physical sensing, and intuitive processes. There was a biological basis within the brain and its organization that supported a similar pattern. Such functions, it was evident, could not reach their optimum levels separately, but only as each was integrated into the whole. Dichotomies did not exist. The human brain showed itself to be both specific and non-specific, the major part of its mass involved in association and composed of associative tissue. As the physicists were claiming, reality was not "either-or"; it was "and-also."

From this insight and with information from all these disciplines, I found that a model of education, of learning and teaching, could be constructed. I felt a need to reflect this more holistic view as thinkers from the past and current researchers again and again showed evidence of the interactive nature of reality. Integrative Education, which relies on Jung's four function theory and is based on the human brain's four function organization, had begun.

The Integrative Education Model: Using the Total Brain/Mind for Learning

The Integrative Education Model uses data from such diverse fields as physics, psychology, and the neurosciences. This interactive system involves the learner's thoughts, feelings, senses, and intuitions. As the model evolved from a theory to actual practice, key components became apparent. By recounting the evolution of the Model as it occurred in the New Age School Project, I hope to help others implement the model in their own school.

First, it became clear that there were strategies students could use to become more successful learners. These methods involved communication and increased physical sensing. Through these methods students acquired purpose and positive self-concept. Still others supported their cognition integrating several ways of knowing and allowing students to use their most effective learning modes as well as giving them opportunities to recognize and develop new ways of learning. It was found that the abilities of intuitive processing lay dormant in most children. Creating safe spaces for this uniquely human function enriched everyone.

The Integrative Education Model focuses on an interactive system that involves the learner's thoughts, feelings, senses, and intuitions (artwork by Steve Pikala).

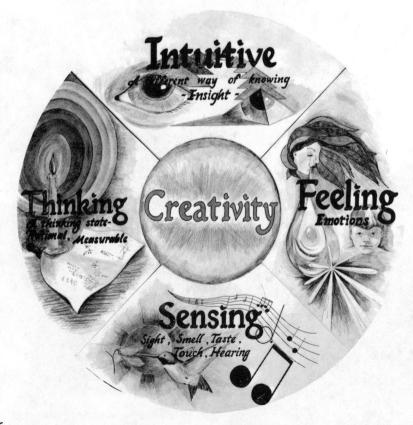

Figure 3.1. *Integrative education: a model for developing human potential.*

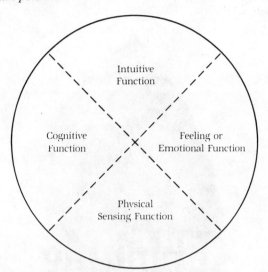

Third, *where* learning occurs was found to have enormous impact. The climate of the setting directly enhances or inhibits the quantity and quality of what the students discover.

DEFINITION

In every subject area, the Integrative Education Model combines thinking with feeling, the senses, and intuition. Through this model each function of the brain is allowed to support the others, resulting in a very coherent, powerful learning experience.

The Thinking Function (Cognitive)

This function includes the analytic, problem solving, sequential, evaluative specialization of the left cortical hemisphere of the brain as well as the more spatially oriented, gestalt specialization of the right cortical hemisphere. Higher intelligence requires accelerated synaptic activity and an increased density of the dendrites, which allow complex networks of thought. Stimulating environments promote the advanced capacity to generalize, conceptualize, and reason abstractly.

The Feeling or Emotional Function (Affective)

This is the function that is expressed in emotions and feelings and, while affecting every part of the brain/mind system, it is primarily regulated from the limbic area by biochemical mechanisms housed there. This function more than supports thinking processes; it does, in fact, provide the gateway to enhance or limit higher cognitive function. Worthwhile academic programs integrate emotional growth.

The thinking function includes analyzing, problem solving, sequencing, evaluating, and orienting spatially (artwork by Steve Pikala).

The Physical Function (Sensing)

This function includes movement, physical encoding, sight, hearing, smell, taste, and touch. We know the world through our senses, so how our bodies and minds integrate sensory cues determines how we perceive reality. Integration of the body and the mind becomes an essential part of an integrative program.

The Intuitive Function (Insightful, Creative)

According to Jung, intuition "does not denote something contrary to reason, but something outside the province of reason" (Jung, 1933, p. 454). He considered intuition vital to understanding. This function, which each person has but uses in varying

Emotions provide a gateway to enhance—or limit—higher cognitive function (artwork by Steve Pikala).

degrees, represents a different way of knowing. This ability is in use when it is felt that something is known, but it cannot be told how it was known. It is a sense of total understanding, of directly and immediately gaining a concept in its whole, living existence, and is in part the result of a high level of synthesis of all the brain functions. People often repress and devaluate the intuitive function because it does not operate in the rational manner western minds have been taught to expect. Activating intuition gives a person a sense of completeness, of true integration. This powerful tool can lead to a better understanding of concepts and people.

Capra (1975) states that rational knowing is useless if not accompanied and enhanced by intuition. He equates intuition with new, creative insights:

These insights tend to come suddenly and, characteristically, not when sitting at a desk working out the equations, but when relaxing in the bath, during a

How our bodies and minds integrate sensory cues determines how we perceive reality (artwork by Steve Pikala).

Intuition is a sense of total understanding. It involves gaining a concept in its whole, combining the known and the unknown, and it results from a high level of brain function synthesis (artwork by Steve Pikala).

walk in the woods, on the beach, etc. During these periods of relaxation after concentrated intellectual activity, the intuitive mind seems to take over and can produce the sudden clarifying insights which give so much joy and delight to scientific research. (p. 31)

Those working to include the development of intuition in the educational setting believe that the ability to concentrate, to work at complex tasks with unusual clarity, results from the intuitive function. Identified now as a function of the prefrontal cortex, intuition is a part of planning, future thinking, and insight necessary to the intelligent person.

By use of the Integrative Education Model and strategies incorporating this construct, students can expect to make impressive gains in areas of cognition, self-concept, and social-emotional development. Among the cognitive gains will be accelerated learning, higher levels of retention and recall, and higher interest in content. They can also improve self-esteem, find pleasure in learning, and improve interpersonal relations and teacher-student rapport (Bordan & Schuster, 1976; Galyean, 1977–80; Galyean, 1978–81; Galyean, 1979; Lozanov, 1977; Prichard & Taylor, 1980; Samples, 1975).

The Integrative Education Model, while employing all of the modifications traditionally used in good educational programming, does not focus solely on cognitive learning. Rather, the Model combines previously used structures with new brain/mind information, resulting in a dynamic incorporation of learning experiences.

Learners of all ability levels and interest can be served within the Integrative Education Model because of its decentralized and personalized organization. The Model has been used successfully in a variety of settings including self-contained elementary and secondary level classes, resource room settings, and in a demonstration school setting.

It is important to include in the curricula such diverse elements as guided imagery, dreams, mind/body integrative activities, and activities nurturing intuitive development. Variety in teaching techniques as well as in personal instruction is needed if the integration of brain functions is to be achieved, and Table 3.1 outlines several basic changes new brain/mind data have found necessary to begin use of the Model.

Table 3.1. Direct implications from new brain/mind data for change in the classroom

Instead of	The New Data Demand
a focus on logical, rational thought as the center of educational experiences	a focus on an integration of all human functions including the logical, rational thought; the important avenues of sensing; the emotional, feeling functions; and the power of intuitive knowing. This focus assures use of the whole brain, and optimizes the learner's ability to learn. This approach is known as the Integrative Education Model.
using external tension for motivation and control	use of relaxation and tension reduction techniques to develop higher levels of learning, as relaxation has been found to be the first step in thinking and synchronizing brain function.
using the classroom environment as the container for the learning process	use within the classroom of color, sound, light, etc., as well as the community and surrounding areas, as important learning tools.
a focus on group work	a focus on individual learning needs, styles, and processes in small group or individual instruction.

(Table 3.1., *continued*)

Instead of	The New Data Demand
a focus on set curriculum given to all	a response to the interest and ability of each learner in developing the curriculum.
knowledge of content the only necessary tool of the teacher and learner	content communicated by interaction between teacher and learner.
a focus on known facts being given by authorities	the teacher presents new ways of viewing facts, and eliciting new questions for as yet unresolved issues.
a focus on controlling the student	a focus on empowering the student to be responsible for self, e.g. use of the inner locus of control which includes preparing the student for learning including relaxation and anxiety reduction; discovering and changing negative attitudes and preconceptions regarding self and the learning experience; awareness of the suggestive impact of teacher words and attitudes; and teaching students about their learning resources and how to use them.

COMPONENTS OF THE INTEGRATIVE EDUCATION MODEL: SEVEN KEYS TO OPTIMIZING LEARNING

The Integrative Education Model can be described through its seven major components. While parts of the Model can be used effectively without all components in place, the most effective use will include all seven.

Key I   The Responsive Learning Environment

This component requires educators and parents to develop new, supportive attitudes toward learning. The roots of this organizational plan are buried deeply in the works of Plato, Socrates, Froebel, Pestalozzi, Dewey, Montessori, Piaget, and other innovative educators, and strives for a unique learning experience for each individual. Participation, necessary to learning, is encouraged to insure the assimilation of concepts. While the responsive learning environment has a different format for each group of learners, there are some basic characteristics:

1. There is an open, respectful, and cooperative relationship among teachers, students, and parents, a relationship that includes planning, implementing, and evaluating the learning experience.
2. The environment is much like a laboratory or workshop: rich in materials with simultaneous access to many learning activities. The emphasis is on experimentation and involvement.
3. The curriculum is flexible and integrative. The needs and interests of the student provide the base from which the curriculum develops.
4. There is a minimum of total group lessons, with most instruction occurring in small groups or between individuals. Groups centered around needs or interests can be formed by teachers or students.

5. The student is an active participant in the learning process. Movement, decision making, self-directed learning, invention, and inquiry are encouraged both inside and outside the classroom. Students may work alone, with a partner, or in groups. Peer teaching is important.
6. Assessment, contracting, and evaluation are all used as tools to aid in the growth of the student. Frequent conferences keep student, teacher, and parents informed of progress and provide guidance for future planning.
7. Cognitive, affective, physical, and intuitive activities are all valued parts of the classroom experience.
8. The atmosphere is one of trust, acceptance, and respect.

The responsive learning environment is highly structured and presents a complex learning organization to the student. This environment has the ability to meet all learners at their present level of cognitive, social-emotional, physical, and intuitive development and to help them move from that point.

Key II   Relaxation and Tension Reduction

If the integration of mind and body is to succeed, relaxation techniques must be learned to allow the body to cooperate with the mind's energy. At least six systems of relaxation are available: Autogenics (Schulz & Luthe, 1959), hypnotic suggestion, biofeedback, Progressive Relaxation (Jacobson, 1957), Yoga breathing, and meditation. Students gain by exposure to several methods, and they can choose the one that works best for them.

While Autogenics and Progressive Relaxation both have a particular methodology, they use the basic concept of tension awareness followed by relaxation. For example, a teacher might say, *Close your right hand into a fist. Hold your arm perpendicular to the body, and push out as you tighten your fist. Continue until you feel discomfort, then suddenly let go completely, relaxing all of the arm and hand muscles. Now relax the arm one level further. Again further. Still further.* This process can be used throughout the body.

Physical environment, too, can play an important part in facilitating or inhibiting the reduction of tension. The use of calming music and colors can aid in reducing anxiety and tension. Also order in a classroom is meaningful and especially appreciated by children who are sensitive to their environments.

Hans Selye (1956), a Canadian scientist whose research on stress has won him the Nobel Prize, regards stress as a necessary part of the life cycle, and believes that stress and relaxation should balance if one is to function properly. However, when one is overstressed or denied relaxation for too long, the system cannot adapt. As educator Joseph Chilton Pearce (1977) says,

> What the body learns in such a state is negative. . . . Failure to assimilate and accommodate to new information breeds the confusion and anxiety of unresolved stress. To enter into an unpredictable situation and accept it openly is to flow with its energy, be augmented in your own energy, and relax its tensions and stresses accordingly. . . . Stress-relaxation is an ability of the mind-brain, and muscular-mindedness must be developed, just as body musculature must be developed. Intellectual strength is a muscular-mindedness by which

greater and more complex unknown-unpredictable situations can be entered into, assimilated by the brain system, and accommodated by a proper response (p. 35).

There are many other ways of creating a reduced-tension learning environment, but it is the professional educator who can best decide how to incorporate these techniques. What is important is that stress be reduced.

Key III   Movement and Physical Encoding

One of the most curious observations made by brain researchers is that physical movement is important to learning (Restak, 1979). A child's movement is quite natural until entering school, where there is less and less opportunity to integrate movement and physical sensing into the learning experience. Among the few disciplines that retain this important aspect of learning are the arts and the physical sciences. Laboratories are used for physics and chemistry, but not in mathematics or history. Why? Though some efforts have been made by psychology and sociology teachers to incorporate experimentation and real life involvement, the teaching process has relied on students sitting at desks listening to a lecture or watching a demonstration in order to develop knowledge of the area being taught.

If we are to better educate students then we must acknowledge the importance of movement. The purposeful change of place, position or posture as part of the learning process, and physical encoding—the learning process which uses the physical body to transfer information from the abstract or symbolic level to a more concrete level—are integral to this movement, and can produce more precise learning with a higher rate of retention. Encoding techniques might consist of the use of rhythms, role playing, physically manipulating materials, and the creation of simulations of actual events.

Key IV   Empowering Language and Behavior

When a student says, *I can't figure this out, so what do I do next?* a teacher who asks, *What would be some of the possibilities?* or *What could you do that might help?* will allow the learner to retain the power and enable this student to experience thought processes while feeling supported. This is an example of empowering language. Giving a student undivided attention and indicating you are listening when that student is sharing a concern or achievement is an example of empowering behavior. Sparling (1984) tells us that these verbal, nonverbal, and overt physical responses result in competence, support, closeness, appreciation, and helpful feedback.

Empowering language becomes an important part of classroom communication between teachers, between student and teacher, and between students. Students who are given opportunities to work in an environment in which empowering language is valued become more responsible, more motivated, and exhibit a positive self-concept. All of these characteristics can be shown to enhance academic achievement (Aspy, 1969; Aspy & Bahler, 1975; Brookover, 1969; Purkey, 1970).

If empowering language and behavior become a part of the entire learning experience, attitudes toward school and self become more positive. The risks involved in creativity are taken, the highest levels of cognitive production made possible. The results of attention to this component of the Integrative Education Model enrich all phases of the students' world.

Key V   Choice and Perceived Control

Values provide the purpose for a person's life. Research shows that without a clear set of values students are unmotivated and lack direction, resulting in unprincipled, confused, and even delinquent behavior (Raths, Harmin & Simon, 1966). Often young people have problems establishing values by which they can live, and they may be expected to accept the values of others as their own without examination or personal affirmation. Too often the result is a rejection of all values.

The concern is not with decisions regarding particular values, but with the process used to develop those values. It is important our values work effectively and lead us to a satisfying, fulfilling life.

During the past decade many researchers have found that choice and the resulting perception of control are significant factors in student academic achievement and self-concept (Arlin & Whitley, 1978; Barnett & Kaiser, 1978; Calsyn, 1973; Matheny & Edwards, 1974; Stipek & Weisz, 1981; Thomas, 1980; Wang & Stiles, 1976). Interestingly it is not just the choice or control allowed students that makes the difference, but their perception of that choice. The possibilities for choice exist, but unless students clearly see those choices and believe that they can really make an acceptable decision, the positive effect will be missing. Good decision making must begin with opportunities for choice and alternative thinking. To become skilled at making appropriate and positive decisions students must have opportunities for guided practice.

Key VI   Complex and Challenging Cognitive Activity

One of the components of the Integrative Education Model that has been given the most attention by educators is the concern for the development of complex and challenging cognitive activities. Many models have been developed to aid in meeting this concern.

There remains, however, a most important matter. Since cognition can no longer include only the specialization of only half of our cortical function, we must integrate the other cortical specialization: the spatial, gestalt processes. Of even more concern is the theoretic construct which encourages only one of four brain functions to be developed. Cognition, even in its expanded definition, only involves the function of the cortex, leaving the brain stem (physical/sensing) and the midbrain, limbic area (feelings), as well as the prefrontal cortex (intuition), completely out of the learning process. Integration of all functions must be accomplished to allow the most effective development of the human potential.

By including all the models now available, planning for optimizing education has an excellent starting point, a cadre of valuable tools with which to begin. If we include all human functions in our concept of learning, we can plan for more effective and meaningful learning experiences.

Key VII   Intuition and Integration

This last component of the Integrative Education Model involves both an area of brain function and a total brain process. As mentioned, the brain is organized in a highly integrated manner, most of its area composed of associative tissue. The brain system is biologically designed for high levels of synthesis, and as educators incorporate these processes into their educational systems, learning experiences will become more effective and efficient, the students more motivated and successful.

The intuitive function has been the least recognized by educators, but attitudes toward intuition seem to be changing. Since it has been shown that brain functions are biologically different, a new effort is being made to bring the right brain's holistic, integrative, inventive ways of knowing into the learning process to provide a more balanced education. Breakthroughs in brain research and physics have caused the very nature of reality to be reconsidered. New findings on human energy, meditation, personal space, fantasy, imagery, and dreams have much to offer educational programs. If, as Barbara Brown (1974) insists, all learning is subconscious, intuitive abilities need to be developed.

Though some of these integrative activities, strategies and tools have been discussed earlier in the chapter, they are mentioned here again to emphasize their importance to the learning process.

1. Relaxation. Teaching techniques which can be used to reduce tension allow more interaction between the cortical hemispheres and better integration of their specializations. Relaxing allows a student to gain access to higher centers of the brain/mind system and to produce biochemical support within the brain for the learning process. The brain does not function well under conditions of high anxiety. The processing of data is slowed until the pressure is removed (Hart, 1978; Restak, 1979).

2. Centering. Centering can be defined as the balanced interaction of the mind and the body that allows access to total human function. Useful not only for physical activities but also for intellectual and emotional balance, centering is the ability to relax, focus energy, and move within a person's natural rhythm. Nearly all human activity improves when movement or action is from a centered position as opposed to a fragmented or tense stance. Centering allows the integration of mind and body that results in synergistic thinking. It is exciting for students to have the feeling of being completely aware, of discovering that solutions exist for problems not consciously being processed. Resources for centering activities can be found in Hendricks and Wills (1975); Hendricks and Roberts (1977); and Galyean (1983a).

3. Imagery. This strategy is a very valuable tool that triggers intuition, a process considered to be unique to the human brain/mind system. Imagery is an activity of the prefrontal cortex and involves the integrative use of the total brain/mind system. Imagery allows the student to walk beside a calming lake, to see first hand the ancient world or to become an electron when trying to understand the nature of electricity.

4. Verbal and physical affirmation. Affirmation is the process of responding positively to one's own or another's capabilities. Such comments as *I can do that* or *I really appreciate the patience you have shown just now,* help establish a positive self-image. Centering and consciously balancing oneself before beginning a difficult task or smiling and giving an appreciative pat to another are physical forms of affirmation. These simple acts have been shown to be important to the earliest physical and intellectual growth of humans and clearly contribute to emotional well-being throughout life. Such actions seem to create their effect by stimulating the limbic area of the brain.

5. Positive energy. This tool refers to the environment's effect on the brain/mind system; negative feelings and conditions weaken the system, whereas positive feelings and conditions strengthen it. Again, the effect is created from the action of the limbic system and its biochemical output to the brain's higher centers.

6. Complex and challenging cognitive experiences. Students are encouraged to take responsibility for finding appropriate challenges. This activity leads to an expansion of the neural structure resulting in accelerated and complex thought processing and more effective use of the entire brain/mind system. In other words, *use it, or lose it.*
7. Intuitive ability. Techniques that increase awareness of and involvement in this ability are important to optimizing learning. Intuitive activities include: completing a picture from partial information; exploring the open-ended solutions of "what if" problems; acting on a hunch; or stretching the mind into the future.

These seven keys allow a view of the Integrative Education Model from several vantage points, including the physical and emotional setting, the attitudes and communication skills of teachers and learners, brain compatible strategies and techniques, and the demand for function integration. From these components come tools students can use to help them become better learners.

INTEGRATIVE EDUCATION IN THE CLASSROOM

In the Spring of 1979 a new class convened at California State University, Los Angeles, a class which brought together current Master's candidates and graduates from the area of gifted education. In this advanced studies course the students explored current brain research implications and the new theories for education of the gifted. At the end of the quarter the group did not want to end their inquiry, and continued to meet informally throughout the following summer and into the next academic year. By late fall these students decided that it was necessary to try out these new teaching strategies for gifted children. The environment, they decided, would have to be one of total teacher and student support, and would have to forgo traditional educational structures and limits. In June of the following year the first session of the New Age School (NAS) was held, a six week summer project for gifted and highly able learners sponsored by Cal State Los Angeles and staffed by the group of Master's degree graduates.

Since then the project has been repeated each summer, and from this experience the Integrative Education Model and its components have evolved. To closer meet the goals of the Model and the needs of the children structures and strategies have been modified with each summer. An ongoing evaluation of the Model takes place as NAS faculty members take ideas developed during the summer back into their classrooms to use during their regular academic year assignment.

Over sixty other M.A. program graduates have joined the faculty to comprise an umbrella organization, the Center for Educational Excellence for Gifted and Highly Able Learners (CEEGHAL). This group arranges in-service meetings for their own enrichment and conducts in-service workshops for interested educators throughout the country, and has given sessions on the New Age Program at many national conferences. The group also conducts a brain research conference in the spring to update educators on the latest learning information and to raise money for NAS Project scholarships. Tuition supports the Project with research on the Model a joint venture of all participating faculty. Along with the Project an on-site training institute is held in which graduate students in gifted education can take classes toward their degree and participate in the excitement of the New Age School. It is in this setting and in the regular classrooms that faculty assess the merits of the Integrative Education Model. Educators visiting the Project have taken the structure and strategies found here into classrooms in this country and abroad and send us many exciting reports of their success.

Because of this genesis the formative data collection of the Model will be described in two subsections: Integrative Education in the New Age School, and Integrative Education in a Variety of School Settings. This information, it is hoped, will help clarify and encourage the implementation of these integrative concepts.

Integrative Education at the New Age School

Designing the most effective learning environment possible was first a job of articulating long held dreams. Whatever factor the group believed to be important and could be shown to have a reasonable theoretic basis could be included. The only limits were those of the creators. There were, of course, funding constraints, but the most difficult limitations to overcome were the old teaching and learning habits that held all these creators subtly in their bounds. To devise teaching techniques to fit previously untested educational beliefs was not an easy task. The goal was to implement all of the key components of the Integrative Education Model, and to focus on the process of learning, giving students tools with which they could become successful and responsible learners. While content was still important it was deemed imperative to give the students ideas and activities that would help them best educate themselves in any subject area.

To give more flexibility and choice to the students a cross-age grouping was devised. After several alternative patterns were explored, this grouping was adopted: Toddlers (ages 2 to 3), Early Age (ages 3 to 6), and Cross Age (ages 6 to 16). Each unit is organized in parallel structures with a decentralized plan appropriate to the age group involved and all units have faculty teaching teams. Team teaching, the NAS faculty has found, provides maximum opportunities for choice and enriched experiences for teachers and students alike.

The administration

The administration of the school has evolved into a participatory, shared management model very much like one suggested by Capra (1982). He states that throughout nature living systems tend to form multileveled structures with differing levels of complexity. At each level the systems are integrated, self-organizing wholes consisting of smaller parts while at the same time being parts of larger wholes. Capra shows that such multileveled systems have been found to evolve more rapidly and have a much better chance of survival than hierarchies or non-stratified systems. "At each level," he writes, "there is a dynamic balance between self-assertive and integrative tendencies and all holons [author's note: a holon is an autonomous system that is at the same time a component of a larger system] act as interfaces and relay stations between system levels" (pp. 281–282).

This suggests that integrative learning is a far more workable model or organization for school than the usual hierarchical model, which is defined as a fairly rigid system of domination and control in which orders are transmitted from the top down. A multileveled organization allows transactions between all levels, ascending as well as descending, the important aspect being not the transfer of control, but the organization of complexity. In the New Age School the levels are represented by the students, the classes, the teachers, the teams, the director and the trustees. Each level operates independently as well as with support and interaction with all other levels, and decisions are made and responsibilities shared at each level. Management is shared by groups at each level and operates by consensus. The result is an educational structure that increases the worth of each individual and which easily benefits from the unique talents of all.

The Toddler Program

This program includes parents as a daily part of the teaching team. The classroom is made up of activity centers for each area of brain function. Spaces and activities are designed for large group, small group, and individual instruction. Process skills are of major concern and content includes experiences that will prepare these little ones for school skills. The curriculum ranges from singing to pre-reading, from communication skills to animal care. While there are many teacher-designed materials and learning experiences, flexibility is built in to assure that student interests are also included. This program meets one and a half hours daily and also provides a half hour of instruction for parents.

The Early Age Program

This program continues the decentralization format with a more complex structure and a wider range of experiences. The classroom is arranged into learning stations and time is given to directed learning as well as to free exploration. The environment is colorful and presents a variety of learning areas. Once again spaces and activities are designed to accommodate large groups, small groups, and individual instruction. The focus is on the development of student independence and responsibility. The curriculum offerings include math, science, reading, art, music, and other subjects in which the teacher or the children have an interest, e.g. calligraphy, Japanese language lessons, archeology, and wood construction. Each week the lessons offered focus on a different theme. Themes that have been used include careers, animals, rainbows, likeness/difference, and the human body.

Children in the Early Age classroom develop their independence skills, responsibility, and self-esteem by learning to operate successfully in an environment that allows choice, variety, and challenge. Each child receives a "choice ticket" which gives the child a system for choosing the offering of most interest. Each teacher signs the child's ticket and indicates the amount of time the child is with that learning experience. By reviewing the tickets each day the teacher can tell in which activities the child is most involved and which need to be included to balance the child's experience. All of the brain functions are built into each lesson at each learning station. As the children grow in their skills faculty members help them to take more responsibility and to have more control of their own learning. This program is a morning program meeting from 8:30 A.M. to 12:30 P.M.

The Cross Age Program

This program parallels the structure of the other two programs, but the choices are now wider and include work in several laboratory settings staffed by different faculty teams. Sample settings are a science lab, such as biology, neurophysiology or physics;

a writing lab, which could include writing and producing plays, novels, and poetry, learning the art of illustrating and calligraphy, making paper, and developing the skills of the critic;

wilderness classes in which the children learn to live in nature and understand the role of humans in the natural ecology, a study culminating in a four day trip to the High Sierras or to a nearby island in the Pacific Ocean;

a math lab that allows students to pursue a wide variety of math usage at their own level and pace.

All offerings include experiences that integrate the four brain functions, each lab decentralized with a variety of levels of activity available. Children between 6 and 16 are free to choose any offering they wish to pursue. This wide age range allows the teachers to flexibly group students depending on learning needs and allows students to move at their own pace. Students, faculty have found, enjoy the mixing of ages and there seem to be many benefits to such a cross age structure.

The Cross Age Program meets from 8:30 A.M. to 2:30 P.M. and follows a set daily structure. From 8:30 to 9:00 is Community and Families, a meeting of all children age 6 to 16 in the auditorium. Here announcements are made, a thought for the day is discussed, a brain teaser is presented (and the children present the solution to the one given the day before), and a group relaxation activity is conducted. The group then separates into Families, i.e., like age groups. These groups spend 15 minutes to a half hour building social-emotional and communication skills, discussing personal experiences, and learning skills to develop strong, positive self-concepts.

From 9:00 to 10:00 Session I provides students with the first academic class they have chosen from the many labs offered. The students reconvene in families from 10:00 to 10:20 for sharing. After a break Session II meets from 10:45 to 11:45 for the students' next academic choice or a synthesis of those already investigated. From 11:45 to 12:00 the students again meet together with an opportunity for scheduled students to share their expertise with the group. Lunch is from 12:00 to 12:40, from 12:40 to 1:00 the students are involved in thinking skill-building games and experiments. Session III meets from 1:00 to 2:15 and includes art, music, drama, and wilderness classes. The students end their day in their family grouping, talk about the events of the day, and join together for a closing activity. The plan for the week includes:

Monday—the two morning sessions provide one-shot experiences. Students are presented with a wide range of activities which will be available only one time, such as a mini-workshop with a visiting novelist, an open science lab with a visiting heart surgeon, a craft class in soap carving, a music composition class with a professional composer, a class in creating computer games, etc.

Tuesday, Wednesday, and Thursday—academic choices that follow a six week format.

Friday—trip day. All students who wish may attend field trips designed to involve the community in the learning experience. The botany class may go on a trip to a nature reserve, or the drama class might attend a dress rehearsal of the Music Center Repertory Company, or perhaps the math class will visit a session of the Stock Exchange in the financial district. Many special events involve the entire population of the school, including parents. There are overnights at a beach or mountain campsite, four day trips into the High Sierras for the wilderness class, parent night, and a play day. By the last day the students, faculty, and parents are a cohesive, caring community of learners. In six short weeks much change and much learning occurs. Most important, however, is how much the students have grown.

An unusual amount of positive change takes place as the faculty focuses on the intuitive, affective, physical, and cognitive growth of the students. The Project's supportive environment allows this integrative philosophy to become a part of every activity and every experience. Several years ago a research team from a nearby University of California campus concluded that one of the strengths of the program was the loving environment that resulted from this focus. When those who attend or visit NAS compare the Project to other educational systems they have known, they consistently make the following observations:

> the students are more relaxed, more at ease with themselves and others;
> they are more caring and respectful of each other and of the faculty;
> they are more creative, try more unusual solutions, and engage in more alternative and higher level cognitive activities;
> they initiate more learning activities and are more enthusiastic about their learning;
> they are more highly motivated toward learning;
> they are more independent and responsible.

Individual students have shown dramatic change. Several years ago a 12-year-old boy who refused to talk came to the program for the summer. Larry's mother assured the faculty that he was highly gifted, but that he had for the past two years refused to talk at school. As a result he had been placed in the learning handicapped program where he continued to remain speechless and uncooperative. She was most concerned and asked if NAS would help. The faculty agreed to try.

About the third day of the program the students and faculty were together in the Community meeting discussing a quotation regarding the difference between an educated person and a learned person. Larry raised his hand to share his ideas. He stood and began to tell the group that an educated person was like a person who was in a box, and who knew the floor, the walls, and the ceiling of the box very well. A learned person also knew all about the box and, in addition, could go outside the box. This person knew about the whole universe and understood how people were connected to the universe and were a part of it. Larry suddenly stopped and looked around him, a look of real fear on his face. But then he saw students' faces turned toward him in interest, listening. He relaxed, smiled, and continued his thought. After the Community was over and as students moved off to their first session, Larry stopped directly in front of me. He took hold of my shoulders, looked me in the eyes, and said, *This school is going to be all right.* From that time on Larry shared freely and enthusiastically with faculty and students alike.

Later it was revealed that years before, when Larry had been "expounding" on his ideas in a class, the teacher had informed him that he was again being irrelevant and that if he could not stay on the topic he was to "shut up." For the next few years similar events happened over and over with different words, different teachers, but with the same message: *Sit down and shut up. What you have to say isn't important.* So he did; he stopped talking at school. At NAS he found students like himself, others with questions and unusual ideas, and he found the opportunity to share with them. He discovered a safe place, and he grew. There are many others who have come to the NAS Program who were, as one student said, *not flourishing* in their regular school setting. Again and again this environment, this structure, this Model, has allowed growth and a renewal of the excitement of learning.

In the years to follow more emphasis will be placed on the collection of summative and evaluative data. To this time formative data collection has been the major focus. As more evaluation is made of which of the components are more powerful for the students and which of the faculty behaviors are most essential, more will be learned about what is necessary to create optimal learning. For now, the student's experience includes all seven components of the Model in the proportions each faculty member finds appropriate to each learning experience. What has happened at NAS is exciting, and future investigation is most promising.

Integrative Education in a Variety of School Settings

During the academic year NAS Project faculty teach from pre-school to senior high school and in a variety of cultural and socio-economic settings. All have adapted the Integrative Education Model to their individual circumstances and the variety of implementations has been extensive. Though there are limits imposed by the administration, the community, and other circumstances, teachers continue to make opportunities for optimizing learning.

In one senior high school in a barrio community of Los Angeles a biology teacher who had taught at NAS found his students were having difficulty passing tests even though they seemed to understand the concepts being tested. He had been gradually introducing integrative techniques throughout the year and the students were familiar with all seven components. Finally he decided to use integrative techniques in the testing experience.

As he passed the examination papers to the students he placed the sheets face down on the desks. He then asked the students to close their eyes and relax. They were to imagine themselves turning the exam paper over and reading the questions. He suggested that they notice that the questions asked only for information the students had studied, and to be aware of how pleased they felt. He then asked them to imagine writing the correct answers to each question.

As he led them through this test-taking imagery he continuously reminded them of their ability to succeed and of the positive feelings they were experiencing. He then asked them to open their eyes, turn their papers over, and begin. At the mid-point of the exam he had each student stand and massage the shoulders of the person next to him or her. The students then returned to the test, refreshed and less tense. The results were very rewarding. Many students raised their exam results one grade level, some as much as two. As he continued providing these experiences during exam periods, he found the students' success rate increasing. He had found a very useful, practical way to incorporate integrative education.

PART II
Using Integrative Education

4

Creating the Climate

KEY I—THE RESPONSIVE LEARNING ENVIRONMENT

The first key component, The Responsive Learning Environment, is used to establish the social-emotional and physical climates of the educational setting. This key is highly structured, presenting the student with a complex learning organization. This environment has the ability to meet all learners at their present levels of cognitive, social-emotional, physical, and intuitive development and to help them to move from that point. The teacher, the student, and the parent form a team in this learning setting.

A recent study directed by Bloom (1982) found that of those persons studied who had achieved exceptional accomplishment of international note, all had received individualized instruction both at the early stages and in their specific fields of accomplishment. This individualization is one of the most conspicuous differences between instruction offered the exceptionally accomplished and instruction found in the traditional schooling experience.

Individualization can be defined as a way of organizing learning experiences so that the rate, content, schedule, experiences, and depth of exploration available to all students stems from their assessed achievement and interests. Varying degrees of individualization are possible:

Level 1—The teacher assesses each student's needs, resulting in an individualized level and pace of instruction.

Level 2—The instruction becomes more personalized when in addition to individualized level and pace the student becomes involved in the selection of goals.

Level 3—Once Levels 1 and 2 have been achieved, the student can begin to incorporate self-directed or independent study skills, as well as the responsibility to self-select learning activities and materials.

Level 4—Total individualization allows teacher and student to cooperatively assess and select goals, learning materials, activities, and instructional techniques. This also allows the student to self-pace, self-level, and self-evaluate using the teacher as a consultant and resource.

In this learning environment students can pursue interests in depth and with a minimum of time limitations. Students are no longer held to the group's pace or achievement level, and they can be grouped flexibly with other students as their learning needs demand or, when appropriate, they can work individually. Learners can function as teachers, researchers, apprentices, resident experts, or as learning managers. The classroom, now more closely related to the real world, becomes a laboratory for learning. In fact, students may often find projects and inquiries which enable them to become more profitably engaged outside of the classroom. Optimum learning will occur when the environment allows students to:

assume some responsibility for their own learning;
become independent learners;
learn at their own pace;
learn via material related to their own style;
learn on a level appropriate to their abilities;
be graded in terms of their own achievement;
experience a sense of perceived control, achievement, and self-esteem.

A large body of literature is available to aid in the understanding of the format and structure of this type of organization (see page 78).

Some strategies for individualization are

Programmed learning—includes assessment, an educational plan based on the assessment, and an individualized rate and level of instruction.

Instructional packages—includes assessment; an educational plan based on the assessment; self-paced, multi-sensory resources and activities; and a self-evaluation.

Contracts—includes assessment, goals, resource alternatives, activity alternatives and reporting alternatives, self-evaluation, teacher evaluation, and enrichment and review activities.

Mentorships—use of another student, teacher, parent, or community expert to work with students in their area of interest at their level of ability.

Community projects—use of resources within the community in planned projects developed from student interests and at their level of ability.

The environment must provide at least three conditions if it is to take advantage of new data on learning. First, the environment must provide accommodations for differences in learning style, pace, and level; brain data indicate that such differences are evident in all learners. The second condition which can be enhanced or inhibited by the environment is motivation, in part the result of participation, shared responsibility, and choice in the learning process. The third condition involves challenge and stimulation; both are necessary for optimal learning and both can become a part of an appropriately planned environment.

THE ENVIRONMENT

Creating the Environment for Toddlers (2–3)

A responsive environment is most important in creating the optimal learning environment for the early learner. The stage or sequence of development is not our most important focus, but the individual differences in ability to perform as well as profit from the experiences provided that appear with that development (Jeffrey, 1980). Age is an inadequate index of neurological and physical maturation as both are changed by the child's genetic program and environment.

Early theories on how children develop suggested that parents and teachers wait until children ask for an activity, but this now seems too wasteful of their abilities and resources. Children have the ability to choose from among a variety of activities those that are most appropriate for their development. The environment should be filled with a variety of objects and activities, and there should be an observant, responsive caregiver present with whom the child can interact. The availability of many resources, including parents and teachers, will allow children to stretch beyond known areas, experiment with new materials and ideas, and develop at their own pace and in their own style. Dubos (1969) states that human potential has a better chance of developing when the social environment is sufficiently diversified to provide a variety of stimulating experiences.

The Social-Emotional Environment

At age two children are interested in the world and in other children. Two-year-olds participate in parallel play but do not readily share toys (Owen, 1984). Their mental powers show rapid growth; speech, mobility, and increasing social involvement all add to their fast-paced intellectual development. All play materials from previous periods are useful, but now in different ways. Two-year-olds create, draw, pretend, and imagine, but only if allowed to and if provisions for these activities have been made. Space for them to explore and time to "do it myself" are needed. The child is now a thinker.

At two and one-half children may seem inflexible and are often very vocal about their demands. Their energy is abundant and their curiosity is high. Children at this age often enjoy routine, as they have difficulty making up their minds (Ilg & Ames, 1972).

Three-year-olds seem to feel much more secure about their world. As language and motor abilities rapidly develop and social skills increase, this age group needs caregivers to explain and model behaviors such as generosity, altruism, and care for others (Ilg & Ames, 1972; Owen, 1984; Stollak, 1978). Robin Soto, a teacher in the New Age School Toddler class, reminds us that although teachers may not be primary caregivers, their behavior toward their students is extremely important. Citing the work of Stollak (1978) she suggests that the following attributes of the environment show a high correlation with positive child development:

1. affection and responsiveness to the child's needs;
2. a stimulating and varied environment;
3. encouragement of exploration and independence;
4. fair discipline.

During this time of rapid growth it is important that all modes of learning—the cognitive, the physical/sensing, the emotional, and the intuitive—be nurtured. Many high ability characteristics already may be evident and should be supported. Curriculum for all preschool children must be rich in variety and stimulating in process. For those who are developing faster and who show higher levels of intelligence such variety and stimulation is even more necessary. We can include in their learning experiences more activities that allow self-direction, exposure to more abstract concepts, and tools and skills to help them better understand reading, mathematics, science, research, art, music, writing, and other aspects of the world in which they live.

The Physical Environment

A home or classroom that seeks to better educate young children will incorporate the same individualized learning elements mentioned at the beginning of this chapter. Individual differences in environments will be in timing, strategies, and the amount of support necessary. Decentralization is appropriate for academic and artistic activity centers. Decision making can be developed and used by children as young as age two and gives them a sense of competency and achievement. Even very young children can learn to adhere to limits on the number of participants in a given area at a given time, and can respond appropriately to signals indicating when and where these activities are to occur. It takes complex planning and structuring to allow young children the freedom and independence they need in order to attain higher levels of intelligence.

One such structure, designed by Alice Hayward (1985) for the Toddler Program at the New Age School (NAS), can be seen in Figure 4.1. Hayward has developed the environment so that parents and children can become familiar with Integrative Education by experiencing each component of it individually, including centers that address thinking, feeling, physical/sensing, and intuitive function. Language development is stressed at every center.

Parents and students are introduced to the components in the following ways:

Cognitive function: science center, math center, reading center;
Physical/sensory function: physical/sensory center, drama center, outside area;
Emotional function: art center, drama center;
Intuitive function: intuition center, drama center, art center.

Whether the toddler's learning environment is at school or at home, Hayward makes the following suggestions:

Make use of famous works of art Change the pictures in the child's room once a month. Have available varied pictures, posters, charts, etc. Traditional children's pictures can be mixed with reproductions of famous works of art (usually available on loan from libraries, museums, or universities). Hang some of the reproductions at the child's eye level. Hayward states, *A two-year-old child I knew would often get out of her bed at nap time and sleep on the floor underneath a picture that she adored which was taped about two and one-half feet above the floor. The picture was a Miro reproduction.*

Have a surprise bag Change the object once or twice a week. Without looking inside the bag the child puts his or her hand inside, then feels the surprise and tries to guess what it is. Begin with objects that are easy to identify; as the child's ability to observe and analyze increases use objects that are less readily distinguishable. Treat the child's mistakes as helpful clues and encourage risktaking.

Hang educational charts Have charts of the alphabet, animals, the development of a seed into a plant, etc., on the wall for the child to observe and discuss (these charts are available at educational supply stores). Clear contact paper extends the life expectancy of pictures or paper materials that children will be handling.

Use child-sized bookshelves Bookshelves low enough to allow children to reach books, magazines, catalogues, department store flyers, and other various reading materials are an important part of the child's environment.

Use the yard as a laboratory The yard can be a marvelous laboratory wherein the child can observe and experiment. Such things as where puddles go, why shadows change their size and shape, how rocks can be so many different colors, etc., can be fascinating. You can even do some experiments listed in children's science books.

Use the community for learning Libraries, museums, children's theaters, concerts, tide pools, markets, and businesses all enrich the child's experience. Prepare for the "field trip" by discussing and reading about the whats and whys of the place you will be visiting. Have the child ready to look for some specific thing or event when you go. Be sure to discuss the trip when you return, and allow the child to do something to record or remember the important things that were observed. An increasing number of resources and classes to help children develop important skills are now available for the toddler.

Hayward remarks that the most important thing in early learning is not the information taught but the processes learned and the attitudes developed. Developing the

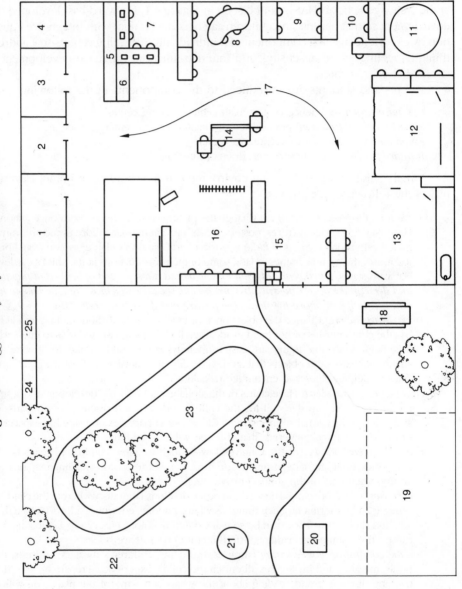

Figure 4.1 *Suggested layout for toddler environment*

The preschool layout (ages 2–3) includes:

1. Storage for inside materials,
2. A boys' restroom,
3. A kitchenette (stove/microwave, refrigerator, washer, and dryer),
4. A girls' restroom,
5. Children's individual storage (cubbyholes and hanging section at toddler height),
6. A parent table (outline of the day's activities, materials to take home, and communication and evaluation forms),
7. A computer center (two tables at student's height, four terminals, one printer to be used mainly for pattern printouts, and a library of software),
8. A science center (two student tables for setup of current skill activities, one kidney or round table for experimentation, and a visible storage area for materials previously presented for students to re-select),
9. A math center (two tables at students' height for current skill activities, a visible storage area for materials previously presented for students to re-select, and an acrylic-on-floor area to mark patterns, numerals, shapes, etc.),
10. A reading center for physical coordination development (two student tables, a visible storage area [see #9], and a chart area for large patterns),
11. A reading center for concept formation development (two student tables for current activities, an area rug, shelves for books to be displayed [cover out facing the children, and one book section to be changed weekly], a slide show area [to be used by individuals, not for whole groups], and a visible resource center fo slide materials),
12. An individual or small group instruction center (area rug, chalkboard, chart racks, sentence strip board, felt board, and a small table that has room for one person sitting on each side [most instruction is done on the floor on a one-to-one basis]),

13. An art center (sink and drinking fountain, secured storage area, visible storage area for selected materials, two small tables [see #12] for selected activities, one small materials table for the day's activities, and easels with clips and paint trays [see outdoor art area #18]),
14. An intuition center (one large table for current activities, two small tables, dividers, and a visible storage area [see #9]),
15. A physical/sensory center (box of large wood blocks, stack of plastic building blocks [18 by 18 inches], one student table for sensory activities, visible storage area [see #9], and balance beams, etc., as needed),
16. A drama/language development center (one student table for current drama activities, one student table for other language activities, visible storage area [see #9], puppet stage, raised platform, clothes rack with costumes [it's important that there be as many "interesting" male options as female options], mask box, and playhouse [furniture, pots and pans, etc.]),
17. A central rug area where materials from the previous week's lessons are taken to be used,
18. An outside art area that can double as an eating area (large table [for large art projects or group projects], and two benches),
19. Large muscle development equipment (jungle gym, slide, horizontal ladder, tunnels [may be moved to grassy area], and horizontal ladder [short]),
20. A sandbox (large box on wheels for sand equipment),
21. A water play pool (large box on wheels for water equipment),
22. A garden (pre-planted with whatever specimens are to be studied in science, intuition, physical/sensory, or other areas),
23. A segmented foot and trike paved track,
24. Animal cages, and
25. An outdoor storage area.

intellectual ability of children truly means helping them to develop physically, emotionally, socially, cognitively, and intuitively. Figure 4.1 and the descriptions of each of the numbered areas illustrates one way the environment can be organized for Integrative Education.

For Early Age Learners (4–5)

By age four children are very verbal, and teachers use high levels of this ability to identify very able children. In addition four-year-olds are alert, curious, attentive, active, and, a characteristic of great joy to their teachers, can easily be engaged in the excitement of learning. At this age children show emotions that make it relatively easy for an observant teacher to provide an appropriate learning environment responsive to the child's needs and interests. Each four-year-old seems to be a bundle of sensory motor energy.

This is an exciting time for the intuitive ability area. Teachers in the Early Age class at NAS have often found in these children the ability to "see" the "color" of the room (i.e. the emotional climate) or of a person. One child could "guess" the next card to be turned up in a naming shapes game with such accuracy that no one would play with him because there was no chance for others to be surprised.

One intuitive exercise in which the class engaged was experimenting with the impact human emotions have on the growth of a plant. The children sang to one plant each day while another plant received only growls and negative thoughts. The favored plant grew and flourished while the less fortunate plant appeared unhealthy and noticeably stunted in growth. The intuitive abilities of this age group are extensive. The teacher must only make it safe to do so and value this mode of knowing. Opportunities to use these abilities will be met with enjoyment and enthusiasm.

The Social-Emotional Environment

Four-year-olds are still living in a "me first" world. As with the younger children, discovering how and at what level these children function and then challenging and supporting their growth is the primary job of their teachers both at home and at school. According to Christine Cenci, team leader for the Early Age Program at NAS, this Herculean task begins by simply watching the children. They will let you know everything you need to know in order to enhance and educate them. As she says, *The aware teacher senses what's happening in the class all of the time. Usually classes are active but involved. Those moments when all speak at once, when a couple of live-wires spark at one another, when three need to tell the teacher of some urgent matter, when a cut finger occurs—all of these moments are also learning opportunities. The premise is that every situation, every word, every innuendo is an instructive forum to be used for the benefit of the learner.*

For example, when David comes in and appears to be happy but cannot sit still and will not tune in, the teacher can use a group physical activity to burn off energy. One activity involves having the children sit down and beginning a rhythmic chant: *Cross your arms now one, two, three; place them on your knees now just like me . . .* Directions can also be given in rhythmic chants: *Boys and girls, please come over here. Boys and girls, pick up the ball. Boys and girls, please come to the rug.* Or when one child is tardy in coming the teacher can say, *Janey, Janey, where are you? Janey, Janey, I'm missing you.* When such phrases are given in a sing-song chant the children's attention is captured.

Another good technique for satisfying the child's need before proceeding to the lesson at hand can be illustrated by a trip the children took to a heavy machinery storage yard as part of the project's curricula. In the yard were thirty large machines and a man ready to explain how the machines worked. Also in the yard were many rocks of various sizes and shapes, and several of the children began to pick them up. Parents accompanying the children on the field trip began demanding that the children put the rocks down and pay attention. The teacher, who saw so much energy being given over to rock-gathering, said, *Children, would you each pick up five special rocks. Look at them, feel them, smell them. Now share them with a friend. Now share them with two more friends. Show them the colors, the shiny places, the rough places. Now put the rocks down and show me you are ready to see the Caterpillars.* This activity incorporated what the children wanted as well as moving them to the planned activity. Had the demand been continued to *put the rocks down and pay attention* the children may never have given their attention or they may have invented their own activity with the rocks; they may have begun throwing them.

Cenci has some further suggestions as to how a productive, healthy social-emotional climate can be built in the learning setting:

1. Share much of the decision making by placing more of it into the hands of the children.
2. Include the children in resolving their arguments and differences. One procedure is to take both children aside and follow this plan:

   Step 1—Child A is allowed to tell what happened without being interrupted. *Child B* is allowed to tell what happened without being interrupted. *Child A* responds to *B*, then *child B* responds to *A* until what has happened has been exhausted (remember: they are discussing *just what happened*, not what will or what might have).

   Step 2—Child A tells what he or she wants (example: no more being hit in the shoulder by *child B*); *child B* tells what he or she wants (example: *child A* to stop pulling the ball out of *child B's* hands).

   *Step 3—*the teacher asks *A* if *A* can agree to what *B* wants, then asks *B* if *B* can agree to what *A* wants.

   *Step 4—*At agreement, the teacher excuses both children. Most often an agreement is reached, but when one isn't, the teacher reconvenes the meeting to determine upon what they can agree.

3. Work to extinguish or incorporate "off-the-wall" comments made by the children. For example, if there is a discussion of the Mobius Strip going on and someone shouts, *John's peepee is blue,* there are many viable responses the teacher can make. Smiling and saying, *Peepee or urine is not blue but in a moment you will use blue paint to . . . ,* is one alternative response, or *Peepee or urine could change color to show us illness but in this Mobius you could use dark blue to show one-sidedness . . .* The teacher might even say, *Joey is really feeling funny today so I'm eager to see how he uses any color, even blue, to color his Mobius pathway.*

   Another way of utilizing seemingly irrelevant comments is to turn the comment into a useful question. For example, if while discussing machines one child says, *I love whales. I saw lots of whales once,* the teacher might say, *Whales are quite interesting and so very big. It is fun to watch big whales move. Do you know how these big machines move?*

Always take the children from where their minds are and lovingly pull them beyond. In these examples the children were not denied their observations and their outbursts were made useful.

4. Use questions as a tool for growth. For example, if a child who has a cut hears the teacher say, *How can I help?* the child then must decide if a hug, a bandage, an ice cube, etc., is needed. The teacher then moves to help. When a child says, *I can't find anything to do* the teacher can respond with, *What have you missed here today? Let's look. Do you see a center that you've forgotten? How about trying that one? How long would you say is fair? Will you let me know how it works out?*

On occasion, however, questions have a deleterious effect and must be redirected. Often when a child is revealing something sensitive in a trust group, expressing a loss or a joy, or needing to relate an experience, the child's intense look should remind the teacher *No questions, this child needs to unload this.* Patient, eye-to-eye contact helps teachers know when to ask questions.

5. Watch the child's body posture. The body can provide valuable assessment data. Small children's bodies will often reflect what is in their thoughts. Watch for slumping, skipping, head down, eyes away, a red face, quietness, fast talking, or bubbly actions. Small children turn away from an activity if they are losing interest, and just as a child is turning to grab another child the teacher can say, *Gentle hands, use gentle hands.* Recognizing these and other body actions can allow the teacher to approach the next learning opportunity better informed, and can in many cases provide an early warning system.

6. Use *I* statements. As with children and adults of all ages *I* statements empower both the teacher and the learner. When a teacher says, *You need to help me, You need to try harder,* or *You need to go out now,* the statements are not only misleading, but also may be untrue. What is actually being revealed is the teacher's need, and statements such as *I need you to help me, I need you to try harder,* and *I need you to go out now* set an honest emotional climate, inviting much more cooperation.

7. Promote the spontaneous spark. As the child rushes to the board with *I can do it!* do not insist on a raised hand or a *wait-your-turn* lesson. Listen, evaluate, approve, encourage, and then invite the children to carry the idea further *after* they have returned to their seats. For example, a lecture/demonstration of the instruments of a symphony orchestra is given by a guest speaker, and then the children are invited to experience the instruments at centers around the room. Roger walks thoughtfully to the center where the drums, cymbals, bells and the baton have been placed. He picks up the baton and with great authority raps for attention from all the "musicians" in the room. He then carefully conducts a symphony of his own for the next ten minutes. The rules of rotation and taking turns can be suspended for those ten minutes with a non-verbal understanding between the teacher and the children.

The Physical Environment

Setting up a classroom that will support student-teacher shared learning requires some degree of skill, but what is most important is care. When properly arranged the classroom can provide exploration, stimulation, and challenge for students and can become an inviting, nurturing place for teachers. The first step is to look at the empty classroom and decide where learning areas should be. Cenci offers some suggestions for establishing teaching areas:

The rug area For this age group the rug area will be a primary learning center. Ideally it should be placed in a corner or off to one side so that it will be accoustically supportive rather than being in the center of the room where sound is dispersed and children will have more difficulty hearing. A rug large enough to seat all of the children and teachers in a circle will be needed. Placing masking tape Xs where you would like each child to sit will give you a good guide for spacing and enable the children to organize quickly for rugtime (to be described later in this chapter). These Xs give the children the security of having a set place, and also allow the teacher to quickly check for missing children. This area is where the day begins and ends and is the place for whole group lessons, singing and rhythmic activities, guessing games, assessment, demonstrations, sharing, guest speakers, and evaluation activities. This area is also used for private conferences, moments of personal sharing, and intimate gatherings for storytelling or reading.

Center areas A number of learning areas can be designated by hanging geometric symbols over each center. These symbols correspond with those on the child's *choice ticket,* a device used to allow children more control over their learning (this device will be discussed later in this chapter). The hanging symbols provide center recognition for non-readers and help children begin to establish experience with geometric shapes (see Figure 4.2).

Areas used at NAS are

1. Art and School Skills—needed are a project table large enough for a group of six children and a teacher, and supplies for lessons in art and school-related skills.
2. Science—needed are a table large enough for six students, a teacher, and science supplies, and a smaller table for two children doing experiments. At NAS this center is located on the patio outside the classroom.
3. Math—lessons for small groups can be taught at a table for four children and the teacher. Large group math lessons can be presented in the rug area.
4. Reading—a kidney-shaped table is perfect for reading instruction with small children. Circular or semi-circular tables can also be used. This kind of space allows the teacher to better facilitate children with reading materials.
5. Private Spaces—these can be obtained by placing small tables or desks so that they face the wall. These areas can house activities that include private writing, brain-teaser game playing, imagining, individual reading, creating, and individual conferencing.

Figure 4.2 *Geometric labels for learning centers*

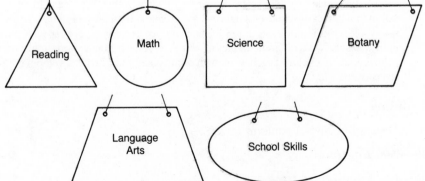

6. Playhouse—this area is useful not only for playing house but for small group guided fantasies, small group brainstorming, special surprises, dramatic plays, production rehearsals, and as a resting place.

Each center should have an abundant supply of various materials. Often these materials can be obtained from paper, can, lumber, printing, dairy, and plastics companies (on pages 79 and 80 is a list of material resource possibilities).

Next evaluate the classroom's wasted space. Where can materials and projects be displayed? The backs of bookcases, the ends of tables and the walls are just fine, but you can also hang art items and small projects from the ceiling on long strings. Try covering wall spaces with cheerful print fabric that will be strong enough to tape up student work and lightweight pictures. Pathways to doors can be made interesting by display tables, hanging designs, or brain-teaser puzzles. Ice cream cartons piled on their sides in rows along one wall are ideal places for personal storage of each child's materials and projects. Whether or not to leave space for individual desks is up to you, but the NAS teachers have found desks unnecessary. A layout of the room designed at NAS can be seen in Figure 4.3.

Setting Up the Integrative Classroom

The following is a time-line developed by Christine Cenci for establishing the Responsive Learning Environment in the Early Age classroom.

Before the children come:

1. Move the furniture to create center spaces, rug spaces, role playing spaces, class library space, display spaces, etc.
2. Hang center signs, puzzles, mobiles, interest items, art, etc., from lights or ceiling tiles.
3. Put up wall displays, basic charts (handwriting, multiplication facts, etc.), one study chart, and one or two bulletin boards for children's work. Put up charts and bulletin boards that are useful now. None should stay up longer than a month (this includes the chart rack and all materials).
4. Bring in necessary equipment: set out the record player, cassette tape recorder, overhead projector, etc.
5. Bring in animals and plants, using as many as the school, the classroom, and time will allow.
6. Check outside spaces for potential for learning enrichment.
7. Develop in detail your teaching plans and center contents for only the first day schedule, and then plan a simple day-by-day for the first week. This allows (and forces) you to stay in touch with the children's interests, paces, and needs. Be sure to have rugtime for the whole group, academic time for small groups at centers, and creative time for individuals. At NAS a different theme (machines, color, the human body, transportation, animals, etc.) is explored each week with each center and activity developing different facets of the theme.

Scheduling

Here is a sample daily schedule from NAS:

8:30—9:00 Rugtime

9:00—10:15 Academic time

Figure 4.3 *Suggested layout for Early Age environment*

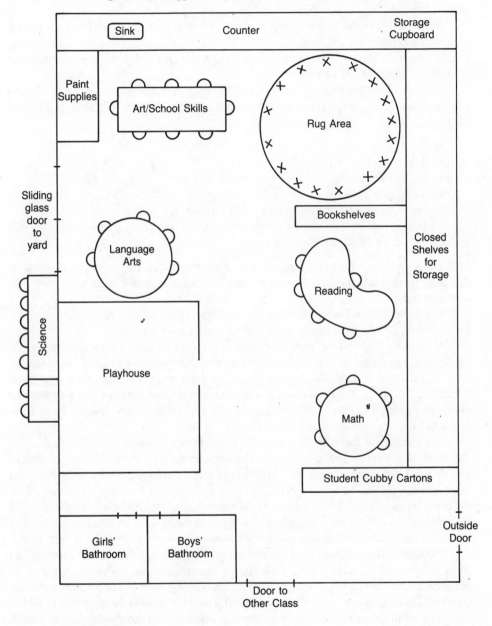

10:15—10:35 Lunch

10:35—11:00 Rhythms

11:00—12:00 Exploration time

12:15—12:30 Closing

8:30—9:00 Rugtime Rugtime is the hub of each day's activities. An average rugtime will incorporate the following:

Welcome A critical factor in self-empowerment is that each child feel important and wanted. Start the day with a personal, positive touch, a welcome establishing physical contact. Begin school with just looking at the child, and end the year with the warmth of hugging each student.

The Schedule Write on a chart or chalkboard a message for the day that chosen students read. Include the date and any special activities for that day. Here is a typical message:

Hello!
Hello!
Today is Tuesday.
Today is July 11, 1985.
Today we will have 2 new centers and a guest, Mr. Suzuki.
Today we will be cooking our own exceptional, gustatory treats so that we can evaluate what we liked and did not like.

Notice the repetition for beginning readers. Also notice that the sentences increase in difficulty to the last paragraph. Those who are ready will ask what *gustatory* and *evaluate* mean.

The Schedule helps students know what to expect for the day, helps them to focus attention, and gives them a chance to model for each other.

Assessment Physical or verbal activities are used to assess remediation or enhancement needs of the child. One example is the Follow-the-Leader assessment. Here the teacher chants, *Reach your hands up high now one, two, three, put your hands on the rug here, just like me, touch your elbows like this and you will see that knees are as happy as can be.* While chanting the teacher leads the children by moving and touching appropriate body parts.

The rhythm of the teacher's chant is a subtle but powerful tool that holds the children's attention and keeps the pace. Throughout the exercise the teacher is watching for hand/eye coordination, for the child's ability to cross the medial body line, and for the child's ability to follow verbal directions. The chant is changed daily to allow for many types of assessment. From this rugtime component the teacher receives vital information on what content the group will need at the centers as well as what kind of sensory, coordination, rhythmic, and body balance experiences should be introduced.

The lesson The following is a typical sequence for the theme *Transportation:* (*a*) show pictures of vehicles for the children to identify, (*b*) ask the group for sounds made by different vehicles, (*c*) sing a transportation song such as *The wheels on the car go bump, bump, bump . . . , (d*) send around a *touch and pass* mystery bag in which there is a small car or plane or boat; as the bag goes around the children chant *Touch and pass,* an easy pacing device so that no child can hold the bag for too long, (*e*) finally, ask each child to volunteer to sit in a vehicle, the structure of which has been set up before class by arranging chairs to represent an airplane, a boat, a train, etc. An appropriate hat to wear while in each vehicle enhances the fun. The children are encouraged to stay in each vehicle two to three minutes before moving to another and each child serves as a passenger three times and a driver once. A timer is useful here to remind the children when it is time to change. After four changes the group is called back to the rug to evaluate what it feels like to be a train, etc., and the teacher may give every other child two train stickers, one to keep and one to share. In this way an opportunity to learn to share is built into the lesson.

Sharing The children come daily with words or items to show and tell, and each is allowed to teach everyone including the teacher. If the child is too shy to stand on a *sharing spot* (a colored posterboard circle), it may be necessary for the teacher to hold the student on his or her lap for the first few times. Later the teacher may encourage the child to stand while the teacher places an arm around the child's waist for comfort and encouragement. At the appropriate time the teacher lets go and the child stands talking to the others. Standing is important as it gives a sense of power and encourages children to take the risk of speaking to a group of peers, a task many adults fear. The fun of sharing is the surprise of what each child will say. The creative task of the teacher is to make the transitions from one student to the next, from the student to the day's study theme, or, perhaps, to mollify the listeners because the sharer used profanity to explain the item brought, when in fact those words might have been acceptable home language.

Guest speakers A different guest speaker visits each week. This person, as do all adults, sits on the rug with the children for the content demonstration. Some excellent speakers can be found among the parents or friends of the children.

Choice time At the end of rugtime children choose their study centers. The children are invited, one at a time, to pick up their *choice ticket* and move to one of five or six locations where an activity is waiting. Rugtime has taken between 20 and 30 minutes and has set the tone for the day.

Guest speakers enrich the classroom curriculum.

Figure 4.4 *Early Age Program choice ticket*

Name:	Johnny				
Week of:	July 1-5				
Theme:	Transportation				
Centers:					
	M	T	W	TH	F
Reading	ℓℓ	ℓℓ	ℓℓ	ℓℓ	ℓℓ
Math					
School Skills				MV	
Botany					
Animals	JM				JM
Science					
Language Arts	IV	IV		IV	IV
Library					
Creating	BC	BC	BC	BC	BC

9:00—10:15 Academic time   The academic time allows the children to choose one or several center activities that focus on the weekly theme. Children bring to the center their *choice ticket,* which allows them to be in charge of their own learning while providing the teacher a constant check of the child's activity choices. The choice ticket is made of colored construction paper on which the week's center selections have been duplicated. While the choice ticket can vary with the teacher's needs, Figure 4.4 shows one version used at NAS. In the spaces provided the adult (if there is one; if not, the children sign their own ticket) signs the tickets of children who have worked in their center.

The ticket is critical in developing responsibility in the child. The children have their ticket with them at all times at each center. If they do not they are sent immediately to find it. The ticket is therefore the pass into a center. In addition the ticket

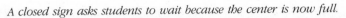

A closed sign asks students to wait because the center is now full.

provides the teacher with very useful information. The ticket in Figure 4.4 indicates to the teacher a concentration on the reading, language arts, and creativity centers. The teacher must learn if the child simply enjoys those areas more than others or if the child is avoiding certain content areas. As the weeks progress the series of choice

Open signs invite students to a center.

Figure 4.5 *Soda pop bottle signs for open and closed learning centers*

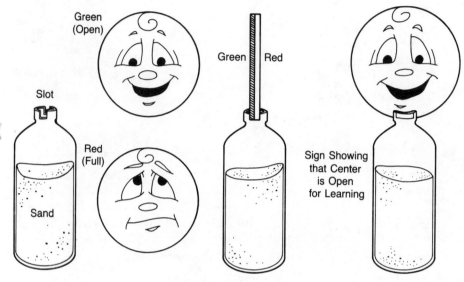

tickets will be an incredible asset in guiding the child and in parent conferences concerning home support.

Also helpful in building responsibility are the *open* and *closed* signs placed at each center. This sign is made by filling a large, plastic pop bottle with sand, cutting slits in the top, and inserting a cardboard circle into the slits. One side of the cardboard is red, the other green (see Figure 4.5). By simply turning the red or green side out, the students show whether the center is full or open. This allows children to learn about taking turns and waiting without the teacher having to remind them. Again the responsibility is on the child.

The content of each center should range from below grade level to two to three years beyond. Remedial students need to be brought to grade level while other children need to be challenged to move on to higher levels. Cenci suggests that a center's content should include 30% specific factual information, 50% process time, 10% product emphasis, and 10% evaluation time. This age group needs much experimenting with and manipulating of concrete items. The content can have an academic focus as long as the above percentages are maintained. Dissection, computers, poetry analysis, coordinate graphing, metric addition/subtraction, and hydroponic gardening are all very viable center content.

10:15—10:35 Lunch

10:35—11:00 Rhythms

11:00—12:00 Exploration time Exploration can be an extension of the learning center or it can be new enrichment activities. Some of Cenci's suggestions are

> *Guided fantasy*—These experiences can be initiated immediately after lunch (see Chapter 5 for information concerning this activity).

Gentle/positive—Plan something to promote friendship (compliment time, favor time, etc.).

Role play—Do one role play of something pertinent to children; the teacher is present only for interaction purposes.

Short story—Read an interesting short story to the children.

Physical movement activity—Do a short exercise/body movement between time slots in the daily schedule.

Walking trip—Plan a walking trip to support an area of curricular study (biology, botany, health, personal relations, etc.).

Show/Teach—Ask a member of the class to show or teach something to the other children (e.g. skill in math, reading, spelling, etc.).

12:15—12:30 Snack

12:30 Closing

Parents can be important participants in the early learner's educational program. One hour of inservice can provide the teacher with immense help at centers; given a text, the educational goals, some pertinent language clues, and the support and gratitude of the teacher, parents can take over a learning area and relieve the teacher of responsibility for a center all year. Parents who drive and can serve as guides are a great help on field trips. A side benefit is a teacher-parent rapport that gives the teacher additional support with administrators and the community.

Cenci offers the following list of skills that parents can develop as participants in their children's educational program:

1. Question the children rather than answer them.
2. Use appropriate language, e.g. no baby talk with small children or *cool* language with high school students.
3. Own the request, e.g. *I need you to open the book now* rather than *You must open the book now.*
4. Direct any verbal or physical action in a positive direction, e.g. if the student says, *I'm gonna hit Johnny!* the parent's response should be, *You may not hit Johnny, but you may hit the tree or the ball or the patio wall.*
5. Check to find the true intent of the child, e.g. if the child says, *You can't do that!* what may be meant is, *I have an easier way to do that!*
6. Support all of the teacher's requests; question them in private later.

Cenci also suggests that a newsletter sent home once a week is an excellent way to keep parents informed of what is happening at school. She also has found parent conferences to be a valuable tool for helping parents obtain information concerning the academic progress of their child, the dynamics of their child within the group, and the current status of their child. Cenci believes that parent back-to-school nights or open houses are necessary to give parents visiting opportunities other than those offered at conferences as well as to share with other parents.

Creating the Environment for Elementary Students (6–11)

As the child enters the formal classroom the support and flexibility given early learners is often unavailable, though the needs of the learner have not changed. If anything, the need for personalized instruction is greater as the child becomes a more curious, more competent learner. The Responsive Learning Environment is ideal for this age learner.

The Social-Emotional Environment

In an environment where each student is considered a unique individual, self-concept can easily be developed. Accomplishments and values can be shared, and students can gain recognition without seeming to dominate. They learn responsibility through the many opportunities given them; they strengthen their inner sense of control by learning things they value and that meet their needs. Any problems encountered by the group can be resolved by the group, giving a natural setting for the development of leadership skills.

The first step in developing an environment that can promote social-emotional growth is the establishment of trust. A trusting environment does not just happen; it is deliberately planned. Classrooms that have used the Integrative Education Model have included use of language and behavior that allows students to feel competent, activities that are more cooperative than competitive, and time for building positive interpersonal interactions.

The group of teachers who planned the New Age School Project found that one of the most important environmental components was the interrelationship of the faculty. We spent two days and an overnight together prior to the beginning of our school to finalize our curriculum planning, and soon we found that we were actually there to get to know each other better and to learn how we could support one another. As we discussed our own goals and ideas we began to care about *each other's,* and about making sure that each of us was able to reach his or her special goals. This genuine caring among the faculty, we later discovered, was to be one of the most powerful examples we could give the students. The environment we were able to provide because of this loving interrelationship created a non-threatening, non-competitive learning setting where the students could take risks, try out new behaviors, and truly grow. Best of all, the faculty grew. Teachers who find themselves non-threatened by each other and totally supported in a non-competitive setting will meet their maximum potential. Each person becomes a viable resource for the others and willingly shares expertise, materials, criticisms, and praise. Opportunities become positive realities.

A most important part of the educational team is the parent. While it may take some time initially to educate parents to the needs of the classroom and how they can best help children learn, they can become invaluable as mentors, resource experts, learning center directors, guest speakers, aides, and drivers.

If you will plan and carry out activities that build relationships, the positive effects of these activities will be extensive and on-going. A pattern that seems to work well is to begin and end each day with an activity or discussion that attends to the social-emotional needs of the students. The activity can be as simple as a short relaxation together at the beginning and an evaluation circle at the end of the period. At the beginning of the year more time may be allotted to these activities in order to help students understand and recognize the importance of their social-emotional needs to the learning process. Occasionally blocks of time can be used to develop communication skills, the trust group, and classroom agreements (see Chapter 6). Strategies to use for openings and closings follow.

Openings

Relaxation and Tension Reduction Strategies When tension becomes too great the limbic area of the brain simply sends the cortex or higher brain biochemical signals to shut down, but to optimize learning the brain must be able to call upon all of its complex functioning. To create the most appropriate learning environment it is best to start the day with a tension reduction exercise.

Exercise 4.1. Basic Body Relaxation

Purpose and expected outcomes: to relax and focus the students; to teach them how specific muscles hold tension and how they can reduce that tension; to introduce the concepts of the body's gravity center and energy flow available when the body is relaxed. At the end of the exercise the students will be relaxed, their brain/minds will be more coherent, and they will be able to focus on their learning, use more integration in the learning process, and retain more of what they have been taught.

Time involved: 7–10 minutes

Material needed: relaxing music optional

Preferred structure of classroom: students sitting in seats or on the floor

Teaching function: director/total group leader

Procedure: Direct students to *Close your eyes and get in touch with your breathing. . . . Just notice . . . do not try to change your breathing. . . . Allow it to happen. . . . We each have our own rhythm of breathing. You will find that your breathing will begin to deepen, to become slower; soon you will be breathing with your whole body. . . . Now I am going to ask you to focus on some of the muscles throughout your body that may be holding tension. A muscle is supposed to tense, act, and relax. Sometimes all the tension is not released. Focus on the muscles across your forehead, just above your eyebrows. These muscles may feel tight. As you breathe in, let air go into that area, and as you breathe out, let the tension out. . . . Now focus on your jaw muscles.*

Continue talking to your students about other muscles: those on either side of the neck, the shoulder muscles, the back muscles, down the legs, down the arms. When they have relaxed all the muscles suggest *If there were a line from the top of your head to the tip of your toes, intersecting that line halfway would put you at the gravity center of your body. . . . Slowly allow your focus to move to the gravity center of your body. . . . It is at this center that you can feel your energy. . . . Energy that is available to you now that you are relaxed. . . . Be aware that you can be very relaxed and yet very aware. . . . Feel the energy flowing through your body . . . your toes and your fingers . . . your legs and your arms . . . all through your body . . . up into your shoulders . . . your head . . . flowing, alert, yet relaxed.*

Ask them to again be in touch with their breathing. Tell them that you will soon ask them to come back to their place in the room. Allow time for them to adjust. You might ask them to imagine what the room looked like when they closed their eyes, then have them imagine themselves back in the room. Tell them that when they are ready they may open their eyes and return to the room. Allow time for them to come back. They may want to share their experiences.

Other openings While relaxation and tension reduction activities can be used to begin a day, other activities can also be included.

Exercise 4.2. A Thought for the Day

Purpose and expected outcomes: to give the students an opportunity to come in contact with great thinking from their own perspectives and to share with each other insights into their own lives. At the end of the activity students will have been exposed to a great thought and a great thinker and will understand how such a thought relates to their lives.

Time involved: 5–10 minutes

Material needed: a quote from a great thinker/philosopher

Preferred structure of the classroom: total group

Teaching function: input, discussion leader

Procedure: Put a quote from a great thinker on the board or on a poster. Ask the students to read the thought to themselves and then ask one student to read it aloud. Ask a second student to read it aloud, this time reading it slowly and dramatically. Encourage a discussion of what the author might have meant and what such an idea would mean in the children's lives now.

Some thoughts used at the New Age School were:

Intelligence can come only when there is freedom—freedom to think, to observe, to question. Krishnamurti

After you understand about the sun and the stars and the rotation of the earth, you may still miss the radiance of the sunset. Alfred North Whitehead

No man [or woman] *can reveal to you aught but that which already lies half asleep in the dawning of your knowledge.* Kahlil Gibran

Your belief system explains only what your limits are—not what the limits are. Belief systems limit experience. Impossible things are things you don't believe in. James Fadiman

Exercise 4.3. A Puzzle for the Day

Purpose and expected outcomes: to challenge students to solve brain teasers; to help students have an experience with alternative thinking; to help them find many answers for a single problem, moving them away from the limiting dichotomy of *right* or *wrong*.

Time involved: 5–7 minutes

Material needed: brain teaser

Preferred structure: total group

Teaching function: input, discussion leader

Procedure: Put a brain teaser on the board or on a chart. Ask one student to read the puzzle aloud. Invite the students to ask for any clarification they might need to solve the puzzle. Tell the students that before class begins tomorrow they will be given a chance to share their solution. They are allowed to use any resources they wish in seeking the solution. On the day following the introduction of the puzzle, allow all students with a solution to share. Some answers may be quite divergent. Use this fact to point out that many situations have alternative solutions and few problems have only one possible solution. Some of the brain teasers used at the New Age School were:

If a snail is at the bottom of a 12 foot well and if he climbs 4 feet each day and slides back 3 feet each night how long will it take for him to climb out of the well?

How can you take 1 away from 9 and get 10?

A man once set up a camp from which to go exploring for bears to tag for a scientific study. Leaving his camp, he walked 10 miles due south, then 10 miles west. At this point he found a bear, tranquilized it, and tagged it. He then walked back to his camp, a distance of exactly 10 miles. What color was the bear?

Asking them to share their solutions for the puzzle for the day helps students to find many answers for a single problem.

Fun with letters:
$cc—Here comes the boss.
!iii—Harry always was a nonconformist.
tf—You curled your hair.
Can you think of one to add?

At the New Age School all three of these strategies—relaxation, a thought for the day, and puzzle for the day—are used at the beginning of each day. Students are invited to bring in their own "thoughts" or "puzzles." After a short time some students will enjoy developing and sharing original relaxation exercises. As the students begin the day these types of activities give them a community feeling of belonging and create a positive environment for learning.

Closings

There are many types of closings that can continue to build trust, leaving the student with a positive feeling about the learning experiences provided throughout the day. Closing class together gives the class a feeling of community. The students have an opportunity to clarify new information, review what has been learned, and examine what worked and what didn't work for them during the day. Positive self-concept, heightened responsibility for their part in the classroom and a sense of closure can be achieved. The following are only a few strategies for closing the day that have been used successfully from preschool through graduate classes.

1. *Summarize the day's activities.* Give the students a chance to share one new idea they will take from the day's work. One way to accomplish this is to ask students to join hands in a circle before leaving the class (this works for *all* ages). Ask the students to close their eyes and go back over their day (or class). Ask them to recall one new idea they found interesting or that they want to remember. Tell them that when they have the idea they may slowly open their eyes. Begin the sharing with one idea you found interesting and then go to your right or left around the circle. Students are allowed to pass, but I have seldom had anyone wish to pass. This activity not only reviews the day for each individual student, but reminds others of ideas they may have forgotten.

2. *Critique and clarify the learning experiences for the day.* Sit in a circle if possible so that each student has a chance to share with the class, not just with the teacher. Ask each student *What worked for you today?* This refers to what they did that felt good, succeeded, or turned out the way they wanted it to. After each has shared ask *What didn't work for you today?* After each answer ask *What could we help you do that would work better next time?* This allows students to focus on ways they might improve their learning experience. It also creates a cooperative feeling among students as they suggest ways others could aid them. Most of all students are encouraged to see learning as their responsibility; with this encouragement they will perceive that they have more control. As discussed in Chapter 6 the data shows perceived control to be an important factor in school achievement.

3. *Re-establish the class as a learning community.* This is important to all facets of the learning experience. As students feel accepted and cared for by the group they will work to achieve not only the goals of the group but also those of individuals within the group. One way of re-establishing the feeling of community again involves having the students hold hands to form a circle. The students then look to their right (or left) and see who is standing there. The teacher asks the students to gently close their eyes and see that person again. Ask them to notice how they feel about that person and think of one reason they are glad this person is a part of the class. Ask them to go back over the day and recall one event that showed that this person was important to the class: something they did or said or some way they may have assisted someone in learning. Tell the students that when they have one event or idea in mind to open their eyes. Begin by turning to the student on your right (or left) and giving a reason that you are glad the student is a part of the class. Stress something specific the student did that day. Continue around the circle until each student has had a chance to share. The students leave with a very energetic and positive feeling about the class, the people in it, and themselves.

Activities that build trust

You might also choose to end a class with a trust activity, though the time of day has little to do with the importance of trusting one another. Only when there is trust within the class can students feel safe to take the risk of learning. Trying things you don't know and things at which you may not succeed, making mistakes, and noticing that you learn differently than others all require a safe environment. It may take a long time to build the trust needed to enhance a learning experience, but the time and effort taken to establish such an environment is time well spent. Here are some suggested strategies for building a trusting environment.

Exercise 4.4. Mutual Interviews

Purpose and expected outcomes: students will know each other better and can therefore feel safer with each other, bringing them to feel more a part of a learning community.

Time involved: 20 minutes
Material needed: none
Preferred structure: pairs of students, then a group meeting
Teaching function: facilitator
Procedures: Ask all of the students to look around the room and find someone they do not know well (if it is the first day of class this will be easy). Each student is to go to that person and find a place to sit. For the next ten minutes they are to do three things: share themselves with each other, listen as they are sharing, and notice how each feels about the experience. Tell them that at the end of the ten minute period you will ask them to introduce this person to the class. I always remind my students that if they do not want to be the last person chosen they should be the first person to choose. After about ten minutes call the pairs back into a single group and ask that they close their eyes for a moment. With their eyes closed ask them to think again about the experience. What do they now know about this person? What did they find interesting or surprising? How do they feel about this person? What would they like others to know about this person? Ask them to gently open their eyes and allow each student to introduce the person they interviewed, sharing the partner's name, something they want everyone to know about the partner, and how they feel about the partner.

Exercise 4.5. Five Tasks

Purpose and expected outcomes: students will know each other better and have an appreciation for some of each other's strengths; they will feel more positive about their self-image. At the end of the activity students will feel closer to a group of their classmates and will leave class feeling energized and with enhanced feelings of self.
Time involved: 20 minutes
Material needed: none
Preferred structure: groups of five
Teaching function: facilitator
Procedures: Ask the students to choose four others with whom they would like to work and have the five sit in a circle. Then tell them, *I am going to give you five tasks to do as a group.* [Make sure to give them plenty of time for thinking between directions]. *The first task is to make contact with everyone in your group* [this could mean simply smiling at each other or nodding to each other]. *Your second task is to give your name to everyone in your group. Now put a one word descriptor in front of your name and share that with the group* [give the students an example such as excited Ann]. *Close your eyes and imagine yourself as far back as you can remember. Now remember from then to age 10* [if the students are younger ask for an age several years earlier]. *Remember something during that period of time that you were very good at doing, something you felt very successful doing. Maybe you received a prize for this, maybe only you knew how really good you were, but let that event or thing come into your mind. Notice how you feel about it and how you feel about yourself. Go over the whole event. Experience yourself doing it again. When you have it well in mind gently open your eyes and share it with your group* [Allow each student in each group to share]. *Now close your eyes again. Allow yourself to be aware of something very successful that you did this week. Notice how that feels. When you have it share it with your group* [Allow each person to share]. *Your last task is to choose one person in your group to be a silent member. This person may not speak or react. Each person in the group is to take turns saying something they appreciate about the silent member directly to them, then the silent member can begin the next round of appreciation statements. The person on their right then becomes the silent member. Continue in this way until each member of the group has been the silent member. You have now completed all five tasks.*

Exercise 4.6. Trust Circles and Lines

Purpose and expected outcomes: to help students feel more trusting of each other, thereby building greater community feeling within the class. At the end of the activity the students will feel a sense of closeness and cooperation with their classmates.
Time involved: 10 to 20 minutes
Material needed: none
Preferred structure: students seated in circles of ten, legs extended (for trust circles); students standing in lines facing a partner, arms extended toward each other (for trust lines)
Teaching function: facilitator
Procedure: Trust Circles: have the students take their shoes off and then sit shoulder-to-shoulder in a circle on the floor. One person stands in the center and all the others place their feet on this person's feet and ankles. Those in the circle now raise their hands and arms in front of them, ready to catch and pass the center person around the circle. When all in the circle are ready, the center person, feet securely on the floor and supported by all the other feet, falls back into the circle. By bending only at the knees and relaxing, the center person can be easily passed from hand to hand around the circle. Be sure students are close enough so that several will be supporting the center person at all times.
Trust Lines: form parallel lines so that one person can be passed shoulder high between the rows. The weight or height of the person is unimportant, as at least four pairs of hands will support him or her at all times. Try it yourself. Your students will enjoy your trust.

Other useful activities can be found in resources developed by Stevens (1971), Ott (1973), Simon (1974), Hendricks and Wills (1975), Sisk (1975), Canfield and Wells (1976), Hendricks and Roberts (1977), and Clark (1983).

The Physical Environment

The learning setting can facilitate or limit the learning program. The classroom environment has far more impact than we previously assumed; it affects even the energy the students have to expend on learning goals.

To best use the Responsive Learning Environment the teacher must first develop a decentralized setting. The classroom needs sufficient "people space." So many educational settings are overfilled with desks, tables, chairs, and equipment that space for people to move about and actively participate in their own learning is restricted. This necessary space can be obtained in a number of ways:

1. *Take out furniture.* If students are engaged in a variety of activities, rarely will everyone need to be sitting and writing at the same time; individual desks are unnecessary. Writing can be done on the remaining tables, at centers, or on portable clipboards. Each student's materials can be stored in racks, boxes, or cartons stacked against the wall.
2. *Carpet some areas.* Carpeted areas provide good group spaces and can easily be used for seating people. Carpet also reduces the noise of movement, causing a room's atmosphere to become more interactive, less tense, and more pleasant. Students seem to show more pride in their surroundings and exercise care when in a carpeted facility. At the university, I often teach several sections of the same class. I have noted that there is far less discussion and interaction among the students when we meet in a traditional classroom than occurs when we meet in the carpeted room. Here are found moveable tables instead of desks, soft floor spaces instead of hard linoleum. A different quality of learning occurs.

3. *Use walls, windows, closets, and drawers for teaching areas.* A reclaimed teacher's desk makes a fine media center. The drawers provide storage space for projectors, films, slides, and filmstrips. The knee-hole makes a good projection area with a screen located at the far end of the opening as it is somewhat protected from light. A small group seated on the floor can participate quite effectively in a self-directed media presentation. Don't overlook the backs and insides of drawers and the bottoms of tables for use as learning center areas. Number facts become much more interesting for third grade students when they must work them while lying on the floor with a flashlight and reading them from off the bottom of a table. Even in secondary and university settings, more flexible use of space is most beneficial.

4. *Bring in comfortable, moveable furniture.* A couch or overstuffed chairs can provide attractive reading and meeting spaces. Floor pillows or small padded stools can also provide highly flexible seating spaces. This type of seating has made a significant instructional difference in our university classroom.

5. *Let the students help.* Students may at first find it difficult to imagine how a classroom can be different. Let them help improve the learning environment by giving them a few options for changing their space. They will be more responsible and involved in the classroom if they have a part in creating it.

Imagine a classroom with many activity areas and quiet, comfortable reading and study areas. Discussion areas are also available to students and teacher/student groups. There are conference and large group areas, and movement is easy because of a minimum of desks and chairs. The walls display alternative activities and materials for self-directed study; closets and cupboard doors provide media centers.

The physical environment must support learning in the cross-age classroom.

Movement in and out of the classroom to the library or other learning centers is not inhibited, and special grouping for specific interests is common. Individual contracts and projects make it possible to learn at your own pace; no one is asked to wait for the group to catch up or to do busy work to pass the time.

At the beginning of the year teacher-initiated activities and materials dominate; by the end of the year the environment represents the learners within it. The responsive learning environment is a place where individuals can meet their unique needs on a full-time basis.

Now that classroom space has been considered, think a moment about light and color. Researchers believe that the brain's pineal gland plays an important part in helping the body adjust to its environment. Light affects that adjustment (Meer, 1985). Ismael (1973) suggests that soft lighting makes people less self-conscious and more receptive. She reports a new sense of ease in teaching and communicating and increased interaction and cooperation among students. According to Meer (1985) the issue of perceived control (discussed more fully in Chapter 6) affects how people feel about lighting systems. He reports that in institutionalized settings lighting control is gained by breaking unwanted bulbs when on and off switches are not available to residents.

Ott (1973) found that natural full spectrum light is important to the proper use of human energy. Fluorescent light omits needed ultraviolet rays, and pink fluorescent light increases irritability, hyper-aggressiveness, and negative feelings. There are fluorescent bulbs now on the market that provide a full-range light spectrum. Psychologists suggest that such bulbs improve visual acuity, make work less fatiguing, and provide important health benefits (Meer, 1985).

Color can be used for a variety of purposes. Heline (1969) reports that reds, oranges, and yellows stimulate, invigorate, and energize; greens, blues, and violets are restful, soothing, and calming. Using color in relationship to the activity you are planning may enhance the result. Visualizing color is reported to have a dramatic impact upon the health and well-being of participants in an experimental program conducted by psychologist Robert Gerard. He believes that thinking of a color is much more reliable in its effects than the use of an actual color (Meer, 1985).

What about sound? Noise can be quite distracting; but because the type of exciting, involved learning that we are discussing requires movement, we must consider the sound that this produces. Carpets, simple movement patterns within the room, and less furniture all help to eliminate unwanted sound. Direction and advice from the teacher, however, can create a source of noise if not handled well. Try creating a sign-up space such as an "I need you" list on the chalkboard where students can list their names when they need help in a project or lesson. Check the board and then visit each individual in order as soon as possible. This practice works very well and measurably reduces noise and frustration.

Listening posts for films, slides, filmstrips, and video and audio tape systems are an excellent way to reduce noise and provide easy, simultaneous access to learning centers and media. Not only should lessons be recorded on tape but also natural sounds. Tapes of running brooks, birds, ocean sounds, and wind in the trees can make excellent contributions to the learning environment. Music can calm or inspire, enliven and energize. Just as you provided spaces for differing intensities of light you must also provide for quiet, thoughtful activities as well as louder, busier learning.

Teachers in classrooms that must be shared with other classes have a different and more difficult problem. For some elementary teachers the environment belongs to them only part of the day; another teacher and another class regularly move into the space. In many departmentalized secondary schools teachers change rooms each period. These situations create difficulties, but they can be worked out. Create portable environments by designing boxes that have all the props you will need for a center. Free-standing cardboard folders designed around a unit or theme with pockets holding materials can instantly convert a table into a learning area. These folders can be stored in file cabinets. A large variety of skills and subject areas can be readied for individualized instruction in this way.

Store your media equipment and materials in closets or nearby offices. Build basic flexibility into your rooms: use moveable tables and chairs, carpeted flooring, and attractive wall display areas. You may be able to share these latter areas with the other classes, but always return the furniture to its usual arrangement. I have discovered that I could do anything in my classroom as long as the teacher following me did not have to put it back in its "proper" order.

While you are working out your way of sharing, start working toward finding your own room. Convince scheduling or the administration of the importance of the environment to creating effective learning; keep trying to get your own space.

Scheduling

At NAS the structure for the day in the Cross Age Program (6–16) in many ways parallels that of the Early Age students.

8:30—9:00 Community and family time

9:00—10:00 Academic time

10:00—10:20 Sharing

10:20—10:45 Outdoor skill building

10:45—11:45 Synthesis and extensions

11:45—12:00 Sharing with experts

12:00—12:40 Lunch

12:40—1:00 Thinking games and experiment

1:00—2:15 Arts, music, drama, and wilderness

2:15—2:30 Closing

8:30—9:00 Community and family time During this time the "Thought for the Day," the "Puzzle for the Day," and a group relaxation are presented to all Cross Age students. Examples of these can be found in the section on the social-emotional environment found earlier in this chapter. Effective skill building is the focus of the Family Time: each faculty member meets with small groups of students for approximately 15 minutes.

9:00—10:00 Academic time Just as in the Early Age Program this part of the Cross

Cross-age grouping makes learning exciting for everyone.

Age Program is organized into learning centers, small group instruction, large group instruction, and individual learning time.

Learning centers Learning centers aid in structuring the environment for individualization. These areas can be set up as learning stations, assessment centers, game areas, media centers, or interest centers. They can be teacher-created, student-created, or the result of a cooperative venture; they may have a specific purpose or may be for exploration and discovery. They can be located anywhere in the room, using tables, desks, walls, doors, drawers, or whatever space is available.

Pflum and Waterman (1974) conclude that every learning center regardless of its purpose must have the following components:

Directions They should be simply and clearly stated; they may be written or taped.

Purpose The purpose of a center must be obvious. Not only must the students understand what the center is for, but also what is expected of them while they are participating in it.

Content This is why the center exists. The center can use manipulative materials, media, books, other people, etc., to communicate the content.

Activities There should be a variety of ways the students can apply what they have learned.

Evaluation This allows the student to let you know what they have learned. Evaluation can be simple or involved and does not have to be limited to testing alone. Some centers do not require any evaluation other than the student's reaction to working there. When evaluation is centered on growth, record keeping can become a joint effort of the teacher and the learner. Evaluation used as an aid instead of a threat can enhance the learning process while contributing to the positive self-concept of the student.

Kaplan, Kaplan, Madsen, and Taylor (1973) suggest that record keeping can serve many functions:

Records can show the parents what the students have accomplished in the classroom, where they are growing, and in what ways they have yet to grow.

Records help students develop the responsibility for planning and following through with a course of study. Students are made more aware of their own learning processes, accomplishments, and other learning possibilities.

Records provide the teacher with a permanent account of the student's progress and allow for assessment and further planning. Records provide a way of sharing the student's growth.

According to Voight (1971) learning centers should:

1. Actively involve each student.
2. Confront the student with essential skill-developing activities.
3. Tempt students to stretch their imaginations and creativity in the pursuit of divergent reactions to problems that offer no one solution.
4. Provoke the interest of students so that they find themselves engrossed in processes or systems of fundamental significance such as cause and effect, etc.
5. Immerse students in conditions that will lead to the development of concepts or generalizations inferred from facts.
6. Tease the student's sense of humor.
7. Team students with one or more classmates in a joint-action task where cooperation and interaction present opportunities for the development of human relations skills.
8. Offer free or controlled choices from among many challenging and intriguing locations around the classroom.
9. Intensify learning activities through the use of listening and recording devices or with viewing and projection equipment, or both.

To establish a learning center Hassett and Weisberg (1972) suggest a sequence of activities that, with modification, may be useful to you:

1. Plan carefully for the selection of materials and for the organization of the students.
   How many groups can I handle comfortably?
   What materials will interest my students and are on their level of operation?
   What materials are readily available?
   What do I hope the students will accomplish through the use of the materials?
   What specific outcomes do I anticipate?
2. Systematically help your students develop a working relationship with manipulative materials.
   Exposure #1—Go through the routines of choosing a material, working with it for a short time, and cleaning up. End with a group evaluation of the students' performances, their feelings, and their problems.
   Exposure #2—Set up routines for changing materials and provisions so that students can move about easily from group to group. Establishing these routines requires discussion, demonstration, and acting out so that students can learn to work well together.

Exposure #3—Give the students the responsibility of recording their own progress and responses to the program (e.g. individual logs, cooperative stories, charts, graphs, pictures, diagrams, etc.).

Exposure #4—Continue practicing individualized learning skills; deal with any problems cooperatively as they occur.

3. Physically rearrange your room.
4. Plan continuous and consistent evaluation of the students' progress.

Voight (1971) suggests the following steps to continue your success:

Before students begin working discuss with the entire class the learning center's assignments; indicate at which centers students can work together.

Stop from time to time to have conferences with students who have common problems; make group experience assignments based on the outcome of those discussions.

On a chart list group experiences that students have a choice of doing.

Plan total group programs that require group interaction.

Assume school-wide responsibilities and organize these responsibilities as a group project.

Some sources for ideas and purposes for learning centers are: Allen (1968); Christianson (1969); Voight (1971); Kaplan, Kaplan, Madsen, and Taylor (1973); Kahl and Gas (1974); and Kaplan, Kaplan, Madsen, and Gould (1975). Books for helping change the educational environment and learning spaces in secondary schools include: James (1968); Mason (1972); Truesdell and Newman (1975); and Beach (1977).

10:00—10:20 Sharing   This small group activity allows students to discuss how what they have investigated relates to the findings of others. Synthesis and multidisciplinary thinking result from such discussions.

10:20—10:45 Outdoor skill building

10:45—11:45 Synthesis and extensions   Building on the academic lessons presented earlier in the day gives students an opportunity to deepen and broaden their understanding of the content. All four areas of function will be a part of the lesson; centers and small groups may be used for this activity.

11:45—12:00 Sharing with experts   Students are given the opportunity to share an area of expertise with their peers. Dates for presentations are planned in advance and only students who wish to become experts may choose to share.

12:00—12:40 Lunch

12:40—1:00 Thinking games/experiments   During this time students are encouraged to stretch their minds and explore unknown areas. Teachers present strategies for developing more effective thinking.

1:00—2:15 Arts, music, drama, wilderness   Discussion of the wilderness class can be found at the end of this chapter in *Beyond the Classroom*.

2:15—2:30 Closing

An open learning structure will utilize enormous quantities of materials because of the diversity of interests that must be met, the limitless learning that occurs, and the students' need to explore directly their environment. This demand for materials should not be seen as a burden but as another way to enrich student learning

Cross-age classrooms should have readily available materials for a variety of subject areas.

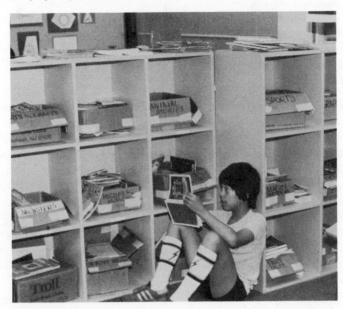

experiences. The following are possible resources for class materials:

your school
junk (send out notes to parents, other teachers, community businesses)
construction sites
lists of free and inexpensive materials (these lists can be found in bookstores, teacher
    journals, and libraries)
school and office supply catalogs (many of these materials can be duplicated using scrap
    material)
flea markets
the telephone company
the beach
nature conservation clubs
· docks and shipyards
the electric company
billboard companies
radio shops
cabinet makers
military bases
state surplus warehouses
landscape contractors
bakeries
grain and feed stores
appliance stores
butcher shops
florists
park service

railroad yards

newspapers

electronic supply houses

crates (these can be obtained from foreign car importers, motorcycle shops, window companies, mattress companies, fruit and vegetable growers, or any shippers)

Creating the Environment for Secondary Learners (12–17)

Adolescence is a particularly challenging period of growth. Transitions are occurring in every area of the lives of these students. Some of these youngsters' goals include achieving independence, discovering their identity, establishing personal values and philosophy, developing self-esteem, exploring and accepting their sexuality, developing meaningful interpersonal relationships, and exploring reality structures through use of personal experience. These ambitions along with an intense physical transition make this a very dramatic and important phase of life. If ever a student needs empowerment it is at this time.

At NAS the Cross Age Program includes students age 6 through 16. The choice of classes and learning experiences in this setting are based not on age but rather on the level of experience and ability of the learners. Age, as we have seen in Chapter 2, has little to do with learning.

The typical secondary school setting makes it difficult to achieve the individualization and flexibility needed for Integrative Education. Not only are high schools

Secondary school settings must allow for individualization and flexibility in order to provide successful integrative education.

*Effective secondary school environments have a two- or three-
period academic core, set up centers or areas, and use flexible
grouping to allow students to learn.*

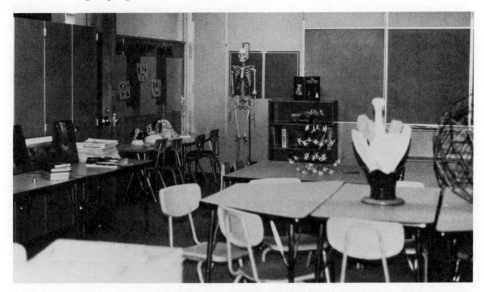

organized by age, they also present separate disciplines in 45–55 minute time blocks. While most of the national reports on American high schools in the 1980s suggest using multidisciplinary learning and doing away with the short 55 minute modules, such reorganization has yet to occur. Until such a dramatic change takes place it may be possible to achieve the flexibility needed for optimal learning in at least a couple of ways:

1. Team with other teachers. Find one or two colleagues within your discipline or in allied fields who would like to pool their time blocks and students. Studying an area of history from several perspectives (the music of the period compared to today's music, the science of the period and its evolution into today's technology, the language as used then and now) would make a most interesting and challenging project for both students and teachers. The teaching team might develop a two or three period academic core, set up centers or areas, and use flexible grouping to allow students to learn. Education would then transcend district requirements for the grade level and serve to enrich the student's learning skills.
2. Transform a self-contained classroom into a laboratory. The information given on the Cross Age Program's daily schedule (pages 75–78) can help decentralize any subject area.

    Other possibilities for creating flexibility within the traditional high school system might be: flexible scheduling, interdisciplinary courses or themes, community-based internships, special-topic courses, and special study centers.

Advances in brain/mind research make the same demands for change on the secondary teacher as they make on the elementary teacher. While cognitive development is important at the secondary level, the other brain functions—feeling, intuition, and physical sensing—are just as critical to optimal learning and development as they ever were. The Integrative Education Model and the environment in which it can best be implemented do not change. What does change is the way the implementation appears. Just as a decentralized laboratory setting in language arts looks different from a science laboratory, so the individualized setting looks different when a school has a core curriculum or a six period day.

THE RESPONSIVE LEARNING ENVIRONMENT— A CHECKLIST

You know you have a Responsive Learning Environment when:

1. the emotional climate is warm and accepting;
2. the class operates within clear guidelines decided upon cooperatively;
3. the students are deeply involved in what they are doing;
4. student activities, products, and ideas are reflected abundantly around the classroom;
5. there is cooperative planning between teacher, student, and parents;
6. the teacher bases instruction on each individual student and his or her interaction with the materials and equipment;
7. for assessment purposes the teacher closely observes specific work or concerns of the student and asks immediate questions;
8. the teacher keeps notes and histories of each student's intellectual, emotional, physical, and intuitive development;
9. the teacher keeps a collection of the student's work for use in evaluating development;
10. the teacher uses evaluation as information for the student and to guide the student's instruction;
11. the teaching day is divided into large blocks of time within which students and teacher cooperatively determine their own routine;
12. students work at various activities both individually and in small groups;
13. many activities go on simultaneously;
14. the teacher groups students for lessons directed at specific needs;
15. students voluntarily group and regroup themselves;
16. there is a diversity of materials, including many levels and manipulatives (concrete materials that can, by the student's handling, create a clearer understanding of abstract ideas, e.g. objects to be grouped to clarify set theory);
17. materials are readily accessible to the students;
18. students work directly with manipulative materials;
19. the environment includes materials developed by the teacher;
20. the environment includes materials developed and supplied by the students;
21. books are supplied in diversity and profusion;
22. students use "books" written by classmates;
23. all students have their own personal storage space (not necessarily their own desks);
24. students can use other areas of the building, the yard, and the community for learning;
25. the teacher expects students to use time productively and expects that their work and learning will be of value.

The teacher is central to creating the environment, and sets the tone as well as establishing the organization, the sense of coherency, and the attitude toward learning. The teacher helps define personal and class goals and helps students find motivation for learning. Aspy and Bahler (1975) have found that it is the teacher's concept of self that affects the achievement of students even more than will their own concept of self. The teacher who wishes to establish a Responsive Learning Environment must be able to

> assess the level of ability, interests, and needs of the students;
> develop the scope and sequence of what is to be taught;
> plan a variety of materials and levels of content;
> plan with choice (see Chapter 6);
> plan with students;
> present a variety of levels and activities using strategies for facilitating learning (see Chapter 9);
> evaluate a variety of levels and activities;
> share responsibility for learning with the students (see Chapter 6).

Students taking part in the Responsive Learning Environment will also need skills if optimal learning is to take place. These students must demonstrate an ability to

> plan learning experiences, both independently and with the teacher or peer;
> work in a decentralized environment;
> learn in small groups;
> learn independently;
> use resources and appropriate equipment;
> make choices;
> self-assess and evaluate;
> conference with the teacher;
> share the responsibility for learning;
> use the tools of the Integrative Education Model.

In summary, the emotional-social environment must provide the students with the support and safety needed for them to feel empowered, motivated, cared for, and caring, feelings that will allow them to become truly effective learners. The physical environment must provide for large and small groupings as well as room for individuals to learn. The environment should designate spaces for a variety of materials and content at a range of ability levels. It should use color, sound, and texture to support the learning process. While Integrative Education can take place without the support of the Responsive Learning Environment, the use of such an environment will make the job of the teacher and the learner much easier, more efficient, and far more effective.

BEYOND THE CLASSROOM

When learning is extended beyond the classroom into the community or nearby nature areas, Integrative Education becomes very natural and effective. The learning expedition, which is a step beyond the standard field trip, can yield enormous educational benefits. By planning and participating in such overnights or extended field trips the class becomes a cooperative unit and gains experiences not available in a classroom setting.

Extending learning beyond the classroom makes Integrative Education natural and effective.

The learning expedition, a step beyond the standard field trip, can yield enormous educational benefits.

The following unit has been carefully designed by Toby Manzanares, team leader for the Cross Age Program (6–16) at the New Age School and a science teacher at Schurr High School in Montebello, California. This set of activities allows teachers and students to share in an outdoor learning experience and provides an excellent example of Integrative Education.

The Learning Expedition

Purpose and expected outcomes: Allowing students to plan the learning expedition from beginning to end gives them an opportunity to experience the natural consequences of their planning and organization. This is learning at its best. Students are also provided with endless opportunities for leadership at all levels and gain self-esteem from having taken responsibilities and personal risks. The success of this endeavor is made possible by allowing students to operate within a high level of trust, interacting openly and honestly. In such an environment it is possible to accomplish rather impressive goals.

There are four broad objectives Manzanares has for organizing learning expeditions:

1. to support cognitive growth in the content area(s);
2. to further develop and reinforce throughout the experience student thinking skills such as inferring, analyzing, hypothesizing, predicting, verifying, and integrating;
3. to develop an environment wherein the discussion of values and attitudes is natural and productive;
4. to provide experiential activities that support personal growth, trust, openness, responsibility, independence, interdependence, honesty, integrity, self-confidence, and the personal commitment to excellence.

Time involved:

Pre-trip—10 hours (this can vary depending on your objectives and destination)
Trip—two days, one night (this also may vary)
Post-trip—1 to 30 hours depending on follow-up and spin-off activities

Material needed: See materials list at the end of the chapter

Preferred structure/organization: Total group, small group, flexible

Teaching function: Organizer, facilitator

Procedure: Manzanares uses an interdisciplinary approach. The content includes archaeology, art, astronomy, botany, ecology, geology, geography, history, journal writing, marine biology, nutrition, psychology, and zoology. Depending on the objectives for the learning expedition some areas of content can be deleted and others can be added.

Step 1: The teacher selects the objectives and content for the learning expedition as well as a location within two hours driving time of the school. This location must have the following characteristics:

a. an interesting interpretive program, historical monument, nature center, nature trail, and/or museum;

Effective "beyond the classroom" experiences transport students to community and nature areas.

b. a campground with adequate group facilities, e.g. tables, bathrooms, water, telephone, etc;

c. aesthetic qualities, e.g. a scenic canyon, beach, state or national park, mountains, or any other natural setting.

Manzanares recommends that the teacher initially select a site that is the subject of previously developed written material. This will make it easier to reproduce material for students without necessitating a large amount of original research. Most state and national parks have a park headquarters office that carries material developed by rangers and naturalists about that specific area.

Step 2: The organizing teacher should personally visit the site and build a file on its potential. During the pre-trip visit the teacher should

a. look for a Visitor's Center in the area or park. Often this facility will have regularly scheduled programs both at the Center and at the campground that might be relevant to the needs of your group. Be sure to sit in on any programs given and stay after to ask questions that will further the development of your site file.

b. talk with campground office clerks, park rangers, naturalists, park superintendents, and anyone else specifically connected with the site.

    c. ask for brochures, handouts, lists of area flora and fauna, trail guides, park regulations, instructions for group reservations, books, pamphlets, prepared slides, and maps of the area.

    d. determine if park rangers or naturalists can be reserved to speak on selected topics to your group. Inform these officials that you are a teacher and that you plan to bring a group of students to study the area. Often rangers will be most helpful in organizing material and resources for your school use.

    e. take a camera loaded with slide film. Put together a photo-journal of the area; take notes or dictate the information into a cassette tape recorder as you go along.

Step 3: Based on the resources and material acquired on the pre-trip visit to the site prepare handouts for the first meeting of your students regarding the learning expedition. Organize the slides taken on your pre-trip visit into a presentation both for your students and for a later meeting with their parents. Include in the handout:

    a. a tentative calendar that includes all relevant dates from the parent orientation meeting to the post-trip follow-up meetings;

    b. a parent information sheet with an invitation to come to a meeting explaining the learning expedition (this meeting is mandatory for parents of students planning to participate).

Step 4: Make an appointment to share with your principal all your information regarding the trip. Invite your administrator to your room to see the slide presentation and to review the tentative calendar. High school teachers may need to consult the administrator responsible for the academic calendar so that the dates for your trip can be cleared.

It is important for your administrator to be aware of your extensive planning and organization. Do this by investigating the forms required by the district for this type of project. Included here is a list of forms required by the Los Angeles, Montebello, and Pasadena Unified School Districts. Your administration may not require all of these forms, but these give you an example of what might be expected. Sample forms can be found at the end of this chapter.

    a. Board Report—requests authorization to accompany a group of students on an over-night field trip. This report must be submitted quite early, usually six to eight weeks in advance.

    b. Trip Slip and Liability Waiver—this form usually includes an emergency medical authorization to be signed by the parents.

    c. Transportation Waiver—to be used when students are to be transported in vehicles other than school buses.

    d. Irregular Program—a form for secondary level students to be signed by other teachers on the students' schedules thus informing teachers of their students' upcoming absence from classes.

    e. Roster of Participants—this is often required by the secondary school attendance office.

    f. Department of Motor Vehicles Report on Drivers—the Montebello Unified Schools requires this form to alert the District to drivers with a bad driving record. This step is required only when private transportation is to be used.

Step 5: Meet with your principal. If you need moral support invite a colleague who is helping you with the planning.

a. Present the objectives of the learning expedition (see *Purpose*) and relate these to your school or classroom goals.

b. Discuss your rationale for selecting the site and then present a short slide presentation of the area. Point out the academic advantages of the trip.

c. Clear the calendar dates.

d. Discuss the required forms.

e. Inquire about a target date for the Board Report.

f. Inquire about the district's policy on "Tripster" insurance. Although not mandatory, most district office administrators are greatly relieved if the teacher arranges for the additional coverage. This coverage is quite inexpensive (approximately fifty cents per student per day), and the extra effort on your part communicates to the administrator that you are aware and supportive of his or her needs.

g. Discuss the supervision ratio. Manzanares recommends the following schedule:

    One adult to one child for kindergarten through grade 2

    One to three adults for grade 3 through grade 5

    One to six adults for grade 6 through grade 8

    1 to 10 adults for high school

Adult supervision can come from a variety of sources including interested parents, campus aides, other interested teachers on campus, retired teachers, community volunteers, relatives of the students, personal friends, and responsible colleagues of the parents.

h. Discuss the transportation options available. If funding is available within the school or district budget, then request a school bus for your trip and inquire about the procedure for ordering it. If no funding is available, then suggest private transportation or discuss fundraising activities to pay for a bus.

i. Request substitute coverage for your classes while you are on the field trip. If there is no money in the school budget for substitutes, then plan the trip on a weekend so that a substitute is not required.

j. Discuss your plans to raise funds to pay for related costs while in the field. Many state education codes require that the student not be charged for admissions or other items related to school field trips; however, most codes allow for students to pay for their food expenses while on a trip. There is a wide range of possibilities for raising funds: jogathons, food sales, seasonal sales like flowers in February and mistletoe at Christmastime. Manzanares has organized "hikeajogawalkabackpackathons" to help pay for mileage incurred by the participant both before and during the trip. With this technique needed money can be collected in advance.

At the follow-up meeting with your administrator be sure to:

a. submit copies of your itinerary and student roster to all relevant administrative and office personnel;

b. inquire as to your administrator's preference for a daily status report while you are in the field. If one is requested, arrange an appropriate time to make the telephone connection. This is simply a matter of courtesy and most principals want to be contacted only if there is a change in plans.

Step 6: Plan an orientation meeting with your class and use the relevant items from Step 5. In addition give the slide presentation to create enthusiasm and to provide clarification of what you expect. Distribute the handouts mentioned earlier and discuss with your class the importance of the parent meeting.

Step 7: Send home with each student an announcement about the parent meeting. Include on the announcement a tear-off portion that the parent can sign and return. As a courtesy to working parents make sure to give sufficient notice. Two to three weeks should be plenty of time.

The parent meeting is essential to the success of your trip. Manzanares makes the meeting mandatory (at least one parent present for each student) although he allows those not able to attend to speak with him by telephone. Holding an alternate meeting is another way to provide for those who find it impossible to attend the first meeting.

Sound planning of this event will help avoid excessive parental concern. Your goal is to communicate to the parents the extensive nature of your planning and your reliability as a responsible professional. Careful preparation for this meeting will show the parents that the health and safety of their children are your priorities and that you have given a great deal of time and effort to meeting this concern. Manzanares suggests listing the concerns you would have as a parent about any teacher planning to take your son or daughter on an overnight trip. Many parents would not authorize their children to go on a trip with a teacher they did not trust completely. Manzanares feels that this is a reasonable attitude.

The parent meeting is also your best opportunity to acquire a large body of volunteers for tasks that must be accomplished before, during, and after the trip.

Step 8. Prepare handouts for the parent meeting. Give special attention to these because parents will view them as representative of the quality of your planning and organization. Some suggested handouts for the parent meeting are:

a. A parent information sheet to include the trip itinerary and a day-by-day, activity-by-activity description of the trip (see end of chapter). Manzanares suggests including appropriate telephone numbers that parents might use to contact their child in an emergency.
b. The calendar and schedule of activities leading up to and following the trip (see end of chapter).
c. A list of equipment and clothing required for the trip (see end of chapter).
d. Volunteer sign-up forms.

Step 9: Hold the parent meeting. A suggested agenda:

1. Welcome/refreshments (arrange for volunteer students to be responsible for these as part of their contribution to the organization and execution of the experience).
2. Rationale (see *Purpose*).
3. Goals (academic, affective, physical, and intuitive).
4. Calendar.
5. Equipment and clothing list.
6. Organization of parent fundraising committee.

Step 10: Develop a pre-trip countdown schedule, but use it only as a reference. Be prepared to modify the schedule to meet specific situations.

Give students who plan to attend responsibility for the completion of the tasks on this schedule, even if this approach takes more time. If the group is very young the teacher or other adults may need to complete some or all of these tasks, but the experience of contributing to the expedition is an important one and helps give the student a greater sense of satisfaction and self-esteem.

Allowing students to plan their learning expedition gives them an opportunity to experience the natural consequences of their planning and organization.

Organize task completion committees. Each committee can be chaired by a student selected by the teacher or elected by the members of the committee. Every participant must be on at least one committee. One way to fill the committees is by simply setting the maximum number of students for each committee and then allowing the students to self-select. Committees often needed are:

- *a.* Organizing
- *b.* Transportation
- *c.* Communication
- *d.* Food/menu/shopping
- *e.* Documentary
    1. photography (prints and slides)
    2. cinematography (super 8 mm movie film)
    3. soundtrack (interviews and theme music)
- *f.* First aid
- *g.* Equipment
- *h.* Book
- *i.* Student activities
- *j.* Mobile library

Each committee then meets to develop their needs and responsibilities as well as a timeline indicating when their tasks will be completed.

Form 4.1. is an example of a countdown schedule the teacher may wish to use once task committees have been assigned.

Step 11: Conduct a chaperone meeting. It is essential that support persons (parents, teachers, and other volunteers) participating in the trip completely understand

Form 4.1. Example countdown schedule

Task	Person in Charge	Due Date	Completed
1. Reservation: Campground			
2. Reservation: Museum/tour, etc.			
3. Appointment for guest speaker			
4. Guide for nature walk			
5. Plan Menu			
6. Select food			
7. Purchase food			
8. Acquire vehicles			
9. Acquire drivers			
10. Chart mileage to determine costs			
11. Purchase film			
12. Purchase recording tape			
13. Copy book articles			
14. Make field guide			
15. Raise funds			
16. Acquire chaperones			
17. Organize food groups			
18. Check group equipment			
19. Check individual equipment			

your goals and teaching philosophy. To insure that these helpers understand the importance of your expectations hold a meeting at least a week prior to departure. The following are items to consider with your trip staff.

1. The students are learners that need to be respected and nourished. Everything that the staff does should reflect this approach. Empowering Language (see Chapter 6) is important for group members to use and will build self-esteem in the students (give the parent group an example).
2. The student should be allowed to experience the process rather than have a parent show the child how it should be done. If support personnel know ahead of time that the students need to be the "doers," then even the older more experienced hands will help the child "do" rather than "take over" what the child is learning.
3. The primary focus of the learning expedition is the students and their learning experience. Adults tend to form groups that the students may see as exclusive. Early morning coffee klatches, for example, can easily be avoided by communicating to the adults the importance of the student.
4. Adults and students must carry an equal share of the daily tasks and duties. Students become keenly aware of this support from the teacher and the parents. This approach empowers the learner and contributes significantly to the success of the expedition.
5. For maximum supervision the adults should sleep in the same area as the student group. Manzanares does not allow the use of tents on the expeditions as supervision is far easier when all are sleeping in the open with sleeping bags. Tube tents are brought in case of inclement weather.
6. All adult participants must hear all of the instructions given to the students all of the time. At regular intervals during the expedition Manzanares convenes a trust circle. Each person on the expedition is to attend; information is then given out and each person must acknowledge that information before the circle is dismissed.

Step 12: Discuss with students how the trip will support course content.

As time for the expedition approaches the teacher discusses with the students how the trip will support the content of the course. Students are expected to record and evaluate their experiences. Manzanares typically has his students keep journals throughout the experience and shows them how to keep one before the trip begins. The journal is likely to include information about the various sites to be visited; places to record the thoughts for the day; puzzles, drawings, poems or other forms of artistic expression; and introductions to lessons to be used on-site. Group journals may result from the material developed by the students in these journals. For field studies students can keep a Naturalist's Field Study Notebook (see end of chapter for a sample journal).

Prior to the trip each student selects and researches a subject that will be a part of the content of the learning expedition. The student is asked to write an article and prepare a five to ten minute lesson to be presented at the appropriate time on the trip. Bound copies of their research articles are then given to the school library and a card is inserted into the card catalog so that other students can share in their expertise.

In the days prior to the trip the teacher must continue to build the group's trust. This trust will take the place of other forms of discipline and will create the best atmosphere for learning and growth. Rules and parameters should be set by the students and the teacher together; when any student violates an agreement while on the expedition a trust group can be called and the group can brainstorm solutions to the problem at hand. The teacher must stress the need for positive, safe behavior during the expedition as the possibility of future trips will depend upon their behavior on this expedition. The teacher must inform the students that the administration has been promised on their behalf that all caution will be exercised. Students should work to eliminate any problems before they occur so that the safety of each person on the trip is assured.

Step 13: Assign staff responsibilities.

Finally staff members are assigned specific responsibilities. Persons are needed to arrange and monitor

1. all equipment and transportation. This includes arranging for all stoves, ice chests, and other equipment needed for the expedition. One important piece of equipment that must be included is a good, complete first aid kit. This staff member is responsible for arranging bus transportation or assigning students to drivers if a car caravan is used. Any and all transportation and equipment are the responsibility of this staff member.
2. all food for the trip. This staff member can supervise any menu planning done by the students. If the students are younger then the menu plan is the staff member's total responsibility. Food purchasing can be done by teams of students under this staff member's supervision. Again, if the students are too young the staff member must be responsible for purchasing all food.
3. all events to take place on the expedition. This includes arranging museum and special event tickets, campsite tickets (if needed), and extra activities if some pre-planned event is not available or must be cancelled at the last minute. It is the responsibility of this staff member to be sure all appropriate forms and trip slips are on file prior to departure.
4. educational center activities. This staff member must locate appropriate sites for the placement of each activity and is responsible for all learning activity materials to be brought on the expedition.

A typical learning expedition might follow this daily schedule:

6:00—6:30 Choice of quiet games, books (a small, selective lending library is included in the equipment provided by the appropriate staff person), puzzles, etc.
6:30—7:00 Breakfast
7:00—7:30 Trust circle, exercises, daily schedule
7:30—8:45 Morning hike
8:45—9:00 Trust circle, choice of centers
9:00—11:00 Center activities (approximately nine centers are brought on an expedition)
11:00—11:30 Trust circle, small group review of morning activities
11:30—12:00 Lunch
12:00—12:30 Student and staff recreation
12:30—12:45 Trust circle, afternoon choices of activities
12:45—2:00 Hike and waterfall play
2:00—2:30 Trust circle, choice of centers
2:30—4:00 Center activities
4:00—5:00 Relays, volleyball, etc.
5:00—5:30 Dinner
5:30—6:30 Nature walk, games
6:30—8:00 Campfire, skits, songs
8:00—9:00 Snacks, quiet talk
9:00 Lights out
9:00—11:00 Staff sharing, planning at campfire (after students are asleep)

The schedule can include student-originated activities but no "free" time. This schedule is posted for all to see and is given to parents prior to the trip as part of the information packet.

On the day of the trip the students and the staff gather in a trust circle, count off, and receive any last minute instructions. Students are given their driver assignments, and from that moment on both the driver and the assigned student must know each other's whereabouts at all times. They are responsible for each other.

The teacher is the expedition leader and as such makes sure that the experience of beginning the trip is a very positive one. This establishes a mind set for students and staff that Manzanares calls "a positive cascade."

The initial trust circle meets before the students leave school for the trip. Students are then reminded that their trust is expected and that they are being trusted. A commitment to the agreements of the trip is asked for and given by each participant. In addition, Manzanares asks that each student know something about three people by the time of the evening campfire. Sharing this information will be a part of the first evening group meeting.

Immediately upon arrival at the site a trust circle is called and a count-off or attendance is taken. The teacher discusses the schedule, sets the physical perimeters of the site, and reviews the agreements. Some of the agreements usually established are: students must have an adult accompanying them whenever they leave the camp perimeters; they must be in attendance at each circle meeting; when on hikes there will be a "point" person and a "sweep" person (no one is ever to get ahead of the point or behind the sweep); and other rules as needed.

Overnight expeditions develop the class into a cooperative unit and enable children to gain experiences not available in a classroom setting.

Manzanares ends the circle by directing students to do something nice for someone else anonymously before noon and write it in their personal journal. They are to include some commentary on how doing it made them feel. With this beginning the learning expedition is off to a very good start.

Step 14: Be aware of the following important areas during elementary-level trips:

1. Some younger children tend to wriggle out of their sleeping bags, and it is your responsibility to survey the children at intervals to tuck them back in.

2. A small number of very young children still may be experiencing an occasional wet bed. This is a more complicated situation while camping than at home. Escort children who have such a problem to the restroom immediately before bedding down and again early in the morning; if necessary awaken them so as to avoid possible embarrassment.

3. One of the agreements required of participants of any age is that they stay within the "in bounds" area at all times unless they have personally notified the group leader. It is particularly important to closely monitor younger children. One useful technique is to keep a record to evaluate how each student handles responsibility. Give each student five points for arriving on time to meetings announced in advance or for completing tasks on time. Students with the lowest totals may need closer supervision as they tend to lose track of time or of what is expected of them. Beginning this responsibility log in advance of the trip enables the teacher to identify the most and least responsible students. On occasion it may be necessary to make alternative arrangements for a child who cannot guarantee abiding by the "in bounds" agreement. Camping with this type of child can be risky; letting this child stay at school with other teachers or requiring a parent on the trip will help insure that the experiences away from school of all of the children will be the safest possible.

Be aware of the following important areas during secondary-level trips:

1. Though the responsibility rating is extremely useful with secondary-level students additional techniques are helpful. Maximize supervision at night as romantic involvements are possible with older students. Design the sleeping arrangements in advance, and have the entire group sleep in an area roughly the size of a normal classroom, thus providing the teacher with a direct line of sight. Separate male and female sleeping zones require double the supervision. Without privacy, serious romance can be curtailed.
2. Allow a "one-hour solo." This has been a popular and meaningful activity for older students. Each student personally selects a place within a well-defined zone at least 50 yards away from the next-closest person. With only a journal and a pencil the student can experience the rare opportunity of being completely alone in an aesthetic natural environment. Urban children have a greater need for this kind of peaceful experience. The products that often result from this activity are poetry, art, or other forms of personal expression that are sometimes poignant and consistently impressive.
3. Secondary students are intensively philosophical and often desperately in search of sound perspectives from adults they deeply respect. Informal talks around a small campfire often lead to discussions about trust, honesty, ethics, and moral action. Students frequently ask very personal questions that are extremely relevant to their world and that would never surface in the classroom. Healthy discussions with an honest adult have the potential of helping young people now experimenting with their roles and actions to make sounder, more thoughtful decisions. In the classroom teachers and students are expected to act in a certain well-defined manner. However, when youngsters live together with their teacher for even just a few days the whole facade of "schoolness" begins to melt away, making room for a much wider frame of reference. In this less restrictive, high-trust environment, students take greater personal risks; often tremendous leaps in personal growth occur in very small periods of time.

Step 15: Debrief and synthesize the experience. Once the learning expedition is over the students are debriefed as a group. For several lunch periods students gather together again to allow an easy reentry into the routine of school. After a few group meetings the students are then willing to go about their usual schedules without needing to hold on any longer.

If the students have put together a group photo-story of the learning expedition they can meet with the staff and parents to share their experience. The principal and members of the School Board should be invited to attend. This makes a very nice closure to the learning expedition and allows the administration and parents to clearly see the benefits of such an experience. The support base has already been developed for the next time such an event is to be planned.

More importantly, the process of making an expedition documentary is a great opportunity for students to further reinforce their thinking skills. For example, students must analyze which slides should go into the documentary, what outcomes are desired, which sequence best yields the desired outcomes, what music best supports the goal of communicating the ambiance of the trip, and which students would make the best narrators. After these decisions are made students can begin the process of writing and editing the script. Rehearsals and a recording session follow. The presentation can then be shown to the group for an evaluation to determine if the desired effect was achieved.

With the information gained during the expedition, students can write, edit, and publish a book or research article. For example, some of Manzanares' students who recently returned from a five-day trip to Yosemite National Park wrote articles on topics such as the geology of the Valley, archaeological sites, recreational impact on the flora and fauna of the region, the discovery of gold in the area, and a history of the Yosemite Indians. These articles became the *Yosemite Book*. This approach keeps the teacher from "force feeding" academic content. Instead, students are enthusiastic about reading research done by their colleagues and are excited about showing their parents a copy of the group effort. Students will do their best because significant others are going to read the product. The teacher edits copy, adding meaningful suggestions rather than grading the work. This type of responsive learning yields learners who are more empowered, intrinsically motivated, and likely to ask, *Where can we go next? How much money will we need to raise? Whose mother or father can chaperone? When . . . ?*

The book project is an excellent way of motivating students to read, research, and write. They do it because it is exciting rather than for the grade they will get. These books become a permanent contribution to the school library and an ongoing source of pride for the students.

In this chapter we have discussed the first key component to the Integrative Education Model. By establishing the Responsive Learning Environment we are developing both the social-emotional and the physical structure that will support optimal learning. Through the use of the learning expedition we can add to that base and enrich the education of all who participate: teachers, parents, and students.

Form 4.1. Sample Board Report Format

<u>MEMORANDUM</u>

November 16, 1984

To: John Cook, Superintendent
Via: Dr. Julian Lopez
From: James Douglas
Subject: Marine Biology Learning Expedition (field study)

Thirty students from Schurr High School currently enrolled in Biology have the opportunity to intensively study the biology and natural history of Morro Bay intertidal zone and associated environs from January 9 through January 13, 1985 (Wednesday through Sunday). Accommodations will be made at official state campgrounds. The approach is interdisciplinary. Anthropology, psychology, ecology, geography, astronomy and biology are all included to develop and apply skills in observing, classifying, comparing/contrasting, generalizing, inferring, analyzing, hypothesizing, predicting and verifying the human environment.

Transportation will be provided by private automobiles driven by parent volunteers who will also assist in supervision of the group along with two faculty sponsors (one male and one female). The group will be accompanied by their Biology teacher, a consultant in science and outdoor field studies programs.

Funding is being provided by student fundraising and student body funds. Emergency release forms will be signed by parents and carried on the trip. Student participation is

(Form 4.1. *continued*)

by application and final selection will be made by December 21, 1984. This finalized list of participants will be forwarded to the Board at this time as required.

We recommend adoption of the following motion:

> That the Board of Education approve a special study trip (learning expedition) for thirty Schurr High School students and their advisors to Morro Bay, California, December 12 through 16, 1984, to further extend their academic background in Biology.

Form 4.2. Sample registration form

REGISTRATION FORM
MEDICAL DATA FORM
PARENT CONSENT

Student Name_____ Grade_____

Address_____

Age_____ Birthdate: Month_____ Day_____ Year_____ Telephone:_____

MEDICAL DATA: IF YOU ANSWER YES TO ANY QUESTION BELOW,
PLEASE SPECIFY ON THE REVERSE SIDE OF THIS FORM.

1. Does the applicant have any severe medical problems? (asthma, allergy to drugs, heart trouble, epilepsy, diabetes, physical handicaps, or dietary restrictions)   yes_____ no_____

2. Is the applicant taking any medication?   yes_____ no_____

3. Should there be any limits on the applicant's physical activity?   yes_____ no_____

4. Has the applicant had any medical illness in the last three years?   yes_____ no_____

5. Is the applicant currently under doctor's care?   yes_____ no_____

6. May we contact the doctor for medical reports? (use the next line)   yes_____ no_____

Doctor's Name_____ Phone:_____

Address_____

7. Is the applicant covered by medical insurance?   yes_____ no_____

Name of company_____

If Medi-Cal, please give ID numbers and have applicant bring current card on trip so that medical care can be billed at time of treatment.   ID number_____

Date of last complete physical examination_____

Date of last Tetanus Toxoid injection_____

(Form 4.2. *continued*)

PARENT CONSENT

If your son or daughter is below the legal age of consent (18), the law requires that we have your permission to give medical service should the need arise.

I authorize medical examination and treatment as may be deemed advisable by the physician in attendance. For minor illnesses or injuries, the Wilderness School adult chaperone will attempt to contact me before my child leaves the medical office. For major illnesses or injuries, the adult chaperone will attempt to contact me before the institution of treatment, unless urgent treatment demands otherwise. If I cannot be reached, I authorize the attending physician to act as medical judgment may dictate.

I also agree to assume any financial responsibility for this care.

This consent shall be in effect from _____ to _____ 1985.

It is hereby agreed that (teacher's name)_____
shall not be held responsible for any injuries which might occur to the applicant at any time or at any place.

Parent/Guardian signature_____ Date_____

Printed signature_____

Telephone number:
home ( )_____ work ( )_____

In case of emergency, please contact the person below if parent/guardian cannot be reached.

Name_____ relationship_____

Telephone:
home ( )_____ work ( )_____

RETURN THIS FORM BY_____

Form 4.3. Sample liability waiver

LIABILITY STATEMENTS

1. As the parent or guardian of the named student or students, I do hereby waive all claims against the Montebello Unified School District, Directors, Organizers, Chaperones, or any other staff member in the event of injury, accident, illness, or death during or by reason of the_____
_____

2. I fully understand that the students are expected to totally abstain from the use of alcoholic beverages, hallucinogenic drugs and marijuana. The directors of the trip reserve the right to discontinue a student's participation in the trip if their (the student) attitude and behavior is incompatible with the ideals and spirit of the trip. If behavior is deemed uncorrectable by the directors, the parents will be informed by telephone or wire and the student will be sent home at the *parents'* expense.

(Form 4.3. *continued*)

I (WE) HAVE READ AND FULLY UNDERSTAND ALL OF THE FOREGOING STATEMENTS.
I (WE) ACCEPT ALL FINANCIAL AND LIABILITY RESPONSIBILITIES AS THEY ARE
STATED.

Dated this_____ day of _____, 1978

_____   _____
        Student's Signature   Parent(s) or Guardian Signature

Form 4.4. Sample transportation waiver

Unified School District
TRANSPORTATION WAIVER FORM

Permission is granted for_____

as a part of his class work in_____
                                              (course)
at _____ High School to participate in the following

school sponsored field trip/s or excursion/s: _____

_____

during the period of: _____

Since no school district transportation is provided, I further authorize my child to use
the following mode of transportation to participate in the above events:

_____
                    (ride or drive in a private car)

In so doing, I hereby expressly waive and release any and all rights or claims of any
nature whatsoever I may have against the Oak Valley Unified School District, the Board
of Education of Oak Valley Unified School District, and its members and employees,
arising out of, in connection with, or resulting from, the above school activities.

_____   _____
Date   Signature of Student

                                         _____
                                         Signature of Father

                                         _____
                                         Signature of Mother

                                         _____
                                         Signature of Guardian or other person
                                         (If signed by Guardian or other person, explain
                                         on reverse side how custody was acquired.)

Form 4.5. Sample irregular program form

To the teachers of:_____

Dear Colleague,

    The student here named has been selected to participate in a unique though somewhat demanding learning experience that will with your approval extend the intensive learning opportunity over a period of five days. The Morro Bay Learning Expedition is an interdisciplinary learning experience. Participants will study the flora and fauna of Montana de Oro and Morro Bay State Parks. In addition, students will specifically participate in seminars relative to marine biology, archaeology, history, ecology, astronomy and geography.

    I share with you a concern regarding attendance and desire that students not fall behind in their assignments. Scheduled on a daily basis is a two to three hour study session designed so that students will have a quiet environment within which to complete assignments for your classes. Each participant has agreed to request advanced work so that upon their return they will be "in tune" with your class as much as possible.

    I encourage your comments and suggestions. If you have any recommendations for supporting the class work of this participant, I will be happy to do all I can to add my support as a teacher. Thank you for your cooperation. I look forward to working further with you for the benefit of our students.

Respectfully,

Toby Manzanares

Toby Manzanares

Oak Valley High School
IRREGULAR PROGRAM

Name_____ has permission to be excused

from period   1._____   2._____   3._____
                Subject   Subject   Subject

4._____   5._____   6._____   7._____
     Subject   Subject   Subject   Subject

to attend the following: *MORRO BAY LEARNING EXPEDITION*_____ to meet *STUDENT LOUNGE*
                     Meeting or Special Activity   Room or Place

Wednesday, January 9 through   Teacher's Signature, Excusing Student
on *Sunday, January 13, 1985*   1._____   5._____
       Date for Meeting Activity

                            2._____   6._____

*TOBY MANZANARES*_____ 3._____   7._____
   Teacher in Charge of Activity

_____ 4._____
       Office Approval

                          After signing, return to teacher in charge of Activity

Form 4.6. Sample fundraising form

HIKAJOGAWALKABACKATHON

A Fundraising Activity for the Morro Bay Learning Expedition

Students will hike, jog, walk and backpack between Montana de Oro and Morro Bay and throughout the adjacent area covering a minimum of 25 miles in the process of participating in this 5 day study tour.

DONATIONS WILL HELP FUND SCHOLARSHIPS FOR LEARNING EXPEDITIONS

	name	address	amount/mile	total
1				
2				
3				
4				
5				
6				
7				
8				
9				
10				
11				
12				
13				
14				
15				
16				
17				
18				
19				
20				
21				
22				

(Form 4.6. *continued*)

23			
24			
25			
26			
27			
28			
29			
30			
Wilderness School at Schurr		TOTAL	

Form 4.7. Sample field study notebook

Naturalist's Field Study Notebook

1. Common name:_____

2. Scientific name:_____

_____

3. Description of the environment:

_____

_____

_____

_____

_____

4. Close relatives:_____

_____

_____

5. Notable behavior/feeding habits/notes:

_____

_____

_____

_____

(Form 4.7. *continued*)

_____

_____

_____

_____

_____

Draw or sketch in detail the plant or animal being studied or observed//label all identifiable structures//use top, side, front views

Form 4.8. Sample itinerary

ITINERARY

THE MORRO BAY LEARNING EXPEDITION

WEDNESDAY, JAN. 9, 1985 Day of departure

    Arrive at school—7:30 AM
    Depart from Oak Valley—8:30
    Lunch and Lagoon seminar at U.C. Santa Barbara—11:00
    Arrive at Montana de Oro State Park—2:30 PM
    Camp orientation, afternoon sessions, dinner, evening sessions
    Campfire and summit meeting

THURSDAY, JAN. 10, 1985 Full day of field studies

    Breakfast and a daily briefing—7:00 AM
    Morning field studies and data collection
    Lunch—11:45
    Tidepool analysis and afternoon sessions
    Afternoon sessions, dinner, evening sessions, campfire and summit meeting

(Form 4.8. *continued*)

FRIDAY, JAN. 11, 1985 Analysis of the Sand Spit and full day hike

Breakfast and briefing—6:30 AM
Early departure for the move to Morro Bay State Park and the day hike analysis of the Sand Spit biological zone
Lunch (to be carried with scientific equipment) on the Sand Spit
Arrive at Morro Bay State Park—4:00 PM
Dinner, evening sessions, campfire and summit meeting

SATURDAY, JAN. 12, 1985 Full day field studies, museum, bird sanctuary, mud flats

Breakfast and briefing—8:00 AM
Marine Biology Museum and Chumash Indian seminars
Lunch on archaeological site focus on Pre-Columbian era
Dig analysis of life zone—intertidal region
Survival celebration dinner, talent show, evening sessions, group interaction discussion

SUNDAY, JAN. 13, 1985 Return trip to Oak Valley—ETA 3:30 PM

Breakfast and briefing 6:30 AM
Break camp, load vehicles and depart by 9:00
Follow-up analysis—Morro Bay and UCSB Lagoon comparison, lunch at Santa Barbara campus
Estimated Time of Arrival in Oak Valley 3:30 PM
Closing activities with a departure of 4:15

Form 4.9. Sample information sheet

Itinerary and Information Sheet
The Morro Bay Learning Expedition

I. Important telephone numbers: (in the event that the group needs to be contacted).

Montana de Oro State Park 805 543-2161
Morro Bay State Park   805 772-2560
San Luis Obispo County Sheriff 805 543-2850 (very responsive to the needs of a school group in an emergency situation)
San Luis Obispo General Hospital 805 543-1500

II. Itinerary:

A. Monday, January 7. All group equipment due at lunch meeting.
B. Tuesday, January 8. Last check of personal equipment.
    Be sure to pack a double meal: a large lunch as well as a large dinner (include drinks).
C. Wednesday, January 9. Day of departure.
    Have a good breakfast!
    Remember to bring:
    a. lunch, dinner, and any necessary items needed for the bus ride in a day pack as luggage will not be accessible.
    b. all your gear in a duffel bag (this is best for this type of trip, although a suitcase or a backpack will do).

(Form 4.9. *continued*)

Lagoon lunch and seminar at the University of California Santa Barbara—about noon.

Arrive at Montana de Oro State Park Campground—about 3:30 PM.

Orientation meeting and activity.

Pre sundown camp set-up and free time.

Spooner's Cove seminar and dinner on the beach.

Trust building activities.

Summit Meeting (Evaluation of the day and the Plan for Tomorrow, music and entertainment, and Crossing Cultural Bridges, campfire, astronomy seminar).

Closing activity or guided fantasy.

D. Thursday, January 10. Bringing up the sun: a celebration @ 6 AM.
  1. Breakfast by 7:00 AM
  2. A Wilderness Drama: Meal prep and clean up responsibilities, or how to avoid the runs.
  3. Day activities to include but not limited to the following list:

a. Group Trust	g. Responsibility	m. On Survival
b. Self Esteem	h. KEEP Visit	n. Solo
c. Value Others	i. Student Activities	o. Botany
d. Interdependence	j. Tidepools/Biology	p. Zoology
e. Openness	k. On Time w/o Time	q. Env. Art
f. Realization	l. History Seminar	r. Scavenger Hunt

  4. Dinner and free time, and talent show rehearsal.
  5. Summit Meeting, campfire, and closing.

E. Friday, January 11. Bringing up the sun for a journey.
  1. Breakfast @ 6:30 AM and packing up the camp, loading.
  2. On leaving it cleaner than when we arrived.
  3. Equipment shuttle to Morro Bay, lunch logistics.
  4. An incredible walk to Morro Bay or "A Fugue in Five Movements."
  5. Lunch on the Sand Spit.
  6. Free time, HOT SHOWERS, camp set up (pre-sunset).
  7. Dinner, summit meeting, closing, moonlight walk.

F. Saturday, January 12. Breakfast @ 8:00 AM.
  1. The Chumash Indians—Archaeology
  2. The Mud Flats or "up to our elbows in _____."
  3. Volcano Walk
  4. The Rookery
  5. An Ancient Oak
  6. An Extraordinary Museum and a film.
  7. Free Time
  8. The Second Solo
  9. Continue Thursday activities.
  10. Wilderness Survivors Outdoor Gourmet Banquet
  11. Talent Show, campfire and summit meeting.
  12. Moonlight Fantasy and closing.

G. Sunday, January 13. Breakfast @ 7:00 AM: The Last Opening.
  1. Clean-up, wash-up, pack-up and
  2. Load-up.
  3. On leaving it better that we've been there.

(Form 4.9. *continued*)

> 4. Depart @ 11:00 AM.
> 5. Santa Barbara Lunch and a last look at the lagoon.
> H. Closing "The Total Group"

Special Note for parents picking up students. The closing ceremony is an essential aspect of the Learning Expedition. You are invited to join us in this activity that I estimate will last 30 minutes. Please plan accordingly so that all participants will be able to stay through to the end of this activity.

ETA (estimated time of arrival) at Schurr High School—3:30 PM
Students may be picked up after the closing activity at 4:15 PM

**Special note: as this schedule evolves it will be important that you keep abreast of any alterations to this itinerary. Keep a separate sheet of paper for notes. Inform your parents of any relevant changes.

Respectfully,

Tobias N. Manzanares

Tobias N. Manzanares

Form 4.10. Sample Equipment List

<u>Morro Bay Learning Expedition—Equipment List</u>

_____ Large duffel bag, backpack with a metal frame, shoulder pads, hip pads

_____ Sleeping bag—down, Fiberfill II, Polygard, Dacron

_____ Stuff bag for your sleeping bag

_____ Sleeping bag straps

_____ Ensolite pad (½ sheet will suffice)

_____ Tube tent (2 person—use as a ground cloth) + 6 clothespins

_____ Nylon cord (50 ft. for use with tube tent—1 unit for two people)

_____ Rain poncho

_____ Small flashlight (with an extra bulb and batteries)

_____ Candle (votive size—in a Coke can lantern) (this is home made)

_____ Compass (maps—one set for each food group)

_____ Canteen (1 quart metal or plastic—wide mouth is most useful)

_____ Personal first aid kit (incl. mole skin, band aids, repellant, etc.)

_____ Plate, light weight metal is best

_____ Spoon or fork

_____ Sierra cup

_____ ½ roll of toilet paper in a zip lock bag (remove core & flatten)

_____ Tooth brush

_____ Tooth paste (smallest tube possible)

_____ Bar of soap (get one that has been used and is nearly gone—it's light)

_____ Wash cloth

_____ Small towel

_____ Vest or jacket (down, polygard, etc. or use multi-layer method)

_____ Levis (one pair)

_____ Long sleeve shirt (one)

_____ Short sleeve shirt (one)

_____ Boots (lug sole boots are recommended—any over-the-ankle boot is fine)

_____ Thick socks (three pair—wool is recommended)

_____ Thin socks (three pair) (wear one pair of each while hiking)

_____ Light camp shoes

_____ Underwear (two sets)

_____ Watch cap

_____ Hat (to protect delicate skin from the sun)

(Form 4.10. *continued*)

_____ Pack cover (large trash can bag cut to fit over backpack)

_____ Optional clean set of clothes for return trip home (in grocery bag)

_____ Swim suit

_____ *Group equipment (one set needed for each food group):*

_____ Pot and pan set

_____ Backpacking grill and bag

_____ Pack stove (two burners minimum for each food group)

_____ Staples bag

_____ Spatula (plastic)

_____ Serving spoon

_____ Salt and pepper (in moisture proof containers)

_____ Matches (in moisture proof containers)

_____ Garlic powder (very small)

_____ Pot scrubber

_____ SOS pad in zip-lock bag

_____ Biodegradable soap in a spill-proof container

_____ Gerry tube of butter

_____ Gerry tube of cooking oil

_____ Coleman lantern

_____ Coleman stove

_____ Ice chest

_____ Optional camera equipment and musical instrument, avoid tubas, pianos, harps, etc.

Regarding backpacking gear—always focus on the lightest possible product and don't hesitate to improvise. Avoid hasty purchase of these items—borrow first, come in and talk it over with us. We may be able to save you a great deal of money.

Form 4.11. Sample calendar of events

Morro Bay Learning Expedition Calendar

SUN.	MON.	TUES.	WEDS.	THS.	FRI.	SAT.
NOVEMBER 18	19	20 *1st meeting*	21	22 *2nd meeting* *Select Research Article*	23	24
25	26	27 *Essay Due* *Application Due* *3rd mtg.* *Begin Fundraising*	28 *Parent mtg.*	29 *Parent Permit Due* *4th mtg.* *Deposit Due*	30	DECEMBER 1
2	3	4 *Irreg. Prog. Due* *5th mtg.*	5	6 *6th mtg.* *Turn in Fund R. collections to date*	7	8
9	10	11 *7th mtg.* *Book Article Due*	12	13 *8th mtg.* *Turn in last fundraiser monies & form*	14	15
16	17	18 *9th mtg.* *Equipment resource network*	19	20 *10th mtg.* *Final Balance Due* *Equip. Check*	21 *Last day of the 1984 school year*	22

(Form 4.11. *continued*)

23	24	25	26	27	28	29
		Christmas Day				

30	31	JANUARY **1**	2	3	4	5
		New Years Day				

6	*Equip. Check* 11th *mtg.* **7** Return to school *Food Comm Shopping Freeze appropriate items*	*12th mtg.* **8** *Final Food Group Equip. Check*	7:30 AM **9** Arrive at school 9:00 Depart for Morro Bay 4:00 PM Arrive Montana de Oro	10	9:00 AM Begin **11** day hike to Morro Bay	12

9:00 AM **13** Depart for Oak Valley *Rest*	School **14** holiday Martin Luther King Jr. *Rest*	*Nutrition* **15** *Follow-Up Meeting* *Bring a Snack*	**16** *Turn in Film for Processing*	17	18	19

20	21	22	*Begin* **23** *Editing Film*	*Second Book* **24** *Article Due*	25	26

5

Integrating the Physical/Sensing Function

The second key component, Relaxation and Tension Reduction, addresses the need for a reduced level of anxiety to optimize access to all levels of brain function. It has been already noted that high levels of anxiety reduce access to higher brain functions (Hart, 1981), interrupt the natural flow of information and processing between the hemispheres (Wittrock, 1980), and make unavailable pre-frontal cortex functions (Goodman, 1978). If we are to allow students the best education possible then we must teach tension-reducing techniques to help prevent excessive stress.

The third key component, Movement and Physical Encoding, discussed later in this chapter, is a most valuable learning tool that can be used to strengthen the content of any subject or discipline. Such strategies can help students better understand complex or abstract concepts and strengthen storage and retrieval capabilities.

Both of these key components support learning by taking advantage of the brain's motor and physical/sensing areas. Movement and physical/sensing areas can be found throughout the brain and are coordinated from the cerebellum as well as the reticular formation and autonomic functions of the brain stem. Reducing tension allows better integration of all such functions.

Young learners learn through physical activity; it seems curious that that activity is by design denied as a support system soon after the learner enters school. Except in a few disciplines—music, physics, chemistry, and art—learning strategies that promote movement and the physical/sensing function disappear from the school. This chapter will present helpful ways to include these neglected key components in a learning setting.

KEY II—RELAXATION AND TENSION REDUCTION

Stress is an unavoidable consequence of the challenges of living. As Albrecht (1979) states, "The great defining characteristics of this period—the first three-quarters of the twentieth century—have been change, impermanence, disruption, newness and obsolescence, and a sense of acceleration in almost every perceptible aspect of American society" (p. 2). Stress is inevitable in such a climate and the need to keep stress within manageable limits has been recognized by psychologists and medical professionals alike.

Selye (1976, 1979) emphasizes that one form of stress, *eustress,* results from achievement, triumph, and exhilaration. Only when stress becomes *distress,* producing a sense of loss of security and adequacy, does it become dangerous to health and well-being. From Selye's seminal work came the discovery that stress produces chemicals within the brain that shut down the system and, over time, create permanent damage. Although the body reacts to protect the system, prolonged or frequent use of this reaction will in fact wear the system out.

Capra (1982) identifies stress as "an imbalance of the organism in response to environmental influences" (p. 324). He believes that some stress is an essential part of living. Only as temporary stress becomes prolonged can it become harmful. Stress then affects the body's immune system and plays a significant role in the development of many illnesses.

Stress can affect learning even when the imbalance is not this severe. Hunt (1982) suggests that under stress we forget things we know well. He explains that part of the reason is that "the stressful input takes up most of the mind's conscious equipment and so impedes the retrieval of information from long term memory" (p. 89).

Of interest to the educator is the finding that ". . . a person's higher level mental faculties are substantially impaired by extreme stress and that they function more effectively when he is comparatively calm and not highly aroused" (Albrecht, 1979, p. 75). For that reason Albrecht and others believe that "one of the most important survival skills for human beings in twentieth-century America is a *neurological skill*— the ability to physically relax, unwind, and demobilize the body for long enough periods to allow it to recuperate and repair itself" (p. 79). Should anyone believe that the concern over stress is that of but a few researchers, there is an International Institute of Stress that claims to have in its library more than 120,000 publications on stress (Selye, 1979).

Ferguson (1980) suggests some clues as to how we might cope with the negative effects of stress:

> Our vulnerability to stress appears to be due more to our interpretation of events than their inherent seriousness. . . . Paying attention to stress in a re-laxed state transforms it. Meditation, biofeedback, relaxation techniques, auto-genic training, running, listening to music—any of these can help elicit the body's recovery phase. Refusal to acknowledge stress means that we pay dou-ble; not only does our alarm not go away, but it goes into the body. (p. 251)

Several researchers suggest that instead of trying to avoid stress altogether the real key is to balance our life styles: balanced amounts of work and play, challenge and ease, stress and relaxation, companionship and solitude (Leonard, 1974, 1978; Pel-letier, 1977; Selye, 1976). Albrecht (1979) believes that "only a few consciously se-lected forms of stress avoidance have the potential for constructively reducing stress" (p. 38). One way to avoid stress and to relax body and mind is to restructure the environment or to move out of it for appropriate periods of time. Relaxing one's body physically allows stress to be reduced to manageable levels.

Restructuring the Environment

Albrecht (1979) gives us four general categories of emotionally induced stress:

1. time stress—anxiety reactions to deadlines, schedules, and lack of closure;
2. anticipatory stress—worry or anxiety about an impending event;
3. situational stress—anxiety as a result of finding one's self in a situation that is threaten-ing and at least partially beyond one's control;
4. encounter stress—anxiety about dealing with one or more people whom one finds unpleasant and possibly unpredictable.

Using this framework educators can assess their environments to see if there are changes that could be made to reduce any of these types of stress. For example, does every assignment have to have a teacher-set deadline? Can schedules be made more flexible? Can more choices be given in the planning and implementation of the learn-ing experience? Is control in the classroom shared or is it maintained by threats of punishment and offers of rewards?

I have found that routine midterm and final examinations are quite stressful to students and create an interruption in the learning curve. I knew that giving students choices reduces anxiety by placing the student more in charge of the learning experience and so I began offering a choice of the type of test the students could take: objective, subjective, student written, or teacher written. This act of choosing helped reduce tension, but I later discovered that what I really wanted was to evaluate the learning. Examination was only one possible way of evaluating; I could also collect data. Once I began collecting pertinent data on each student I found that examinations were unimportant. Students responded most favorably and the quantity and quality of their work increased.

Abraham Maslow (1968) devised a hierarchy of human needs to explain how emotional development is facilitated or inhibited. According to this hierarchy human energy is used to provide for needs at six levels. If needs at any one level remain unmet then energies are drained off at that level; further progress is inhibited and overemphasis is placed on that need level. The balance necessary to limit stress would be missing. Maslow's structure can provide a framework for a productive, less emotionally stressful environment.

Level 1 Basic physical needs. These include food, clothing, and shelter. If this level has not been met then the student's energies will be focused at this level and learning will be minimal.

Level 2 Safety needs. While failure to meet physical safety needs is fairly obvious, failure to meet emotional safety needs is not. The reward-punishment-competition model used by so many educators forces students to spend a great deal of energy insuring their own psychological safety. According to Feldhusen and Klausmeier (1962) this type of anxiety is debilitating and interferes with the learning process.

Level 3 Love and belonging needs. These include the need to love and feel loved, to be in physical contact with one another, to associate with others, and to participate in groups and organizations. Teachers who establish a climate of trust within the classroom allow each student to see each other as a person instead of a stranger. Learners in such an environment can learn from each other as well as from the teacher.

Level 4 Needs for self-esteem and positive responses from others. These provide a sense of well-being and self-satisfaction and allow the student to take the risks required for learning and creating. By encouraging diverse pursuits, internal validation, and the idea that mistakes provide learning experiences, teachers will furnish the opportunity for fulfillment at this need level.

Level 5 Self-actualization, which includes the realization of our highest self, development of our potential. The classroom that values, encourages, and provides opportunities for diversity, self-exploration, introspection, interaction as well as quiet contemplation is the classroom where self-actualization will be most likely to occur. The goal is to have access to all of your life, all of your potential, and to be who you truly are.

Level 6 Transcendence. Maslow died before he could finish his inquiry into the need and meaning of this next level. Others have now continued this inquiry and have found that the transcendence level includes the nurturing of intuitive abilities. To create a world where the oneness of all being is understood and practiced, where the unity with and interdependence of all parts of the cosmos are valued and provide the basis for action, is a noble undertaking. We can live most effectively if we transcend the self by becoming the most each of us can be and by recognizing and valuing this in others while, underlying the uniqueness, we experience the connectedness.

Physical Relaxation

Even the most everyday tasks—driving, teaching, working around the house, or simply walking down the street—involve staying attentive, watchful, and alert. Some of your muscles are ready for action, the capillaries constricted to slow down circulation of the blood. The cells in those muscles are producing energy, available nutriment is being used up, and toxic wastes are being excreted by the cells. To receive the full benefit of a steady flow of blood the cells in and around the constricted muscle need to go through their full cycle of tension, release of energy, and relaxation. Unless they complete the cycle, those cells end up being undernourished and even drugged by the toxins that build up around them. The problem is that many muscles do not complete the cycle but rather operate at "ready" much of the time. This causes the entire body to be in a constant state of tension, making the body more prone to disease.

The first step we must take is to begin to pay closer attention to the physical sensations of our own body. By becoming sensitive to and intimately familiar with the signals from our body it is possible to prevent stress from becoming *distress*.

There are many strategies and forms of relaxation that can be employed to develop the skill of physically reducing tension. This chapter will mention some of those forms and will detail a few strategies that can be used in the classroom.

Progressive Relaxation

This form of relaxation (Jacobson, 1957) is probably the simplest and involves sitting or lying in a comfortable position with your eyes closed. Concentrate on various muscles in your body, relaxing them one at a time. A systematic sequence is suggested; try starting at the top of the head and progressing to the feet, releasing each of the muscle groups in turn. Imagery may enhance the process, e.g. imagining each area is gradually turning to jelly or sinking into the floor. Exercise 4.1. (page 67) is an excellent example of such an exercise.

Autogenic Training

This relaxation technique originated in Germany over 30 years ago (Schultz & Luthe, 1959), and involves the use of tension and release, imagery, and mental concentration. A simple way to experience this form of relaxation is to make a fist with your right hand. As you squeeze your fist shut push your arm away from your body. Continue pushing and squeezing until you feel discomfort in your arm, then quickly release all tension and allow your arm to hang beside your body. Notice how your hand and arm feel. Be aware that you can relax them even more. Allow your hand and arm to relax more deeply. Notice how that feels. Allow your hand to feel very heavy (it may begin to feel even a little warm). You could relax even more; however, bring your hand and arm back to their normal states by gently moving your fingers and arm. Notice the difference between your right hand and arm and the left hand and arm you have not relaxed. To avoid muscle imbalance use the same procedure on the left hand and arm. You can use this tension-relaxation procedure on muscles throughout your body.

Rethinking, Thought Stopping, and Mental Diversion

These are mental techniques used for creating physical relaxation (Albrecht, 1979). Rethinking involves recognizing negative or non-productive thoughts and substituting them with positive, constructive ones. When you say to yourself, *This is terrible!* rethink, *This is just the way it is now. Let's see what I can do about it.* If you find yourself thinking, *He is acting so stupid! I can't stand it!* rethink, *I'm really uncomfortable with the way he is handling this. How shall I deal with him?*

Thought stopping is precisely that: when you find yourself having thoughts that are uselessly depressing or critical try to "hear" in your mind the shouted word *Stop!* Substitute a new and more productive train of thought. This is one way to recognize negative feelings that only add to your tension and reduce your effectiveness.

Mental diversion is the process of consciously choosing to focus your mind on positive thoughts instead of negative ones. When you are anxious about an event or decision and have already done all you can to assure its outcome, begin thinking about a positive topic. Unless you replace one topic with another your mind will continue to hold on to the anxiety already produced.

Mental Rehearsal

Allow your mind to move through anxiety producing events prior to the actual confrontation. Visualize each step and each detail of the coming event. Picture the place, people, and possible happenings. See yourself carrying out the task, dealing with any problems or obstacles that arise, and bringing it to a successful completion. Work out alternative ways of handling the event so that you will have maximum flexibility when the event occurs. By carefully rehearsing the situation in your mind you can reduce the anxiety you feel and prepare yourself to give your best effort.

Students feel most anxious when faced with an examination. Anxiety interferes with the learning process not only by reducing the amount that can be learned but also by blocking the retrieval of information previously learned. The following exercise is a more detailed account of a guided imagery activity mentioned in Chapter 3. High school biology teacher Toby Manzanares uses this mental rehearsal to help his students lower their anxiety prior to an examination.

Exercise 5.1. A Guided Imagery for Testing

Procedure: Give the following directions to the class just before an examination. Allow plenty of time for them to react to your instructions. Never rush this exercise; give the students the benefit of approaching an examination with their minds clear and ready.

I need you to take five cleansing breaths. . . . Inhale quietly through your nose. . . . Exhale quietly through your mouth. . . . Each time you exhale imagine that you are blowing tension out of your body. . . . Allow your eyes to close gently. . . . Feel your body soften as the tension leaves your muscles. . . . Allow any sounds that come into the classroom to float through your consciousness and back out again; you need not hold onto any of these sounds. . . . Again, take another deep cleansing breath . . . and relax. . . . This is a special time for you to find your center. . . . Imagine that you are lying on a hilltop and watch-

ing clouds gently drift across a vivid blue sky. . . . Feel the breeze blow through your hair. . . . Feel its coolness. . . . Watch as the clouds move into different shapes. . . . Notice how relaxed your body is . . . and how comfortable you feel. . . . Imagine yourself as you take the exam. . . . Notice the look of confidence on your face, a look that reflects the confidence in your ability to remember. . . . Everything that you've ever heard is permanently recorded year after year in your brain. . . . The more relaxed you can become the more you can remember and the greater the access to your incredible memory. . . . Notice the smile on your face as you mark the correct answers on your answer sheet, and notice how comfortable your body feels. . . . When you're ready, return to the classroom and open your eyes. . . . Remain relaxed and notice how you feel. . . . You are now in a better mental state to perform well on your exam. . . . Remember that smile of confidence as you begin. If you feel tension building, close your eyes for a moment, take a few cleansing breaths, and blow out the tension as you exhale.

Affirmations and Environmental Cues

Because being aware of our stress is vital to lowering our stress, any techniques that remind us of the need to relax will help reduce tension. Albrecht (1979) suggests that we place a small colored dot in the center of our watch crystal so that whenever we glance at our watch we will be reminded to pause for a second or two, take a deep breath, and relax our bodies. He believes that we should surround ourselves with "positive, uplifting ideas and positive, uplifting people" so that we may more easily maintain a positive frame of mind. "This," he writes, "is an important part of eliminating unnecessary anxiety and maintaining a low-stress style of living, working and thinking" (pp. 250–251).

Other Relaxation Strategies

For Very Young Children:

Exercise 5.2. The Rag Doll

Purpose: to help young children understand relaxation and tension reduction
Time required: 5–10 minutes
Materials needed: a rag doll with flexible joints; a recording of slow, quiet music
Preferred classroom structure: children sitting in a circle on the floor
Teaching function: group leader
Procedure:
Step 1. Hold the rag doll with both hands and show the children how limp it is. Shake it gently and call attention to the way its head, legs, and arms hang loosely.
Step 2. Have the children shake their hands and arms just as do the rag doll's. Then have them let their arms and legs go limp. Have them do the same with their heads and then their entire bodies.
Step 3. Play the recording and have the children move around the room as if they were rag dolls.
Step 4. Have the children lie down. Go around to each child and lift and gently drop an arm or a leg. Say to the students, *Feel like a rag doll. Make your arms and legs heavy and floppy.*

118

To Energize:

Exercise 5.3. Z z z z z

Purpose: to pick up energy in a classroom when everyone seems apathetic and listless (most often during the last hour of the day)
Time required: two minutes
Materials needed: none
Preferred classroom structure: have everyone stop wherever they are and face the teacher
Teaching function: group leader
Procedure:

Step 1. Ask the students to put their hands out in front of their bodies with their palms facing forward.

Step 2. Ask them to push their hands forward and away from their bodies as they make the sound *z z z z z.*

Step 3. Have the students continue to push, push, push; make the *z z z z z* sound for several seconds with every push.

Step 4. Ask the students to stop, put their hands down, and notice how their heads feel. They will feel tingling in their heads because they have just hyperventilated.

Fantasy Trips for Relaxation:

Exercise 5.4. Floating Down the River

Purpose: to relax and focus the energy of the students and to center their thoughts on pleasant, positive experiences. At the end of the exercise students will be refreshed, their brain/minds will be more coherent, and they will be able to focus on their learning and retain more of what they have been taught.
Time required: 7–10 minutes
Materials needed: relaxing background music or environmental sounds
Preferred classroom structure: room on the floor for students to lie down on their backs without touching; in classrooms with no floor space students should get as comfortable as possible in their own chair
Teaching function: group leader
Procedure: Allow the students plenty of time to imagine while you give them the following instructions:

Lie down in a space on the floor where you can be alone and think your own thoughts. Be sure you are not touching another person so that you will not be disturbed. . . . We are going to take a journey. . . . Gently close your eyes and let your body get as comfortable as possible. . . . Let your breathing slow down and deepen until your whole body is breathing. . . . Slowly let your focus move down to your gravity center. . . . Imagine that you can see a door in front of you. . . . It is a large door with a very large handle. . . . Reach out and take the handle into your hand. . . . Open the door and step out. . . . Close the door behind you. . . . You are standing on a gentle hill. . . . In front of you is a short path leading to a lovely pond. . . . All around you are flowers and soft grass. . . . Begin walking slowly down the path toward the pond. . . . Allow yourself to walk into the pond and lie down. . . . The water is pleasant and buoyant. . . . You float so easily. . . . Just allow yourself to relax and float along. . . . The water feels so gentle all around your body, so relaxing. . . . A current begins to move you slowly out into the pond and then into a small stream. . . . Floating slowly and effortlessly, you move through fields of wildflowers and grass. . . . Smell the flowers. . . . Notice the lovely colors. . . . The sky above you is blue, the flowers bright. . . . You are warm and relaxed. . . . Little patterns of shade begin to play

across your face as you slowly drift under the branches of trees. . . . The leaves are gradually becoming thicker and you drift on into the cool, quiet shade of a forest. . . . On either side of you you can hear birds, small animals, the sounds of the forest. . . . You can smell the damp and earthy smells of the forest. . . . Just to your right a gentle deer stops drinking from the steam to watch you float by. . . . Again the shade begins to play in patterns across your face as you slowly float out of the forest and back into the warm sunlight. . . . Ahead there is a large boulder. . . . In a minute you will float around the boulder. . . . When you do you will be able to go anywhere you would like for a little while. . . . I will tell you when to come back. . . . You are now floating around the rock and for a little while you may go anywhere you would like [allow several minutes of silence]. *Let yourself return to the stream once more. . . . You are now floating back to the little pond* [reverse all of the experiences]. *Allow yourself to walk out of the pond and slowly back up the hill to your door. . . . Slowly open the door, move through, and gently close it behind you. . . . You are now once again at your center. . . . In a moment I am going to ask you to come back to this room. . . . You may keep the centered and relaxed feeling you now have as you return. . . . When you are ready and at your own pace, you may slowly return to the room.*
     Allow time for all the students to open their eyes.

For Healing:

Exercise 5.5.   The Healing Screen

Purpose: to relax and focus energy and to allow students to free themselves of minor physical discomforts or distracting thoughts. At the end of the exercise students will be less tense, more mentally focused, and aware of their comfort and well being.
Time required: three to five minutes
Material needed: calming music
Preferred classroom structure: students sitting in seats or on the floor
Teaching function: group leader
Procedure: Allow the students plenty of time to imagine while you give them the following instructions:
Gently close your eyes. . . . Notice your breathing. . . . Allow it to slow down until your whole body is breathing. . . . Center yourself and get as comfortable as possible. . . . Imagine that you are standing in front of a large screen . . . much taller and much wider than you. . . . Notice the color of the screen . . . a very nurturing, very comforting color. . . . It is a color that makes you feel good . . . very peaceful . . . very calm. . . . Notice the pattern of holes in the screen . . . each small hole a part of this unique pattern. . . . Notice the shape of each hole . . . interesting shapes . . . an interesting pattern. . . . This screen is very special. . . . It is especially tuned to the vibrations of your body. . . . You are able to walk right through this screen. . . . The pattern on the screen will allow only the comfort and health of your body to pass through it. . . . Only positive feelings will pass through it. . . . It is a healing screen. . . . Move slowly toward the screen. . . . Again notice the color . . . the pattern . . . and allow yourself to slowly move through the screen. . . . Notice that all discomfort in your body is absorbed into the screen. . . . All your bad feelings flow out and are trapped in the screen. . . . As you move through to the other side you feel calmer, more centered. . . . You are aware of your energy and how good you feel. . . . For just a moment be aware of yourself as a whole, relaxed, calm person. . . . Be aware of how good you feel. . . . Know that any time you feel tense or troubled you can move through your healing screen again and heal yourself, calm yourself, or energize yourself. . . . With this feeling of energy and comfort let yourself move back into this room. . . . When you are ready, gently open your eyes and return.
     Allow time for all students to open their eyes.

KEY III—MOVEMENT AND PHYSICAL ENCODING

When dancers listen to music their minds very often choreograph the music and they "see" dancers moving with each passage they hear. After experiences with physical encoding students report that they can "see" ideas physically represented or encoded even when they have not participated in actual movement. The following exercises are excellent examples of practical, effective techniques to help students grasp ideas and abstract concepts they might otherwise have problems understanding.

In Science:

Tobias Manzanares developed and successfully implemented this lesson in his biology class at Schurr High School, Montebello, California. The use of this strategy resulted in an increase in the understanding and retention of a rather abstract concept.

Exercise 5.6 Phagocytosis

Purpose: to develop an understanding of the body's immune system through an integrative activity, and to reinforce the terminology used in the unit on the circulatory system
Time involved: one fifty-minute class period
Materials needed: handout of a drawing of the process of phagocytosis
Preferred classroom structure: an area representing the human body with space for student movement
Teaching function: instructor/group leader
Procedure:

Step 1. Students should record in their notebooks the diagram they have been given and should note the following:

    a. Many white blood cells are capable of phagocytizing, or eating, large numbers of invading microorganisms.

    b. Specialized cells in the liquid-filled spaces of your tissues are also capable of phagocytizing invading organisms, and are most effective in the specific region of a skin wound.

    c. If the infection moves into the body from the region of entrance, phagocytic cells circulating in the vascular system will ingest the invaders. Additional phagocytic cells are found in the liver and spleen should the infection reach the blood steam.

Step 2. Let each student decide whether he or she wants to be a part of a white blood cell or a member of a three-person invading cell. Three invading cells will be needed; members of these triads can choose to be a virus or a bacterium.

Step 3. The remainder of the class links arms to form a closed circle representing a white blood cell. This group selects a member to act as the nucleus.

Step 4. Instruct the invading triads to leave the room momentarily and that when they return they are to invade the body (the room) through a wound, scratch, or any other method they may choose to describe. (Example: *Giardia lambia* is a protozoan that enters the body through contaminated drinking water.)

Step 5. Instruct the remaining group (the white blood cell) that they are charged with the responsibility of protecting the body by ingesting and thus destroying the invading organisms.

Step 6. As the invading triads (arms linked) enter the room (body), instruct them to move at the speed of a microorganism (very slowly). Instruct the nucleus of the white blood cell to direct the action of the cell in the very best manner and wisdom a nucleus can display.

Step 7. Allow three to five minutes for the phagocyte to phagocytize. As an invading triad is ingested instruct the members to become part of the larger phagocyte by linking arms with that group.

Step 8. Stop the activity momentarily (after ingestion) to have the group focus on their feelings. Ask the phagocyte, *How did you feel as you attacked and ingested an invader? Did you have a sense of power? Did you feel a sense of responsibility? Success?* Ask the invading triads, *Did you feel a sense of exclusion relative to the bigger group? Did you feel differently after becoming part of the larger cell? What kinds of feelings were experienced upon penetration of the body?*

Step 9. Have the class return to their seats and write a metaphor about their immune system.

Step 10. Conduct a guided imagery to raise the students' awareness of their ability to assist their bodies' immune systems. (Clark, 1983, pp. 309–310)

In Math:

Exercise 5.7. Fractionated Groups

Purpose: to understand the concept of fractions
Time involved: 15 minutes
Material needed: none
Preferred classroom structure: students standing with enough space for them to move into and out of small groups
Teaching function: group leader
Procedure:

Ask for volunteers to form a small group (4–6 students), then ask another student to use the group to show one-half of the group; one-third of it, one-fourth of it, etc.

Now ask all the students to form groups of various sizes of their choice. Have them add, subtract, multiply, and divide fraction problems using their group, then ask them to work problems with mixed fractions by using their group and other groups.

Example: A group has six members. They are to find one-half of the group. The group must divide themselves in half. A group of five members will notice the difficulty and the need to have a remainder.

Example: Groups are asked to add one-half and one-third. They must first find one-half of one group and one-third of another and then add them together.

Be sure to discuss each problem with the entire class after a group demonstrates a solution. A guided imagery exercise in which the students imagine groups moving could be the next step. This activity precedes pencil and paper work.

The following exercise was developed and successfully implemented by Christine Cenci at LaMerced Elementary School, Montebello, California.

Exercise 5.8. Clock Math

Purpose: to develop the concept of time and the use of a clock to tell time
Time involved: 5–10 minutes
Material needed: none
Preferred classroom structure: students standing with enough space for them to move around
Teaching function: director/facilitator
Procedure:

Ask children to use their arms (and/or legs) to show three o'clock, six o'clock, 4:30, etc. Variation: The body can also be used to show geometric shapes.

In Geography:

Exercise 5.9. Directionality

Purpose: to develop the concept of directions
Time involved: 15–20 minutes
Material needed: "Treasures" hidden around the room
Preferred classroom structure: students seated with enough space for them to stand and move around
Teaching function: instructor/facilitator
Procedure:

After demonstrating the procedure with one child ask several children to stand and head for the south wall, the north wall, the northwest, etc. Ask them to take turns doing this. Now give each child a card with directions on it to get to a "treasure" e.g. *go three steps east, turn, and go five steps south.*

Variation: To develop abstract thinking give the directions to a treasure in clues that are cryptic e.g. *go three steps toward the hands that hold infinity* (the clock) or *stand below an indoor blind that never shades a window* (the pull down map), etc.

Variation: Bury archeological artifacts and give the students a map to find the "dig site."

In Reading, English and Language Arts:

Exercise 5.10. Integrative Grammar

Purpose: to teach word sequence, noun and verb usage and the need for parallel construction
Time involved: 15 minutes
Materials needed: a card for each participant with a word and its sentence part printed on it
Preferred classroom structure: students standing with enough space for them to move into and out of small groups
Teaching function: director/group leader
Procedure:

Ask for five volunteers and randomly give each a word which when placed together with the words of the other students in the group will make a five-word sentence. Ask the students to line up in any order they wish and have them read the words. Then let them rearrange themselves so that the sentence makes sense.

Now give every person in the group (including the original five) a word card. These words should make up several five-word sentences that have in them singular and plural nouns and present and past tense verbs. Ask the students to wander around randomly for a minute then have them stop and form groups of five with nearby students. Instruct the groups to try to form a correct sentence with their words. They may exchange people (words) with other groups until they can make a correct five-word sentence. Have each group read their completed sentence. Finally, discuss the process, especially the need for parallel number and tense of nouns and verbs.

Exercise 5.11. Integrative Reading for Preschoolers

Purpose: to teach children to read simple verbs and their own names.
Time involved: 15 minutes

Material needed: a card for each child in the class (on each card should be written a child's name); cards with verbs that can be acted out in the room e.g. run, jump, walk, sit, etc.

Preferred classroom structure: students seated on the floor or in chairs with room for movement

Teaching function: director/instructor

Procedure:

Show the children the cards with their names and be sure the children know their own names. Hold up an action card and then a name card. Invite the child named to do whatever the card says. Continue until all children have done several things. The order of the cards can be reversed at times, example: *JUMP JOHN* or *RUN ANN* or *JANE SIT.* Cards can be given to each child to put in a "card pocket" to be carried and demonstrated throughout the day.

These are just some examples of how movement and physical encoding can support the learning process; you will find yourself thinking of many others as you begin to work this way. There does not seem to be an age for which these strategies work best. I have found that physical encoding was of great help in my graduate class on research design. Students who had previously had trouble understanding various design possibilities and their uses found that "becoming" the design and its components allowed them to internalize the structure in a very different way, a way they could then manipulate and remember.

The two components presented in this chapter enable students to begin to become active partners in the Integrative Education Model. Lower levels of anxiety and tension and the use of movement and physical encoding give the learner tools for a move effective and efficient education. Learning becomes more brain compatible when we include the physical/sensing functions of the brain.

We know the importance of the environment to learning. The students have been given techniques designed to help lower anxiety levels and to help them visualize otherwise invisible concepts. The first three key components to optimal learning are now in place.

6

Sharing the Responsibility for Learning

We have begun the process of empowering learners emotionally by developing a trusting environment, a safe place for students to take the risks required during the learning process. Our next concern is with finding ways to share the responsibility for the classroom and allowing students to take more control of their learning. Research shows that this perceived control increases motivation and induces higher achievement (Stipek & Weisz, 1981).

In Chapter 5 the integration of brain function into the learning process began with the physical/sensing functions of the brain; now we must integrate the brain's emotional functions. This second system of the triune brain, known variously as the old mammalian brain, the limbic system, and the emotional mind, is located at mid-brain. Here are found the biochemical systems activated by the emotions of the learner as well as the interactions that enhance or inhibit memory. This area affects such diverse functions as anxiety, rage, sentimentality, and attention span. We rely upon this area of the brain to combine internal and external experience to create our personal identities. This limbic area provides the connecting bridge between our inner and outer worlds to give us our construct of reality, our model of a possible world. This system is often referred to as the gateway to higher thought: the cortical and neocortical functions. By the release of neurotransmitters from the limbic system, the cells of the cortex are either facilitated or inhibited in their functioning. Novelty activates growth in this area (Restak, 1979); feelings of pleasure and joy have been found to increase stimulation to this area (Sagan, 1977); and inadequate levels of touch and movement profoundly affect this area, possibly resulting in an increase in violent behavior (Prescott, 1979).

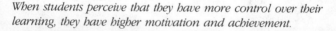

When students perceive that they have more control over their learning, they have higher motivation and achievement.

Most of the systems for developing responsibility in the classroom seem to regard the issue as a dichotomous one: either the class is teacher-centered to extend and protect teacher control, or it is student-centered, structure and content being initiated by the student. As with most dichotomies this one is not useful. Some "teacher accountable" educational evaluation systems give the teacher the entire credit or blame for each student's achievement. Many "effective teaching" approaches rely entirely upon the teacher's manipulation of the student for "student effectiveness"; any failure on the part of the student is seen as incompetence on the part of the teacher. Such systems seem to have no place for the unique talents of the teacher or of the learner. When teacher and student share the responsibility for the control and business of the classroom, both find the dignity and respect needed for effective growth (deCharms, 1984). Both teacher and student profit from the experiences, feelings, and special abilities each has to share. The classroom that can count the teacher (or teachers) and each student as a resource for the class is one that can provide optimal learning for all involved.

Two of the key components of the Integrative Education Model address the issue of how we may share the responsibility for learning: Key IV, Empowering Language and Behavior; and Key V, Choice and Perceived Control. Each key empowers teacher and student and enhances the inner locus of control and self esteem of both.

The term locus of control is used to express the idea that the perceived control can be located either within the individual (as when a choice is made from interest), or externally (as when a reward is given for making the choice). An inner locus of control allows students to focus on their own ability or skill in relation to the task rather than in relation to the abilities or skills of others, allowing them to judge based on how well they feel they have completed the task. Nichols (1984) finds that such students use self-competition to improve their skills and seek out challenging tasks. Students who have a strong inner locus of control express themselves more freely and view errors as feedback and as clues to improving their effort. When they succeed they are far more likely to feel joy and satisfaction. Learning for such students (or teachers) becomes an exciting adventure, and success in later life directly correlates to how much inner locus of control the individual has developed. This perception of responsibility for and control over one's life is the single most important condition for success, achievement, and a sense of well-being (Allen, Giat, & Cherney, 1974; Bar-Tal, Kfir, Bar-Zohar, & Chen, 1980; Dweck & Goetz, 1978; Lao, 1970; Morrison & McIntyre, 1971; Phares, 1975).

Behavior resulting from an external locus of control is dependent on cues from other people or the external environment. Such behavior is seen to be overly conforming and/or rebellious (Anderson & Prawat, 1983). Schools that encourage conforming behavior do not allow students or teachers to become self-directed and responsible. Responsible behavior is dependent on internal cues and does not stop once external cues cease.

Knowledgeable use of language and behavior can support positive emotional development in the classroom. Sparling (1984) tells us that some language and behavior create a sense of competence, support, closeness, ability, and caring; this type of language is *empowering.* Other language and behavior makes one feel depressed, hopeless, worthless, incompetent, and unloved; such language and behavior is *debili-*

tating. Empowering language and behavior in the classroom can make a significant difference in the emotional empowering of both student and teacher.

KEY IV—EMPOWERING LANGUAGE AND BEHAVIOR

One of the functions of the brain is to identify meaningful patterns from the random input provided by the environment, a task which the brain performs effectively and efficiently (Hart, 1983). Our concern then is for what kind of input the brain is receiving from the environment. There seem to be at least two sources of language that can empower or debilitate the learner: verbal and/or non-verbal messages coming from outside sources, and inner language used to direct and mediate experience.

Verbal/Nonverbal Communication

There are two levels of meaning involved in verbal communication: (1) the content—the words you say or hear, and (2) the meaning—what you're actually feeling when you talk or what you perceive the other person to be feeling as you listen. Communication works best when these are the same. However, teachers or students may try to say what is expected of them or what they think the other wants to hear. This use of language does not actually tell how either feels. Rogers (1961, 1969) believes that this type of confusion is so devastating to the communication process that he has suggested "congruence" as one of the basic tenents of his approach to counseling and teaching. He considers congruence—matching verbal communications and actual feelings—so powerful that he believes it can provide a healing climate.

A lack of congruence can often be seen as well as heard. When a person refuses to express feelings directly in words the voice, body position, or movements may give the real meaning intended by the sender. Both the teacher and the student should be more aware of non-verbal messages. Classroom communication can be improved by developing more congruence between these verbal and nonverbal messages.

Empowering language allows the student to hear what is being said. Gibb (1961) asks us to consider language a "people process." He suggests that if we want our students to hear our message, we must be aware of the need to reduce defensive listening. Worse than non-listening, defensive listening reduces the ability of the student to engage in a task either alone or in a group, causes distortion of what is heard, and affects the climate of the classroom by creating more defensiveness among those present. Gibb believes that defensive climates differ from supportive climates in the following ways:

1. a defensive listener perceives the sender to be judging, while a supportive listener perceives the sender to be requesting information, or sharing feelings, ideas, or perceptions;
2. a defensive listener perceives the sender to be attempting to change or control the listener, while a supportive listener recognizes attempts to define a mutual problem for which no solution is now known;
3. a defensive listener perceives the speaker as having a hidden agenda, being dishonest or devious, while the supportive listener perceives the speaker as being honest and straightforward;

4. a defensive listener perceives the speaker as being inconsiderate, seeing the listener as worthless, and inferior, while the supportive listener recognizes attempts to identify with and be concerned about the listener;
5. a defensive listener perceives the speaker as having all the answers, as being inflexible, and as being opinionated, while the supportive listener perceives the speaker's open-minded, honest opinion and willingness to consider the opinions of others.

If students spend their time and energy on defensiveness and resistance there will be little energy or time for learning. One way to contribute to a supportive climate in your classroom would be to affirm your students rather than judge them. Show them that their behavior is the problem, not who they are as people.

Example: Larry noisily enters the room, throws a book on his desk, kicks the chair, and passes loud and profane judgement on the day, the school, and every-one in it.

Affirming response: *Larry, I can see you are really upset. Would you like to step outside and talk about it or would you rather work a while now and discuss it later?*

Judging response: *Larry, you know that kind of behavior is not permitted in this room! What is the matter with you? Can't you grow up? Now sit down and get to work.*

Inner Language

Ellis (1977) has shown that what we say to ourselves about what we observe or that in which we participate determines what we will feel about these events.

Example: Andy sits slumped in a chair and stares into space. In front of him is a word sheet with a matching puzzle developed from his reading words. When the teacher asks what the problem is the student responds, *I can't do these old problems.*

Oh, the teacher replies, *I feel like that sometimes. But look, what is this,* she says with a tone of discovery. She points to a two letter word she is sure the child knows.

Andy looks with some curiosity, and says, *It's to.*

Exactly, says the teacher. *What about this one?* The child begins paying more attention as the teacher comments, *You may be better at this than you thought.* The teacher leaves Andy to work, and returns occasionally to reestablish a positive attitude.

The teacher here is practicing empowering language and allowing the student to replace his debilitating dialogue with more empowering inner speech. This teacher is helping the student become aware of what he can do, not what he can not do.

In a discussion of changing debilitating inner speech patterns Sparling (1984) gives the following clues:

use *I* centered messages:
Instead of saying *You make me so angry!* we can say *I really feel angry.* This change in language lets the student know how we feel without blaming the student for making us feel that way.

avoid such words as *should, shouldn't, must, must not, always,* and *never:*
  Instead of saying *You never get your homework in on time. What's the problem?* we can
  say *You seldom get your homework in on time. Is there a problem?* The word *seldom*
  does not invalidate the few times the student has been successful in meeting the deadline. Eliminating demanding words like *should* and *must* reduces the defensiveness. Try
  simply stating what you would like to have happen, e.g. *You shouldn't do that,* can be
  changed to *I need you to do . . . .*
phrase things positively
provide personal examples of learning errors
avoid praise for easy work
avoid giving excessive help
allow self evaluation
teach strategies that increase empowering language and decrease debilitating language

The following activity may be used to help students understand the abstract concept of debilitating inner language. This exercise makes the abstract idea visible and
concrete for all ages of students.

Exercise 6.1. The Empowering Arm

Purpose and expected outcome: to demonstrate the debilitating effect of negative
inner language
Time involved: five to seven minutes
Material needed: none
Preferred structure: flexible, room to move around
Teaching function: demonstrator/facilitator
Procedure: Ask for a student volunteer. Ask the student, *Which is your strongest arm?*
Position the student in front of the class with the arm extended straight out to the side,
parallel to the floor. Tell the student, *I am going to try to bring your arm down to your
side. Don't let me do it.* Using both hands on the top of the student's arm push down,
gradually increasing your strength to see how much the student can resist. Now ask the
student to say out loud to the class over and over *I can't, I can't, I can't.* When the student
has repeated the statement several times, say, *Keep saying 'I can't' as you put your arm
out to your side again. As you are repeating 'I can't' I am going to try to put your arm
down to your side. Don't let me do it.* As the student repeats the phrase you will find it is
much easier to move the arm downward. Now ask the student to repeat *I can, I can, I can*
over and over. Follow the same procedure and you will find the arm much stronger. Allow
the student to try the same procedure with a partner. Discuss the results.

A supportive classroom climate is a major benefit of empowering language and
behavior. Teachers can use physical and verbal affirmation, humor, reflective questions, and constructive, specific, task-related feedback. Mistakes can be encouraged as
clues to learning and errors valued for the information they give to both the teacher
and the learner. By teaching effective communication skills to our students, empowering language and behavior can become a shared concern, teacher to student, student
to teacher, and among the students themselves.

KEY V—CHOICE AND PERCEIVED CONTROL

If one of our goals is to help students become more responsible learners, opportunities must be provided in which they can experience choice and shared control. It is

even more important that they perceive that choice and control are available to them. Further they must believe that they have the competency or can acquire the competency to make good choices and to achieve their goals. Teachers will be able to share responsibility with their students if they help them maintain this sense of perceived control (Anderson & Prawat, 1983; Rubble & Boggiano, 1980; Weisz 1980).

Choice and perceived control have been the subject of extensive investigation over the past decade and have been found to significantly affect motivation, academic achievement, and self-esteem (Arlin & Whitley, 1978; Barnett & Kaiser, 1978; Calsyn, 1973; Matheny & Edwards, 1974; Thomas, 1980; Weisz, 1980; Wang & Stiles, 1976). Psychologists have long known that human beings are naturally motivated toward growth (Rogers, 1961) and toward seeking new information (Weiner, 1984). The relationship between teacher and student and the design of the classroom activities are most responsible for supporting or inhibiting this natural motivation (Maehr, 1984). To be most effective the classroom organization must include choice. Possible choices must be clear to the students and they must believe that they are in control of their choices. The perception of control is as important as the opportunity to choose. Student decisions must be open, the consequences of each alternative must be known, and there must be alternatives that the student might actually prefer. Another condition of choosing is freedom to choose.

Maehr (1984) has found that when the organization of a classroom or a lesson incorporates competition, grading on external criteria only, or external reward systems, the development of the inner locus of control and freedom of choice is hampered. To succeed in such an environment the student must focus on being better than others. Ames (1984) finds that competition results in a negative interdependence among students. The focus shifts from accomplishing one's best effort to doing better than one's classmates.

Student involvement in the evaluation system allows it to become a tool for self growth. When a student is graded by others on a criteria not set cooperatively, perceived control is lost, motivation diminishes, and achievement is far less satisfying and dependable.

As our society moved toward the goal of mass education, it became impossible for school personnel to know each student. Thus grading and its inherent problems began. Individual ability has disappeared into a more manageable, numeric representation of academic ability. That grade is, essentially, a force *external* to the student. It is hard now to conceive of schools functioning without grades, but we must remember that in many ways grades inhibit and impede learning.

Research over the last fifty years has covered: the practice of grading; how a grade affects learning and the learner; its merits; and the use of grades to predict future grades or success in life. Some of the results are most thought-provoking.

Grades have no inherent or stable meaning and are low in reliability
Teachers differ significantly in their interpretations of grades and in the standards they use. Even the philosophy of grading varies from teacher to teacher: some grade on student effort, some on proximity to goals set by the teacher and student in consultation, some against an outside goal set up for the entire class or grade level. Many teachers grade according to a distribution dictated by the statistical representation of a normal population ("grading on the curve"). Although statisticians will quickly point

out that the size of most classes makes the use of the curve totally inappropriate, it is, nevertheless, quite commonly used, especially in secondary and higher educational systems. Even with adaptations this method of grading can be very unfair to the students and result in arbitrary and capricious grades (LaBenne and Greene, 1969; Pressey, 1925).

A number of studies have pointed out this variation in interpretation and its effect on grading. Teachers from different classes, in some cases from different schools, were asked to grade the same papers (Dexter, 1935; Edwards, 1956; Rosenthal & Jacobsen, 1969; Starch, 1913; Starch & Elliott, 1912; Temple University, 1968; Tiegs, 1952). The range of grades on a single paper was found to be extreme. Some more defensive teachers blamed the results on the material used, believing that the outcome would be different if papers and examinations from the more precise disciplines of math and science were used, but the range in grades was found to be even greater in these areas. Even when graders have received intensive training to insure reliability they disagree significantly. Such things as fatigue, personal values, neatness, organization, and showing or not showing calculations all influence grading. Over a two-month period teachers have been found to be inconsistent in remarking the same paper. It seems that variability in marks is not a function of the subject, but rather of the grader (some teachers even use testing and test grades for punishment, e.g. the "pop quiz" to punish those who might not have studied).

Grades do not predict success in careers, in living, or in level of ability
Numerous studies (Chansky, 1964; Drews, 1972; Hoyt, 1965; Lavin, 1965; Martin & Pacheres, 1962; Pallett, 1965; Wright, 1965) show little or no correlation between grades received in high school or college and future success. Only moderate correlation exists between test scores and grades and long-range academic performance; no correlation exists between grades and postacademic performance. Even in professions highly dependent on skills (engineering, teaching, physics) there is little relationship between grades and later success. The type of schools attended, the number of years of education, and the people studied under and with all seem to have more correlation with success. The only predictive ability grades seem to have is on the basis of entry screening, where GPA is used for hiring, placement, or further study. It is important to point out that GPA is an average or mean figure that flattens any high levels of achievement, leaving outstanding abilities hidden in some cases.

Grades do not motivate most students to learn   For those few successful students who *are* motivated by grades, their teachers run the risk of creating a reward situation that makes learning only a means instead of a fulfilling or exciting pursuit in its own right. For less successful students, grades serve only to further demean and debilitate their self-concepts. Research shows that downgraded students continue to fail (Perrone & Male, 1981); failure and mediocre performance will sometimes cause false effort, academic cheating, or acting out in class to gain peer approval (Covington & Beary, 1976).

Boredom, irrelevant assignments, repetition, meaningless or unrealistic subject matter, and lack of skill-building opportunities all contribute to low grades.

Grades also have been shown to be poor indicators of student learning. Short term memorization, cheating, and other coping strategies result directly from grading practices, while true learning does not (Bowers, 1964; Chansky, 1962; Fala, 1968; Knowlton & Hamerlyneck, 1967; LaBenne & Greene, 1969). Relying upon extrinsic rewards, creating an atmosphere of continual evaluation, and the presence of standards set by someone other than the student results in a breakdown of commitment and self-regulated learning (Bidwell, 1973; Covington & Beary, 1976). When performance is exchanged for grades, many high achievers learn shortcuts to those rewards and regard out-of-class learning as unnecessary (Doyle, 1978). Maehr and Stallings (1972) have found that external evaluation used to maintain or increase performance in the classroom does so at the expense of negative effects on continued motivation.

Evaluation without grades is facilitating to the learning process Allowing students to know their strengths and weaknesses while giving them support and opportunities to develop their skills is important to learning. When mistakes are regarded as learning experiences then exploration and knowledge increase; reduced anxiety promotes long-term retention and increases knowledge. It is the teacher who, using many sources for evaluation, facilitates the students' discovery of their strengths and weaknesses and their interests and abilities, and who guides their growth toward greater fulfillment of their potential.

Grades are quickly read, easy-to-manipulate, and provide a quick way to categorize and group children. Grades are also unfair, misleading, often meaningless, and provoke anxiety in both the teacher and the student. Grades at best are neither explicit nor constructive. But, unfortunately, many parents and teachers regard grades as the most important part of the school's responsibility.

The use of external rewards is another practice resulting in different effects than those desired. Research has shown that external rewards (any reward that is not the natural consequence of an activity) often become goals in and of themselves; learning activities then become only the means to an end and have no value other than the reward. When the reward is taken away the reason for being involved in the learning activity is gone (Deci, 1975).

Example: Mary Jane is told that she can have chocolate pudding if she finishes her carrots. The message she receives is that carrots are not good, and that chocolate pudding is. If she will force herself to put up with eating the nasty carrots, she will get some yummy chocolate pudding. In school teachers often do the same thing with reading and "free" time. If the students will tolerate the nasty reading (or other school work) they will get to choose some exciting activity for "free" time. These children will learn quickly that carrots and reading are not to be valued.

External rewards are helpful to a student only when perceived as feedback rather than control or when the reward is given as the result of an activity in which they have made a personal decision to become involved.

Example: Matthew finds he has a special talent for tennis. After a great deal of work and practice he enters a tournament to test his level of skill. The trophy for winning is not the goal; playing at the peak of his performance and receiving some feedback as to just how good he is are the real goals. Just playing, win or lose, gives him great satisfaction.

External rewards are most damaging when they are viewed by the students as contingent upon their behavior.

Example: When students are given stickers for each book they read, they will see the accumulation of stickers as the goal and the reason for reading the books. If instead the stickers were to be given to every child as a surprise at the end of reading time, this reward would enhance the special feeling of the day, and promote pleasure in the reading activity.

Schools use external rewards—grades, prizes, gold stars, special privileges, threats, and punishments—without considering whether the student is intrinsically motivated or not. It has been found that the more external controls are provided by the home or school environment, the greater will be the loss of the student's inner locus (Deci, 1975). For children who have intrinsic motivation an external reward system can be devastating (Greene, 1974; Lepper, Greene, & Nisbett, 1973). These children will no longer work for the joy of it or notice the satisfaction of accomplishment but will focus on the learning task as being only a means to a different goal, the reward. Once the reward stops being offered, the task ceases to be worthwhile. This is also true for adults as well. Therefore a planned environment that builds inner locus and heightens the perception of choice is important. Intrinsic motivation and internal locus of control help students and teachers function positively in society and find personal satisfaction in whatever they choose to do.

But successful experiences are not enough. If adults or children believe that their successes were given to them then they are not perceiving any control. Failure, then, can be viewed as a positive result if they believe their own increased efforts could lead to success. The world must not be viewed as a place where we are helpless and everything just happens to us, but as a place to be acted upon. Our perception of an internally or externally controlled world is established very early, some researchers believing within the first two months of life (Lewis, 1972). The development of this strong inner locus and perceived control helps to trigger mechanisms for developing higher intelligence levels (Andrews & Debus, 1978; deCharms, 1976; Gordon, 1977).

How then can we plan an environment that increases a sense of perceived control? Here are some suggestions:

1. The environment must be a complex structure that attempts to give every student alternatives at an appropriate level of choice. A flexible, responsive structure is important at home as well.
2. Incorporate lessons that develop responsible decision-making. Students need a great deal of practice in choosing.
3. Give the students real choices; any that are presented must be acceptable to the teacher with no hidden preference.
4. These choices must be accompanied by student-developed alternatives to be considered whenever possible.
5. Teachers must believe that students can and should make most of the decisions about their learning experience. Teachers may provide the organizers, the resources, and the structure to help students to be effective.
6. Students need specific skills to make good choices. Some of these include alternative thinking patterns; an ability to build personal power through relaxation and tension reduction, imagery, and intuitive strategies; and the ability to see and evaluate consequences.
7. Teachers must believe that each student has an irreducible dignity and can help the

students recognize dignity in themselves and others. Such experiences need to be built into a school day.

8. The faculty must model effective interpersonal relationships and personal growth.

Schools need to be organized with flexibility and a structure that provides alternatives. This type of structure is currently rarely available either to teachers or to students. Teachers need to become resources for ever-widening, student-initiated choice. Comfort with ambiguity, and novel, open-ended situations is tremendously important. The behavior of all students is significantly influenced by their locus of control, resulting in success, achievement, and well-being. Exposing students to many ways of viewing problems will allow them to become aware of bias in thinking and to recognize the difference between belief and fact. They will also be able to see that each conflicting viewpoint may be valid, that information sources are vital to learning, that cooperation and consensus is integral to group action, and that many alternatives must be weighed before deciding on solutions.

Teachers must present only alternatives with consequences the students can understand if they are to help students make decisions on their own. If students cannot perceive what will happen as a result of their decisions, then they are not really making a choice. Gradually increasing the number and complexity of alternatives will help students gain confidence in their abilities and make them better decision makers (Jellison & Harvey, 1976).

Activities to Develop the Skills for Choice and Perceived Control

A major focus of the Responsive Learning Environment was the provision for choice at every age level. At NAS a variety of centers were made available to the Toddler and Early Age groups, the latter being given an additional responsibility, the choice ticket. This strategy allows the children more control of their learning and their choices expand to include content and timing. For the Cross Age youngsters choices were a part of the structure and of every lesson. On one-shot days the number of alternatives was increased. For more information on this structure refer again to Chapter 4.

Agreements

An initial activity that we have found helpful at the New Age School in establishing the tone for perceived control is the development of agreements which take the place of class rules to clarify expectations of the teacher and students in the classroom. This activity was initiated by Saundra Sparling and has become a part of her Shared Responsibility Model (discussed at the end of this chapter).

Agreements are developed by the faculty at their annual retreat prior to the opening of school. These agreements are then brought to the students in small group settings to discuss, add to, delete from, or change in any way that allows the student to feel ownership. When the list of agreements has been worked out with the students they are then charted and used during the year or until they need modification. Differences between classroom rules and classroom agreements include:

1. The students develop a sense of ownership for having contributed to the forming of the agreements.

2. During a trust circle with the class each student affirms his or her intent to keep all the agreements. If a student feels that an agreement is one that he or she can not keep, a discussion leading to clarification and modification follows until the student feels satisfied with the agreement.

3. When an agreement is broken the students are reminded rather than reprimanded and are asked for their intent.

    Example: *Mary, I thought you had agreed to listen, share, and respond appropriately with all of us. Has something changed? Did you just forget? What would you like to do about this?*

All class members, including the teacher, operate from the same rules and standards. Because they were cooperatively devised and clarified the rules make clear what is appropriate behavior and what isn't. Students will find it much easier to meet predictable standards of behavior.

With agreements students remain in control and it is their responsibility to suggest solutions to the problems they create. Rules are imposed, not agreed to; therefore, students more naturally resist them.

The Agreements at NAS have been:

1. I will listen, share, and respond appropriately to others.
2. I will find out the alternatives and choose what gets me to my goals.
3. I will treat others as special people.
4. I will take care of myself so that I can be the best I can be.
5. I will handle each problem with the person who can do something about it.
6. I will figure out what I want and ask for it at an appropriate time and in an appropriate manner.

Agreement 1 comes from an inherent need to be listened to, shared with, and responded to when trying to communicate. Giving students examples of the problems associated with violating this agreement makes it possible to help them understand how their own goals are better served if such an agreement is kept. The following is taken from an example given by Sparling of a "Valuing Experience." This activity works well to help students clarify the meaning of expected behavior, in this case listening.

Ask the students to find a partner and tell them that for two minutes they are to share something important with their partners. Before they begin, however, set up the following conditions: (1) One partner will talk while the other partner is actively non-listening. Tell them that they may do anything except leave the room to show that they are not listening. After two minutes the partners are to switch roles. (2) When the teacher gives the signal the partner who was talking now becomes the non-listener and the non-listener becomes the talker. (3) After allowing approximately two minutes for each person to be the talker and for each to be the non-listener ask them to discuss their experience. *What did you do to not listen? How did that feel? How did it feel to not be listened to? What did you do when you found your partner not listening?* (4) Finally, allow the partners to freely talk with each other for another two minutes with each listening carefully to the other. Then discuss which way felt better. This leads nicely into a discussion of the need for Agreement 1.

Agreement 2 is important in an environment where many choices are available. This agreement reminds students that it is necessary to know all of the alternatives and consequences possible in order to become effective decision makers.

Agreement 3 helps students to notice their responsibility for the classroom climate. Each person is important to that climate.

Agreement 4 is one that we find especially meaningful at NAS. Often both faculty and students overextend themselves and try to do more in a day than is possible. This agreement reminds us to take care of ourselves emotionally, physically, and spiritually so that we can have good and positive energy to give to others and can give each task our best effort. It may be worth noting that teachers are often the worst violators of this agreement.

Agreement 5 gives each student an opportunity for self-empowerment. Too often teachers and students complain to others about the actions of other teachers or students. Those who hear the complaints can seldom do anything to alleviate the problem. If, however, the student or teacher addresses the complaint to the person who has caused or who controls the situation the possibility for change exists. This agreement is a very good one for effective teacher modeling.

Agreement 6 again gives the teacher and the student a positive, effective tool for self-empowerment. It allows us to become responsible not only for our own needs, but also focuses our attention on how we might best express those needs. Discussing this agreement can help clarify the expectations of both the teacher and the student and allow each to become more effective in the classroom.

These agreements may be a starting point for your class. Revise them with your group in any way that is needed. I believe you will find that they will make an important difference in the climate and motivation in your classroom.

Even non-negotiable assignments can become more motivating when choice is involved. While there may be no choice involving the subject to be studied, it may be possible to allow the student to choose from among a variety of ways the subject can be studied. "The Integrative Education Planning Sheet," found in Chapter 9, is an example of how to include student choice in the lesson plan.

Saundra Sparling, a teacher for Los Angeles Unified Schools and a part time faculty member of California State University, Los Angeles, has developed a model which very effectively empowers both teacher and student and allows the creation of a positive and productive learning environment. This model incorporates many of the best ideas formulated by psychologists and educators over the past twenty years along with new ideas from brain researchers and educational theorists, and can be used in classrooms at all levels. The following is a brief description of the Shared Responsibility Model. For further information please write to Saundra Sparling, 6126 Condon Ave., Los Angeles, CA 90056.

THE SHARED RESPONSIBILITY MODEL

The Shared Responsibility Model (SRM) by Saundra Sparling was first developed for low-socio-economic students in an urban school setting (Benson, 1978, 1979). Over the past six years it has been used with students from age two to fifty, of ability levels from the learning handicapped to the gifted, and in groups numbering from five to fifty.

The SRM is focused on two goals. One is to provide educators with a way to gradually share with students more of the responsibility for their behavior and learning achievements. The second is to relieve some of the teacher's burden of managing and controlling student behavior. The philosophy of the SRM considers the control of student behavior to be the student's responsibility.

The strategies employed by the Model can be easily modified for the teacher's and the student's level of skill and need for structure. In SRM responsible behavior is conceptualized as falling on a continuum between being totally teacher-controlled and totally student-controlled. What works best is a shared responsibility producing optimum levels of freedom and structure for both (deCharms, 1984).

In the Model it is recognized that teachers may lack skills for sharing responsibility just as students may lack skills for accepting it. Therefore, all activities are designed to help students learn to take responsibility and to help teachers learn to give it away.

Component 1—The Teachers' Task-Involvement

Belief in the feasibility of attaining a goal is a key determinant in a person's motivation to achieve it. To be successful in sharing responsibility teachers must believe that students can behave responsibly and that classroom strategies can support them in that behavior. The Teachers' Task-Involvement is the SRM component that fosters belief and commitment. Teachers often encounter difficulty in creating task-involving activities, but first-hand experiences with these activities will build the necessary teaching skills and aid in developing belief in the power of the process. Once teachers gain confidence in this process they will want to use many more task-involving activities, allowing them to develop and design activities for any situation in unlimited numbers.

Researchers of responsible behavior have found that problem-solving is the most effective way of creating task-involvement (Anderson & Prawat, 1983; Clemes & Bean, 1980; Johnson, 1983a, 1983b; Miller & Oskam, 1984). The SRM includes a problem-solving approach called the Five Question Method. As the name implies, the method consists of five questions:

1. What is the problem?
2. What do you want?
3. What are you doing about it?
4. Is it working?
5. What are you willing to do *now* that might work?

Question 1 engages teachers and students in recognizing and admitting that a problem exists; this act alone often causes them to look toward finding solutions. Looking toward solutions directs attention toward hopefulness, a positive attitude. Positive attitudes foster improved performance.

Question 2 focuses attention on making decisions about personally valued goals. Such goals give teachers and students direction. Lack of common direction between teachers and students is one of the barriers to taking responsibility.

Question 3 allows teachers and students to consciously identify the strategies they are currently using to achieve their goals, while question 4 calls for self-evaluation of those strategies. Decisions to continue or change behavior can be made only by recognizing what is wanted, what action is being taken to get it, and the effectiveness of that action. Question 4 addresses effectiveness at each student's level of ability. Self-evaluation and focus on task-mastery are important aspects of task-involvement.

Question 5 helps form solutions to problems and plans for achieving goals as well as addressing the probable effectiveness of each solution or plan. Students should be encouraged to generate at least three alternatives and set deadlines by which they will act upon one of the alternatives.

Anderson and Prawat (1982) have found that an effective problem-solving routine involves the ability to recognize and admit a problem, to generate a number of alternative solutions, and to take action. The Five Question Method develops all three abilities. For that reason, the SRM encourages teachers to use it both with students and with themselves.

The Five Question Method helps induce teacher belief and commitment for sharing responsibility. When used with students it is equally effective in inducing their task-involvement. Student task-involvement leads to a greater sense of self-direction and an increase in positive feelings (Maehr, 1984). Task involvement alone, however, cannot counteract the tremendous amount of negative feelings and attitude students experience every day (Weiner, 1984). To help address this problem the SRM offers additional strategies.

Component 2—Increasing Positive Affect and Attitude: Empowering Language and Behavior

The second component deals with these feelings (affects) and attitudes of students and teachers. Teachers, students, and classroom interaction must be more positive than negative; activities that de-emphasize student competition are one way to increase positive affect. The set of SRM procedures called Empowering Language and Behavior (ELAB) provide a number of additional ways.

Weiner (1984) and Anderson and Prawat (1983) studied the affective experiences of students in the classroom and found negative feelings constituted over 80% of the emotions reported by their subjects. The SRM proposes that these negative emotions arise from the debilitating language and behavior between teachers and students and from the students' own debilitating inner language or "self-talk." Ellis (1977) has shown that what we say to ourselves about events determines what we will feel about them.

Sufficient positive emotional experiences over an appropriate period of time can bring about a positive change in a student's attitude toward learning. Wright and Mischel (1982) demonstrated that positive emotions and attitudes improve student performance on class assignments. The ELAB component of the SRM, then, provides strategies for altering the classroom person-to-person interactions and the student's inner speech patterns from debilitating to more empowering. The use of ELAB helps teachers create a positive context in which their students can safely reach beyond what they already know toward goals the SRM helps identify.

Component 3—Identification of Goals: Helping Students Create Their Own Classroom-Appropriate Direction

The SRM holds that the first step in helping students create their own direction is to make them aware of their personal goals. The second step is to help them see a valuable personal link between those goals and their school activities, thus aligning their behaviors so that all efforts are directed toward optimizing learning.

Goals define the direction behavior will take; irresponsible students have frequently been described as lacking direction. The SRM philosophy believes that the problem is not that students lack direction but that their goals and therefore the direction of their behavior conflict with what teachers want. In order to align the student's goals with the teacher's goals for them the teacher's goals must first be identified and shared with the students. The students must also get to identify and share their goals with teachers. This process helps both to understand the individual and common direction their behavior must take. The SRM includes Goal-Identification Activities, Goals Questionnaires, Skills Assessment Feedback, and Intended Outcomes Information to help facilitate identifying and sharing these goals.

The SRM asserts that every goal has certain inherent demands which must be met if the goal is to be accomplished. In the SRM these actions are referred to as Ground Rules and serve to determine the direction behavior must take and what must be done to achieve a goal.

Ground Rules

Ground rules are defined as the minimal, essential steps toward achieving a goal. Not honoring the ground rules results in not achieving the goal. Suppose your immediate purpose is to sit in a chair across the room. There are certain things you must do to achieve this goal: you must move near enough to make contact with the chair; you must adjust your body position; you must allow your weight to rest on the chair. If you fail to take any one of these actions you will fail to achieve the goal.

The crucial thing about ground rules is that they are not what the teacher, the principal, or the parents impose upon students. They are imposed by the goals themselves. Though it makes sense to students to resist what they feel we impose upon them it does not make sense to resist ground rules. If students fail to honor the ground rules they fail to achieve their goals. The teacher doesn't fail them and the principal doesn't fail them. They fail themselves. The consequences for doing or not doing what works are clearly theirs. Getting students to own the consequences for their behavior is a major argument in favor of having them identify ground rules. The agreements found on page 136 are a set of ground rules for the entire classroom.

Students taking responsibility for monitoring their own progress, or self-monitoring, is another major argument in favor of identifying ground rules. By having students identify goals and then the ground rules for achieving them students can easily determine the appropriateness of their behavior. Self-monitoring decreases the students' needs to have others control and supervise them, but their need for assistance in learning skills and strategies and for obtaining information will not decrease.

As a result of decreased need for control but continued need for assistance our teaching task will gradually change from policing to facilitating.

Having teachers and students identify and share their goals does not insure that those goals will be aligned or that either group will be committed to achieving them. Students and teachers may find all this new behavior as running counter to their formal training and social pressures, sometimes resulting in discouraged participants (Stipek, 1984). Students and teachers may both lose interest in and commitment to achieving their own and others' goals. We have all had the experience of knowing how to achieve a goal (like staying within a budget) but failing to get ourselves to do it and, in failing, becoming discouraged about it. The SRM proposes strategies that establish and maintain willingness and commitment, the antidotes to discouragement. The fourth component, then, must be a process for maintaining this interest and commitment.

Component 4—Establishing and Maintaining Willingness and Commitment: The Valuing Experience (VE)

The SRM includes two processes to meet this need, the Personal Value-Link and the Valuing Experience.

Helping students to clarify their own values and to be aware of the values of others is the first step. Teachers must encourage discussion of open-ended problems and controversial issues, while students must be encouraged to listen carefully to each position or solution expressed, deferring any evaluation of differences between values held by the student and opposing viewpoints. Discussion groups in a trusting environment can help students become aware of the wide range of solutions possible. This awareness can help students define the values they feel are most appropriate for them in their lives as well as an understanding of the values of others. Resources such as Simon, Howe, and Kirschenbaum (1972) will give the teacher activities to use in guiding this clarification.

Often students need guidance in determining which values they can support; decision-making skills now become most useful. The Valuing Experience allows students to experience appropriate and inappropriate values so that they can decide upon and make personal commitments to the action that they believe is most meaningful to them. The teacher tries here to reduce the amount of time spent as a controlling agent and to increase the amount of time spent as an influencing agent, a guide. This allows the student to retain the perception of self-influence, important to the maintenance of an inner locus of control. The effectiveness of the Valuing Experience hinges upon teachers and students becoming aware of: (1) their current, inappropriate behavior in relationship to specific goals; (2) the dissatisfying feelings that often accompany that behavior; (3) more appropriate alternate behavior; and (4) the accompanying, more satisfying feelings of that alternate behavior. Contrasting current and alternate behaviors and feelings will place more personal value upon the behavior for which the students experienced the most satisfaction, committing them to the alternate behavior. Inappropriate behaviors can then be understood in relation to the dissatisfaction they cause.

The Valuing Experience, an example of which is on page 136, is effective for initiating behavior changes relative to the individual goals of students and for establishing general classroom behavior agreements.

Skills and strategies become a concern once teachers and students are positively committed to the goals. The skills and strategies students have available to them vary greatly as do the perceptions students have of those skills and strategies. The students' perception of their own skills and strategies determines whether or not they believe in their control over achieving the results they desire. This perceived control, an essential element in responsible behavior, is the fifth necessary component in the Shared Responsibility Model. This component, along with the ability to choose, make up Key Component V in the Integrative Education Model.

Component 5–Establishing and Maintaining Student Perception of Control

The SRM defines perceived control as sensing that one already has or can attain the competencies necessary to achieve a goal. Teachers will only be able to share responsibility with the students if they help them maintain this sense of control (Anderson & Prawat, 1983; Rubble & Boggiano, 1980; Weisz, 1980). Perceived control occurs when identified goals, ground rules, and valuing experiences are combined to create commitment.

Perceived control also requires that teachers have reasonable but challenging expectations of students. Teachers must also be willing to help students set reasonable but challenging goals for themselves. Getting students to break down seemingly overwhelming tasks into several small manageable steps helps turn their resistance into action. Continuous Reevaluation and a clinical psychology procedure called Baby Steps are used in the SRM. These strategies help teachers and students establish and maintain appropriate levels of reasonableness and challenge in the classroom activities.

Component 6—Development of Skills and Strategies

Developing the belief that students can acquire needed skills and strategies requires that they be given the opportunity to do so. There are four types of skills and strategies students will need: strategies for recognizing what will work to achieve their goals; skills for doing what works; strategies for predicting the barriers they will encounter and the consequences they will incur while achieving their goals; and strategies for either overcoming those barriers or accepting the consequences. These strategies together form the sixth component.

Ground Rules are used in the SRM to help students identify what will work to achieve their goals. The teacher must help the students develop the skills they need for doing what works. Because of their task-involvement students perceive skills instruction as valuable assistance for achieving what they want rather than, as with more traditional educational models, the imposition of what the teacher wants.

To help students predict barriers and consequences and develop strategies for overcoming or accepting them the SRM relies heavily on Brainstorming and on the Five Question Method mentioned earlier. Also Renewal Influences—strategies and information that can support students in the achievement of their goals—provide additional help.

The organization of lessons is one of three aspects of classroom activities that determine how students respond. The other two aspects, evaluation and reinforcement, relate to how students know when they have achieved a goal and the payoff they receive for having done so. These are the focus of the seventh component of the SRM.

Component 7—Acknowledgement of Progress and Goal Achievement: Self-Monitoring

Finally, students need appropriate evaluation and feedback so that they can acknowledge their progress, keep themselves working toward the goal, and recognize when they have achieved it. The use of external evaluation and reward must be avoided when fostering the student's task-involvement. Set-Standard Criteria, Individual Criteria, and Self-Monitoring are the evaluation and feedback strategies that make up this component.

Controlling one's behavior involves knowing what behavior is appropriate and what is not. Appropriate behavior will increase as a result of self-evaluation. One of the teacher's tasks is to make the classroom environment and its standards predictable and clear.

Self-Monitoring is a feedback process that lets students know whether or not they are moving toward their goals and when they have arrived. One way is the student-designed checklist. The following is an example of how it works.

Imagine you are the teacher in a fourth grade creative writing class. Your students are working on original manuscripts for picture books. They are to write, illustrate, and bind the books themselves. You have spent the major part of the school year providing them with hands-on experiences involving each of the separate activities. Now they are to combine the separate skills to make a complete book.

To make the creation of these books a self-monitored process students will need to identify all the parts to be included in their completed book and the steps they will need to go through. Their first assignment is to make a list of parts and steps. This is the checklist one student created:

My Book Writing Checklist

I have completed these steps:

1. I have picked my title._____
2. I have written my story._____
   It is fiction._____
   It is one long rhyming poem._____
3. I have done my own editing._____
4. I have gotten the teacher to check for errors._____
5. I have made my story board._____
6. I have penciled in my title page._____
7. I have written the story in pencil on the pages._____
8. I have completed my drawings in pencil._____
   I have made big enough margins._____
9. I have colored in the drawing._____
   I used water colors._____

10. I have inked in the words._____
11. I have backed my pages._____
12. I have bound my book._____
13. I have shared my book with the class._____

You may want to require your approval of the checklist before students begin working. Once the students have designed their checklists they are able to track their progress and know when they have completed the goal, thus allowing you to spend less time monitoring them and more time helping them. You also get the satisfaction of having your students take the responsibility for their own learning.

Summary

The entire SRM consists of seven components, each of which is intended to move students toward more responsible behavior.

1. The Teacher's Task-Involvement: Helps teachers to believe that students can be responsible for their learning and that teachers can do something to elicit that responsibility.
2. Positive Feelings (Affect) and Attitudes: Gives students and teachers a positive environment in which to share responsibility.
3. Identification of Goals: Helps students to gain direction for their behavior and to align with the direction desired by the teacher.
4. Establishment and Maintenance of Willingness and Commitment: Helps students to commit to and maintain the achievement of their goals.
5. Establishment and Maintenance of Student Perception of Control: Helps students to establish and maintain a sense of perceived control over the outcomes they desire.
6. Development of Skills and Strategies: Helps students and teachers build skills and strategies for sharing responsibility.
7. Acknowledgement of Progress and Goal Achievement: Helps students monitor their progress, stay on task, and recognize when goals are completed.

When using the SRM it is wise to remember that sharing responsibility is not a paper and pencil exercise. Time for students to interact with each other in the classroom is mandatory. The atmosphere must allow them to safely observe themselves in that interaction and learn from the mistakes they are making.

The SRM sees prevention as more efficient and less emotionally costly than remediation. It is designed to prevent continued occurrences of irresponsible behavior and to increase occurrences of responsible behavior.

Table 6.1 gives an overview of (1) the barriers to personal valuing and decision-making and, ultimately, to responsible behavior; (2) the seven components proposed in the SRM to address each barrier; (3) the desired teacher and student behaviors; (4) the SRM strategies used to elicit those behaviors; and (5) the predicted outcomes.

In this chapter we have discussed the importance of the emotional function of the brain to optimizing learning. Two Key Components of the Integrative Education Model have been used in this discussion, Key IV—Empowering Language and Behavior, and Key V—Choice and Perceived Control. Now that we have empowered the learner emotionally we are ready to involve the higher learning centers. Chapter 7 will bring together the linear rational and the spatial, gestalt styles of cortical function into the new paradigm we are calling optimal learning.

Table 6.1. Components of the Shared Responsibility Model

	Barriers to Responsible Behavior	Components to Address Barriers	Procedures	Teacher/Student Behaviors	Outcomes
1	Teachers' lack of belief and commitment	Experience with task-involvement sufficient to foster belief	*5-question method	Task-involvement	Increased belief and commitment
2	Teachers' and students' negative affect and attitudes	More positive than negative classroom experiences	*Empowering language and behavior (ELAB)	More positive responses and communication Task-involvement	Increased productivity and responsible behavior
3	Lack of appropriate direction	Recognition of own goals and understanding of expectancies	*Goals-identification activities *Goals questionaire *Assessment-feedback *Information about intended outcomes *Ground rules	Identify personal goals (dreams and desired skills) Identify expectations of others	Increased sense of direction
4	Discouragement	Process for developing and maintaining interest, willingness, and commitment	*Personal value-link *Valuing experiences (VE) *Renewal influences (RI)	Establish and maintain alignment of goals, willingness and commitment	Development of goal alignment, willingness, and commitment
5	Lack of perceived control	Processes for establishing and maintaining perceived control	*Constant reevaluation *Baby steps	Establish and maintain reasonable goals and expectations	Decreased avoidance of challenging activities
6	Poor skills and strategies	Opportunities for building skills and strategies	*Brainstorming *Ground rules *5-question method *Renewal influences	Predict barriers and consequences Identify minimal necessary behavior to achieve goals Develop strategies for achieving goals	Thinking through actions Figuring out what to do Figuring out how to do it
7	Lack of evaluation procedures and accountability	Process for knowing when one has achieved the goal	*Set-standard criteria *Individual criteria, and self-monitoring *=An SRM Procedure	Acknowledge progress, stay goal-directed, recognize goal completion	Development of self-direction and responsible behavior

Saundra Sparling
Copyright © 1985

Integrative Thinking: Using Both Cognitive Processes

Key Component VI—Complex and Challenging Cognitive Activities focuses on thinking processes as it integrates the functions of both the left and the right hemispheres of the brain cortex into the learning process. We have discussed earlier the importance of viewing the brain's specialized functions as supportive of each other rather than as separately functioning entities. Let us now look at how we might take advantage of these specializations and the brain's associative nature to support the learner in the classroom.

Although there is still much that is unknown about the functioning of the cortex, there are some intriguing clues. Wittrock (1980) states that our brain hemispheres may specialize in the strategy of coding used rather than in the type of information encoded. The left brain is most responsible for linear, sequential, analytic, rational thinking. Reading, language, the computational aspects of mathematics, the inquirer, and the critic are located in this hemisphere. Thought of a metaphoric, spatial, holistic nature is the province of the right hemisphere. Here we find involvement with the creation of art, music, the concepts of mathematics, synthesizing, and a more coherent perceptual style. The right brain seems better at passive comprehension, the left at active articulation.

Herrmann (1981) believes that most of us have a dominant style that we are comfortable using, and has developed an instrument for assessing these preferences. His results indicate that when we use our left-brain mode we show preference for written directions, structured places, organized tasks, lists that can be crossed off when things are accomplished, successful results, control, and closure. When we are using our right-brain mode we tolerate a lack of closure and ambiguity, desire lots of space, see the whole problem or situation, appreciate an artistic and aesthetic focus, and enjoy spontaniety.

Some of the dominance seen in the use of brain hemispheres may be linked to the sex of the student or, more accurately, to how the hormones of each sex affect the organization and maturation of the learner's brain. Greater lateralization or specialized activation of spatial function to the right hemisphere in males seems to give them superior ability on tests of spatial skills. However, male lateralization of language to the left hemisphere seems to work against them and results in a more narrow though precise language ability (Witelson, 1976). More important, however, is how soon each hemisphere's particular strategies become mature and competent enough to integrate function. Maturation of the left hemisphere seems to occur earlier and to be more pronounced in girls, which may explain their apparent superiority in verbal learning (Bryden, 1970; Kimura, 1967; Pizzamiglio & Cecchini, 1971; Reid, 1980; Van Duyne & D'Alonzo, 1976). By age four boys surpass girls on tests of spatial function (Levy, 1980) and maintain this superiority at least through middle-age (Davies, 1965; Porteus, 1965). Language develops earlier in girls than in boys (Clarke-Stewart, 1973; Moore, 1967) and remains a superior function into middle-age (Backman, 1972; Rosenberg & Sutton-Smith, 1969; Stevenson, Hale, Klein & Miller, 1968). These tendencies seem to hold across cultures (Porteus, 1965). It seems then to be a function of the brain that the left hemisphere of girls and the right hemisphere of boys mature earlier and that biological differences between the genders are largely responsible (Levy, 1980).

These significant differences suggest that diffuse organization within and between hemispheres is more typical of females and that strongly lateralized organiza-

148

tion is more typical for males. We cannot assume, however, that such biological differences rule out effects of the environment. The environment reinforces and magnifies those aptitudes considered sex-appropriate by the society. It must also be noted that not all males and females fit these data; as with any generalized data, we have only the dominant trend. Traditional and stereotypic masculine and feminine roles still serve to limit a full range of function for both boys and girls.

Herrmann (1981) believes that teaching our brain functions to work together gives us the advantage of our full ability and creativity. If we are concerned about the optimal growth of intelligence we must provide ourselves opportunities for the use of both right- and left-brain processes. As Wittrock (1980) explains, "It seems clear that the sophistication and variety of cortical brain function cannot be reduced to any single dichotomy. The cortex of the brain performs a myriad of different functions within and across its hemispheres" (p. 393).

Most importantly we must recognize not only the specialization of the hemispheres but also the need for interaction and intersupport between the hemispheres. For example, trained musicians listen to music with both left and right brain. More nerve connections exist between the halves of the brain than from the brain to any other part of the body. To reach our potential we must develop both types of functions and integrate our learning experiences. Concentration on the rational, cognitive functions of the brain will paradoxically limit these very functions. Without the support of a well-developed right hemisphere left-brain growth will be inhibited. For years good teachers and parents have intuitively used both right- and left-brain functions in their teaching. The evidence for specialization now validates their teaching ideas.

Accompanying this information on the nature of brain hemispheres are some interesting discoveries concerning the limbic system of the brain, discoveries that directly affect some of our previous assumptions on how learning occurs. You will recall that this limbic system is considered to be the gateway to higher thought and seems to be responsible for the release of neurotransmitters, a process that can enhance or inhibit the cells of the cortex. Complexity, novelty, challenge, and pleasure are triggering mechanisms for neurotransmitters that enhance brain function.

Task analysis, the process of breaking down information into small and simple steps, is one of the most often used methods of teaching difficult concepts. While this may be a justifiable practice for very slow or retarded learners, average and able learners will find this practice incompatible with the way their brain operates. As we now understand brain function, optimal learning requires complexity and challenge (Restak, 1979).

In an attempt to take advantage of these findings a high school math teacher in a nearby district decided to introduce some geometric shapes all at the same time instead of separately, a practice he had found unsuccessful in the past. He reported that the complexity of the lesson seemed to intrigue the students and that they not only showed more motivation but were able to differentiate and conceptualize beyond the material given. By allowing them to analyze the differences and develop their own organizing system for the complex ideas they were confronting the students became more effective learners.

Repetition and drill, other methods often used to help students retain information, also seem to be negated by current brain research. Researchers are consistently finding that the brain processes novel events more efficiently than those encountered repeatedly and will in fact not attend to sameness and routine. As boredom sets in the higher brain processes shut down (Restak, 1979).

A technique that reduces the need for this repetition and drill has been developed from the work of the Bulgarian educator Georgi Lozanov (1977). Though this example employs vocabulary as the material to be learned the same procedure can be used with spelling words, math facts, dates in history, and any other factual information.

Exercise 7.1. An Integrative Vocabulary Lesson

Purpose: to learn vocabulary words and their definitions
Time involved: 15 minutes
Material needed: tape recorder; tape of calming music, e.g. Vivaldi's "Spring"; list of vocabulary words and their definitions
Preferred structure: students seated comfortably, teacher at the front of the group
Teaching function: information giving
Procedure: Ask the students to relax in their chairs, close their eyes, and listen to calming music. While they are listening to the music read vocabulary words and their meanings aloud in the same tempo as the music. Read each word three times using three different degrees of volume, first normal, then louder, and then softer. You may wish to begin with ten to fifteen words; you may increase the number at later sessions as the students become used to this method of learning. Allow the music to play for several seconds after you have finished reading the vocabulary words. Invite the students to gently open their eyes and return to the room.

After an hour or more read the words again and ask the students to give the meanings aloud as a group. During this recall session you may wish to have them watch you write (or, with younger students, print) the words on the chalkboard or show them cards for each word. This exercise should not have a drill quality connected to it. Prerecording this lesson and placing it in a learning center allows students to listen as many times as they wish.

Lozanov suggests that students then use the words learned in active ways: role playing, creating a play, greeting each other, and in conversation. He strongly advises against drill work or homework, insisting that the experience must be pleasant and novel. His research has shown amazing results and continues to be modified for use in many countries around the world.

MODELS FOR COGNITIVE DEVELOPMENT

During the past two decades a number of models have been developed that focus on the thinking process and its place in curriculum planning and implementation. A brief review of some of these models will reveal an immersion in the linear, rational aspects of the brain's function. While these models remain excellent educational tools for the teacher other brain functions need to be incorporated into the learning experience. Integrating the emotional, physical, and intuitive functions, and more of the spatial, gestalt specialization of the cortex will make these models even more effective.

The Taxonomy of Educational Objectives: Cognitive Domain (Bloom, 1956)

Bloom presents and clarifies a taxonomy of learning that illustrates the importance of presenting learning at many levels to meet the needs of a variety of learners. Average and more able students need to have learning presented at the levels of knowledge, comprehension, application, analysis, synthesis, and evaluation. Opportunities to work at more advanced levels are crucial for the more able student. Because the brain must continue to be stimulated or loose its capability the fact that the majority of classrooms have been found to present learning experiences only at the lower levels

Figure 7.1. *Taxonomy circle*

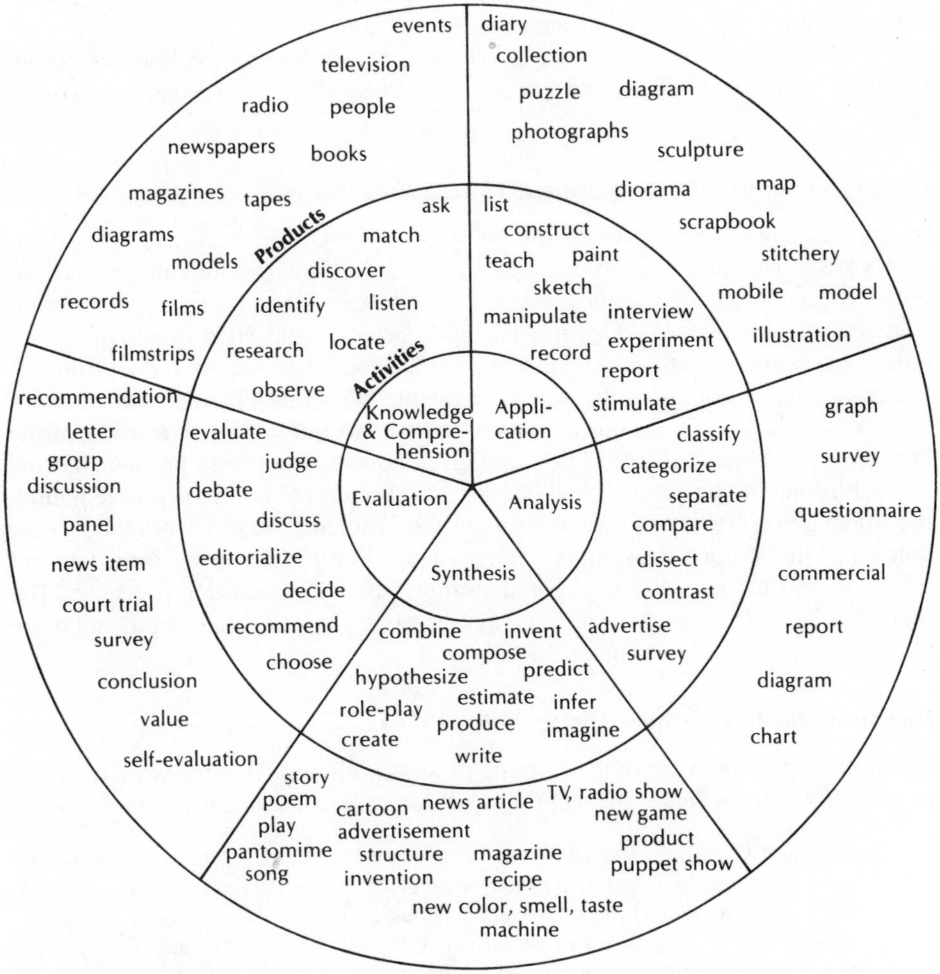

The wheel in Figure 7.1 was developed by my colleague, Barry Ziff, and a class of teachers of the gifted. From *Growing up gifted* (p. 222) by B. Clark, 1983, Columbus, OH: Charles E. Merrill. Reprinted by permission.

is of concern to all teachers who wish to optimize learning. Being aware of and using all the levels of learning that Bloom and his committee identified are important in every classroom (see Figure 7.1).

Structure of Intellect (SOI) (Guilford, 1967)

The SOI Model provided psychology with a multifactor view of intelligence to replace the single factor view previously held. The division of intellectual abilities into three dimensions—contents, operations, and products—and their subdivisions enables this model to show interrelationships between human abilities. Some educators, especially Meeker (1969), extend the use of the SOI Model to serve as a basis for a diagnostic-prescriptive tool in the teaching of thinking skills. Meeker believes that using the SOI Model for curriculum development will allow educators to meet the educational needs of each child more adequately.

While both of these models are too often used as workbook or seatwork assignments integrative methods such as physical encoding (see chapter 5) can be incorporated.

Inquiry (Bruner, 1960; Suchman, 1961, 1962)

Bruner strongly believed that any discipline could be taught at any age if the discipline's basic structure was communicated in ways the student could understand. He urged educators to address themselves to the process of learning, e.g. to present science as the scientist would learn it. This approach certainly lends itself to the use of integrative learning. Suchman did just that by developing an inquiry model from his understanding of the scientific way of thinking. While this model oversimplifies human thought by leaving out important areas it is quite useful in teaching many important processes. Suchman's program gives students practice in problem solving by establishing the properties of all objects or systems involved in the problem, finding which objects or systems are relevant to the problem, and discovering how they function in the solution. Sessions are designed to help students learn to formulate and test their own theories and to become aware of their own learning processes. The outcomes lead not so much to new or right or wrong answers but to fresh and more productive questions (see Figure 7.2).

Instrumental Enrichment (Feuerstein, 1978)

A somewhat different view of the learning process is embodied in the work of Israeli psychologist Reuven Feuerstein. His theory includes the following theoretical aspects:

1. Structural Cognitive Modifiability. Feuerstein (1978) describes this concept as "the unique capacity of human beings to change or modify the structure of their cognitive functioning in order to adapt to changing demands of life situations" (p. 1.1). Cognitive changes can be considered structural when they are self-perpetuating, of an autonomous and self-regulatory nature, and when they show permanence. Human beings are open systems, accessible to change throughout their lives.
2. Mediated Learning Experiences (MLE). Although much is learned through direct experience most of the structural changes that occur in human cognition are the result of

Figure 7.2. *A visualization of the inquiry model*

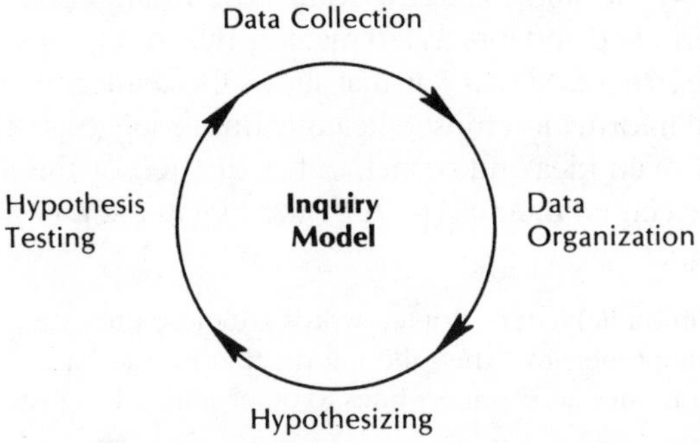

Data Collection

Hypothesis
Testing

**Inquiry
Model**

Data
Organization

Hypothesizing

From *Growing up gifted* (p. 226) by B. Clark, 1983, Columbus, OH: Charles E. Merrill. Reprinted by permission.

MLE. Characteristically these experiences are intentional, have the quality of transcendance, have meaning for the learner, mediate behavior, and mediate a feeling of competence. (Notice the similarity to the conditions suggested in Chapter 6.)

3. Learning Potential. Almost everyone has a great deal more capacity for thought and intelligent behavior than is often exhibited. Assessing this potential requires a dynamic assessment of the learning process rather than a sampling of previously learned material, e.g. instead of asking *How much does a person know?* the question becomes *How can the person learn?*

Feuerstein's learning process moves the student from passive dependence to autonomous, independent learning. This along with the underlying assumptions of Instrumental Enrichment make this model a valuable one for introducing complexity and cognitive challenges. The training which accompanies the use of materials developed by Feuerstein includes attention to the students' feeling, attitudes, and to relating the information to real life circumstances. The following paragraph from a fifth grade student provides an example of this model's outcome.

Instrumental Enrichment and Space
Instrumental Enrichment has taught me to think and recall instead of being impulsive. The instrument dealing with space has shown me how to think vividly and pictorially instead of at a more concrete and symbolic level. Now I use different strategies and use cues and deferred judgement which helps me in life, such as in baseball and math. Now I hypothesize more than I've ever done. I put myself in a position that could happen and think of alternatives. I've learned to internalize. Instrumental Enrichment and Space have probably changed my life from an impulsive person to a *kid with a flowering mind.* (Chang Weisberg, 1984)

Mindmapping (Buzan, 1983)

This method allows students to use both hemispheric specializations to support and to improve their information processing and retention. In addition to many clues that might improve reading skill, memory, and other school skills Buzan offers a strategy for notetaking that he refers to as Mindmapping. Designed to give students an alternative to the traditional linear mode of organizing information, mindmapping asks students to use the multi-dimensional and pattern-making capabilities of their brains to organize and record the information. Because the brain works primarily with key concepts in an interlinked and integrated manner Buzan suggests that notes and word relations should be structured in a way that shows these interrelationships as easily as possible. To record information most efficiently Buzan suggests that "one should start from the centre or main idea and branch out as dictated by the individual ideas and general form of the central theme" (p. 91). Buzan gives the following suggestions for creating a mindmap:

1. Print words in capital letters. Printed words are more photographic, more immediate, and more comprehensive when the information is read back.
2. Print words on lines and connect lines to other lines. This gives the mindmap a basic structure.
3. Print words in units. This leaves each word to be joined to other thoughts and allows note-taking to be more free and flexible.
4. Print the ideas freely and with no concern for order. More will be captured in the mindmap when you allow your mind to recall everything as quickly and as freely as possible. Final order will evolve from the map itself.

The importance of the ideas are clearly indicated when main ideas are in the center and the less important ideas are at the edge, making links between concepts immediately recognizable. New information can easily be added, and recall and review are both more effective and more quickly completed.

Simulation

Simulation, the process of exploring a problem or an idea by simulating or recreating the events within the classroom, develops cognitive abilities and understanding through affective involvement. Simulation requires the learner's active participation and results in a high degree of motivation, interest in research, use of decision making and communication skills, a deeper level of understanding of the content, a change of attitudes, and an integration of curriculum areas. Simulations might include board games (chess, Stocks & Bonds [3M Company]), paper and pencil exercises, environmental and "real life" recreations, such as crises at the United Nations, power status of socio-economic classes, and the signing of the Declaration of Independence.

Simulations can be purchased from companies that develop and sell them or they can be structured and run by teachers and students. The following resources will aid you in developing simulations of your own: Boocock and Schild (1968); Seidner (1976); Sisk's *Teaching Gifted Children;* Taylor and Walford (1972); and Zuckerman and Horn (1973). Other resources for classroom simulations are NASA (Educational Services); Project SIMILE (Western Behavioral Science Institute, 1150 Silverado, LaJolla, CA 92037); Science Research Associates, Inc. (259 E. Erie Street, Chicago, IL 60611); Wiff 'n Proof (P.O. Box 71, New Haven, CT 06501).

Synectics

Synectics, a strategy developed by W. J. Gordon (1961), holds that learning is a combination of focusing, connection making, and application. "To learn," Gordon writes, "students must respond to subject matter by focusing on important points, internalizing those points, expressing their comprehension, and sometimes creatively applying what they have learned. Effective internalization takes place when students connect the subject matter to something they already know about" (Gordon & Poze, 1980, p. 147).

These assumptions are integrated into the curriculum or the problem-solving situation in several steps that utilize analogy and metaphor as tools for learning. The first step is to discover within the concept to be learned or problem to be solved the paradox existing at the core. Gordon shows, for example, that the paradox of double weakness, or that specific needs when taken together can make for strength, lay in the concept of symbiosis. Next, the student is asked to think of an analogy for the paradox. The old tale of Jack Spratt and his wife would provide a good analogy for this paradox. Gordon states that the very use of a connective analogy lends clarity and sophistication to expression of the concept. Personal analogies are later constructed by the students to further clarify the concept, allowing students to work at their own levels of ability. More able students will produce creative extensions of the process, resulting from subliminal connection-making processes which then become conscious, explicit, and within the student's control.

As we consider ways to use more of our brain's capabilities for the learning process we must be very aware that each of us has all of the learning styles or modalities available to us. I believe it would be unfortunate if we were to assess our students as to their preferred style or modality and then restrict them to that style. Research has shown that when people were encouraged to develop a mental area they had previously considered weak, this development, rather than detracting from other areas, seemed to produce a synergetic effect in which all areas of mental performance improved (Buzan, 1983). Figure 7.3 shows a mind map and an outline of a recent speech I gave. The mindmap was a great help to me during the planning stage while the outline aided the organization of my delivery. This exemplifies my belief that the ideal learning process would make available strategies that use both brain specializations and that allow students to choose which strategy works best for them. Presenting students with the opportunity to strengthen both the linear-rational and the spatial-gestalt thinking processes and then allowing them to choose which process to use seems to me to be an important goal. Using this strategy we will truly empower the student cognitively and allow for optimal learning.

Figure 7.3. Individualization mind map

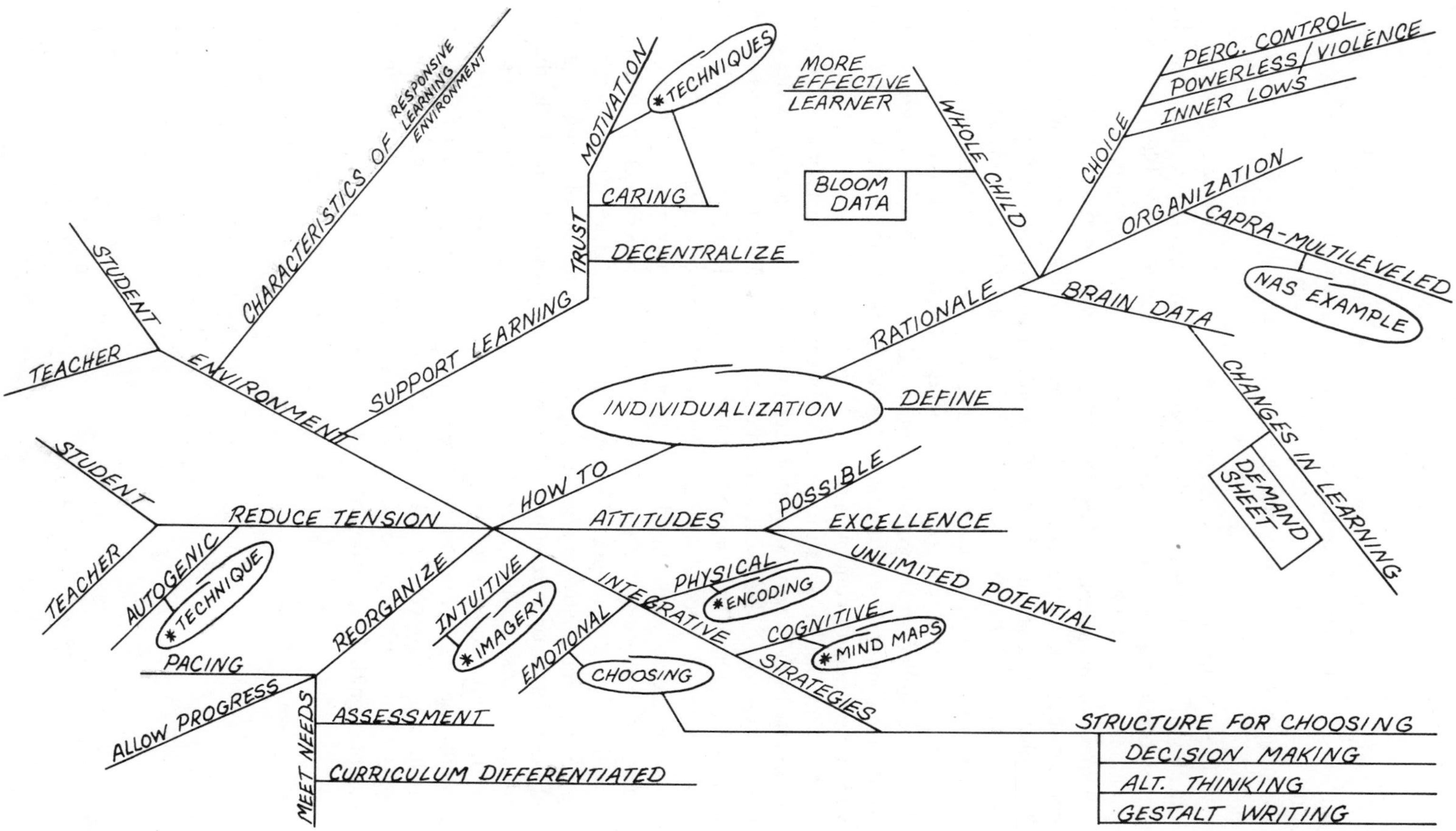

156

Form 7.3. Personalizing education: using individualization

Overview and goals

Definition of individualization:

    Highly structured, complex, decentralized
    Environment supports learning
      Characteristics of Responsive Learning Environment
    Allows variation in pace, level, grouping
    Meets each learner's needs
    Participation and involvement encouraged
    Bloom Study

Rationale for:

    Brain compatible learning
      Brain data
      Demand Sheet
      NAS experience—Multileveled adm., cross age
    Perceived control: teacher and student
      Inner locus/lessens with rewards
      Powerlessness main cause of stress, violence
    Actualize more potential, more motivation, higher level of learning
    Important to all children

How to develop:

    Environment—responsive, trust, complex, highly structured, flexible
    Reduce tension—Autogenic exercise
    Organize for—progress, meeting needs, continuous assessment
    Develop shared responsibility—
      Scope and Sequence
      Choice and perceived control
      Alternative thinking, decision making
      Self-assessment and evaluation
    Develop effective learners—brain compatible
      Integrative Education Model
        Cognitive, affective, physical, intuitive.

Results for students

Importance of attitude

    Change is possible
    Potential is unlimited, each student has a unique contribution to make
    We can be more effective and efficient
    It begins with YOU

8

Using Intuition: Our Highest Level of Synthesis

This chapter will discuss the last Key Component of the Integrative Education Model, Intuition and Integration. The least known and yet the most powerful area of human brain function, intuition is probably the area that promises the most for the continuance and fulfillment of humankind. All other areas of the brain provide support for and are supported by this area of function. As each area evolves to higher levels, more of the intuitive and creative functions become available (Goodman, 1978; MacLean, 1978; Restak, 1979).

A strange paradox exists in this area of function. According to neurobiologists the prefrontal cortex is the most uniquely human area of the brain. It is species specific, that is, humans share this area of the brain with no other life form. The functions of this area, however, are those that are least discussed by researchers, least recognized by educators, and most ridiculed by otherwise intelligent, thoughtful people. One thing is certain: this area of brain function is seldom presented without some kind of emotional response.

The prefrontal cortex's functions seem to include planning, insight, empathy, introspection, and other bases for intuitive thought (MacLean, 1978). It is engaged in firming up intention, deciding on action, and regulating our most complex behaviors (Restak, 1979). The prefrontal cortex is, in fact, the area that energizes and regulates all other parts: it houses our purpose.

The prefrontal lobes of the cortex play a critical role in high level intellectual and emotional operations, curiously probing for and monitoring input, analyzing and synthesizing incoming information, excluding the irrelevant and then referring the new information to memory. Later these areas reconstruct from scraps whole and relevant memories, taking the outward leap of hunches and fantasy, guessing and postulating, carrying the mind into the future, making plans, shaping strategies for goals, forecasting, and then making readjustments to fit new perceptions and new goals. Emotionally they will provide empathy and cues to sociability, the basis for a communal spirit, and a moral sense (Loye, 1983).

Goodman (1978) more specifically places the following functions in the area of the prefrontal cortex, which he believes fully develops between ages twelve and sixteen. Luria (1973) puts maturation of this area between the ages of four and seven.

1. Foresight. The ability to see patterns of change and to extrapolate from present trends to future possibilities. This process uses imagination, prediction, and behavioral planning.
2. Self-regulation of bodily processes through insight, internal commands, and generation of visual images. This is the basis for meditation and biofeedback strategies.
3. Analytic systems thinking. A high form of creativity, this complex analysis of input requires formal logic and metaphor.
4. Holos. A social sense, rational and emotional; the foundation of altruism.

Those most responsible for changing our culture (Plato, Newton, da Vinci, Einstein, etc.); important poets, musicians and artists (Keats, Mozart, Monet, etc.); philosophers, mathematicians, psychologists and educators (Phythagoras, Tesla, Jung, etc.); and modern scientists (Bohm, Prigogine, Pribram, etc.) all write about the use of intuition in their great discoveries and creative contributions. Although these abilities were highly valued by these eminent contributors to our culture schools do nothing to enhance them but rather ignore or actually inhibit their use.

160

The business community, a group whose organizations and techniques are so often used as models for making schools more efficient and effective, now shows an interest in intuition, especially the type of intuitive ability that allows prediction and forecasting. This interest is reflected in the increasing number of articles being written by and for the business community regarding the importance of the hunch in making executive decisions and the correlation between success in business and intuitive ability. Screening tests are now available to help those hiring at the executive level to know just which prospective candidate for an executive position ranks highest in intuitive ability (Goldberg, 1983; Loye, 1983).

Stories of those who have used the intuitive hunch successfully are fast becoming a part of the literature of success in business (Dean, Mihalasky, Ostrander, & Schroeder, 1974). Ray Kroc was advised by his staff, his board, and all those he consulted not to buy a small hamburger chain he was considering purchasing. He had a nagging hunch that he could not dismiss and after several days of personal introspection called his lawyer and ordered him to buy McDonald's. As he said later, "I felt in my funny bone it was a sure thing" (Goldberg, 1983).

WHAT IS INTUITION?

The intuitive process seems to be highly synthetic and dynamic, drawing from and integrating all other brain functions. This integrative characteristic allows the intuitive process to be compared with creativity. It is my belief that these two terms may be referring to the same human ability; the processes are quite similar regardless of which term you choose to use. The integration of all of our human functions—thinking, feeling, and sensing—releases intuition, which is also true of creativity. Restricting any one of these functions restricts intuition, also true of creativity. Intuition requires synthesis of all functioning as well as a spark from another dimension; so does creativity. Creative and intuitive processes seem to be expressions of the highest level of human intelligence. While this discussion will focus on the intuitive process, I ask you to note the similarity to discussions of the concept of creativity. Creativity may be, in fact, a part of the intuitive process.

Different investigators find different ways of viewing and defining intuition. As we have become aware in previous discussions of the Integrative Education Model, Jung (1933) referred to intuition as one of the four basic human functions. Bruner (1960) discusses intuition as an important part of the education process and encouraged its training. Expanding on the work of Loye (1983), and for the purposes of our discussion and the development of implementation strategies, I would like to define intuition as occuring in at least three levels:

1. Rational Intuition—While this may seem to be a contradiction of terms Rational Intuition expresses a level of intuitive behavior that realigns known information in such a way that new insights emerge. We intuit the next step to take in solving a problem, evaluating alternatives, diagnosing a treatment, or resolving a personal crisis. Though we have known the facts we see them in a new light, put them together in a new way, or infer from the past the direction to be taken. This area of intuition relies heavily on the highly synthetic characteristic of the intuitive process. By combining all one's

consciously-known information with information one once processed but which is no longer consciously available new alignments and new patterns seem to emerge.

2. Predictive Intuition—This level enlarges upon the processes of the first by including new information into existing patterns or sequences. Predictive Intuition includes the ability to complete unfinished pictures, see a gestalt from little information, and gain accurate insights not previously available with the given information. This area also builds on the first level by including unknown or only suspected information into the synthesis process. This is the level of the hunch, the "best guess," and the perception of the whole picture when only the parts can be seen by others. Here unconscious impressions or information of unknown source becomes an important part of the new patterns formed, the insights, or the profound conclusions. An individual may arrive at a solution to a problem while remaining unaware of the process involved. For some this process is called creativity (Goldberg, 1983).

This type of intuitive process is responsible for many breakthrough discoveries. The "aha" experience that comes after perhaps months or years of extensive preparation and that appears when the person is relaxed or involved in an entirely different task is a part of this level of intuition. The experience is euphoric, the solution suddenly absolutely clear. At this level the brain perceives matters with a holistic, gestalt awareness rather than with the linear, sequential mode.

This level of intuition is responsible for the forecasting of trends and the intuitive leap so valued in business, diplomacy, science, economics, and personal life decisions. Loye (1983) believes that the very best forecasting is done by those who can access all four functions: thinking, feeling, sensing, and intuiting.

3. Transformational Intuition—The third level of intuitive processing is the most fascinating and the most awesome. When operating at this level a person seems to be using a different kind of sensing that "picks up information through a means that has defied scientific understanding" (Loye, 1983, p. 52). Those who have received information at this level often report that ideas came to them suddenly, unbidden or in a dream, or that what they wrote came through them as if from an outside source. Brier and Tyminski (1970) concluded that such abilities may be common to us all, but for most it is a very weak signal usually missed due to the noise of everyday living.

The story is told of Churchill that, when London was under siege in the fall of 1941, as he was preparing to enter his car by the customary door being held open by his driver he instead stopped and walked around the car and let himself in the far door. Moments later a bomb exploded near the side where he would have been sitting. He would have been injured had he not changed his position. When asked later how he had known to sit where he did he replied, "Something said to me, 'Stop!' before I reached the car door held open for me. It then appeared to me that I was told I was meant to open the door on the other side and get in and sit there, and that's what I did" (Goldberg, 1983, p. 54). Goldberg calls this *operative intuition* and finds that it subtly guides, "sometimes with declarative force, sometimes with gentle grace" (p. 54).

Another way that this level of intuition may appear is as a coincidence, or what Jung calls *synchronicity*. These are happenings where events that have no apparent causal connection occur in such a way as to give meaning or significant impact. You seem to be at the right place at the right time, or you think of someone and very soon they appear.

Finally this level of intuition can be experienced as transcendence. This level can be observed within the brain as a change in the rate of coherence or the correlation between brain waves from separate regions of the brain. This coherence seems to be at its highest during transcendence (Goldberg, 1983). This highest form of knowing occurs when one knows and knows totally the universe, the self, and the connection between. Maslow (1971) began to explore this way of knowing just prior to his death, and his final work predicted that psychology would become more involved in the transpersonal and in transcendence. Eastern mystics seek this elevated state of knowledge as do the religious of all faiths. Variously known as enlightenment, illumination, ecstasy, or by other similar terms, this form of intuition is the ultimate experience, the drawing together of all other forms of intuitive process.

Although a single definition of the intuitive process would be difficult it is possible to show several common characteristics. Intuition at all levels seems to be:

1. a highly synthetic and dynamic process which integrates all other brain functions.
2. most accessible when one is in a relaxed state of mind and body.
3. inhibited by fear, tension, and stress. The harder we try to grasp it the less available it becomes. It is the first area of brain function to drop out when anxiety becomes too high.
4. difficult to communicate in a rational, linear mode, and is often symbolic in nature. Vocabulary for expressing intuitive experiences is limited.
5. free of the need to see the world in dichotomies, but is a merging of opposites. Wrong answers are often the best way to learn the correct information; the view of reality includes unity and separation together, self as a part of the world and at the same time apart from the world.
6. a natural process that can be encouraged and developed, and which seems to improve with use.
7. productive of insights, creative products and solutions, and affective actions.
8. usually following and based on an accumulation of skill or knowledge.
9. complementary to analytical thinking.
10. instantaneously knowing, complete, and often spontaneous. (Bruner, 1960; Capra, 1982; Goldberg, 1983; Loye, 1983; Luria, 1973)

Intuition can be quite fascinating to discuss but of what value is it in the classroom? Again let us look at history for some possible reasons to include intuitive process skills in our concern for optimal learning. Goldberg (1983) shares the following insights on using intuition:

> In the original manuscript describing his sun-centered cosmos, Copernicus mentioned the possibility that planetary motion might be elliptical rather than circular. He crossed it out. History credits the discovery to Johannes Kepler, who also had turned his back on the idea for three years before accepting it. "Why should I mince my words?" Kepler wrote. "The truth of Nature, which I had rejected and chased away, returned by stealth through the back door, disguising itself to be accepted. Ah, what a foolish bird I have been!" Kepler finally opened the door to elliptical motion, but, in turn, he closed it to universal gravitation, leaving that gem for Newton.
>
> When you find yourself leaning away from an intuitive idea, you may be acting like a "foolish bird." (pp. 195–196)

The physicist Capra (1975) tells us that rational knowing is useless if not accompanied and enhanced by intuitive knowing, equating intuition with new creative insights. Many of those working to include intuition in the classroom believe that the ability to concentrate with unusual clarity on complex tasks is a result of the intuitive function.

Students can expect to make impressive gains in areas of cognition, self-concept, and social-emotional development by using intuition-incorporating strategies. Among the cognitive gains are accelerated learning, higher levels of retention and recall, and higher interest in content. Other areas will show improvement in how competent the student feels, pleasure derived from learning, interpersonal relations, and teacher-student rapport (Bordan & Schuster, 1976; Galyean, 1977–80; Galyean, 1978–81; Lozanov, 1977; Prichard & Taylor, 1980; Samples, 1975).

DEVELOPING INTUITION IN THE CLASSROOM

Intuition is always available to us. Huxley (1962) believed that intuitive ability could be developed, and viewed cognition as a conscious, active power and intuition as a complementary, receptive power. "Both kinds of training" he wrote, "are absolutely indispensable. If you neglect either you'll never grow into a fully human being" (p. 255).

Conditions Which Foster Intuition

1. A relaxed state
2. Silence
3. Focused attention
4. A receptive, non-judgemental attitude
5. An ability to synthesize all brain functions
6. Novelty and variety in the environment
7. A teacher who:
   values and encourages intuitive processes;
   provides opportunities for educated guessing, hypothesis setting, probability testing;
   is comfortable with mistakes, both the students' and personal;
   emphasizes personal discovery over memorization of facts;
   models intuitive behavior
   (Bruner, 1960; Galin, 1976; Goldberg, 1983; Loye, 1983; Raudsepp, 1980).

These same researchers note that the following conditions stifle intuition: focusing on mistakes instead of successes; avoiding change; seeking control and predictability; adhering rigidly to rules and set procedures; anticipating disasters instead of miracles; taking ourselves, our work, and our problems too seriously; and relying heavily on analytic procedures.

Clark (1977) gives three basic steps for developing our intuitive abilities: quiet the mind, focus attention, and use a receptive attitude. These simple steps cannot be developed unless teachers regularly allow time for them, practice them, and value the outcomes. This is not a one-time-only exercise or strategy.

The intuitive process seems to be triggered by a number of practices or skills that can be incorporated into the curriculum, allowing students to release more of their intuition and to become more creative.

Relaxation and Tension Reduction

Nervousness, fear, and tension block even learned knowledge; the first step to releasing intuitive ability is to reduce tension (Assagioli, 1973; Roberts & Clark, 1976). Teaching techniques that reduce tension allow more interaction between the cortical hemispheres and better integration of their specializations. Relaxation allows students to gain access to higher centers of the brain/mind system and to produce biochemical support for the learning process (Hart, 1978; Restak, 1979). For information and strategies concerning this area see Key Component I, Chapter 4.

Imagery, Fantasy, and Visualization

Important components in developing intuitive ability are imagery, fantasy, and visualization. Noted scientists Faraday, Galton, and Einstein have reported solving scientific problems in visual images and only afterwards translating their thoughts into words (Hunt, 1982).

> In a famous instance of this, Einstein, unable to reconcile his special theory of relativity with Newtonian physics, pictured a box falling freely down a very long shaft; inside it, an occupant took coins and keys out of his pocket and let them go. The objects, Einstein saw, remained in midair, alongside him, because they were falling at the same rate as he—a situation temporarily identical with being in space, beyond any gravitational field. From this visual construct, Einstein was able to sense some of those seemingly contradictory relationships about movement and rest, acceleration and gravity, that he later put into mathematical and verbal form in his general theory of relativity.
> (p. 215)

Singer (1976) believes that the foundation for serenity and purpose in our lives may lie in fantasy. He found that those who had trouble using fantasy to enrich their lives or to substitute for aggression had serious problems. Children whose games are lacking in fantasy have trouble recalling facts and integrating events. In adolescence these children are dependent on the external environment and may engage in antisocial, delinquent, and aggressive acts as a result of their inability to internalize humanistic attitudes. As adults their problems increase and "their inner experiences seem less insistent than even the most irrelevant physical fact of their immediate environment" (Singer, 1976, p. 34). Alcoholism, obesity, and drug abuse may be the consequences of such an impoverished inner life.

Nurturing the growth of fantasy is easy. Using sound effects and voice changes while reading to children, allowing them to make up plays, to finish open-ended stories, and to play pretending games all provide opportunities for such development. A climate that encourages the sharing of fantasies will allow those fantasies to become the basis for books, reports, poems, and journals.

Fantasy journeys also can be helpful and can provide understanding not available from factual reading. A high school teacher reported using fantasy as a tool for teaching history. After relaxing, the students were asked to go back in their imagination to the 1860s. They were told to see, taste, smell, and hear all that they could. After a time

Children can take a fantasy journey by imagining what it would have been like to be a train engineer long ago.

the students were returned to the present and asked to write down everything they could remember. After compiling all the experiences into a class journal the students were told to validate as much as they could by using library resources, texts, journals, and diaries written during that period. The results were an exciting learning experience that will long be remembered by the students. Using this same technique electronics teachers can send their students as electrons through an entire circuit, and science teachers can guide their students who imagine themselves to be red blood cells through the circulatory system.

The use of inner visualization is growing in therapeutic settings. Evidence suggests that changes in perception, attitude, behavior, and even physiology can be made by visualization procedures (Goldberg, 1983). Hunt (1982) reports that a recent study revealed greater success with a recall exercise when a group of university students were told to visualize the room in which they had originally learned the words. Visualization allowed them to equal the recall of those who were tested in the original room. Students tested in a different room without visualizing were less successful.

Try the following exercise to experience how visualization can change a physical function.

Exercise 8.1. The Lemon Tree

Very gently close your eyes. . . . Imagine that you are just waking up in the morning in Southern California. . . . It is a cool, clear day with just a hint of warmness. . . . Feel the bed covers around you; . . . stretch and begin to think about getting out of bed. . . . Swing your legs over the side of the bed and slowly get to your feet. . . . Put on your robe and walk out of the bedroom, through the living room, and onto the patio. . . . Feel the cool cement of the patio. . . . Walk into the yard and feel the soft grass on your feet, the dampness of the dew on the grass. . . . Ahead of you is a lemon tree. . . . Notice the dark green leaves, the dew on the leaves, the bright yellow lemons nestled among them. . . . Walk up to the tree and reach out and pick the lemon closest to you. . . . Feel the smoothness of the skin of the lemon, the coolness . . . slightly damp with the dew. . . . Now with your thumbnail slice into the skin of the lemon. . . . Notice the spray that comes from the break in the skin; smell the tangy odor of the spray. . . . Begin to pull off a part of the skin of the lemon. . . . You can hear the membranes tear as you pull away pieces of the skin. . . . Now push your thumbnail into the fruit of the lemon. . . . Let the juice of the lemon flow over your hand, cool juice of the lemon flowing down onto your hand. . . . Now stick your tongue into the hole in the lemon. . . . Let the cool lemon juice trickle into your mouth, down your throat, lemon juice flowing into your mouth and throat. . . . What are your salivary glands doing? Open your eyes. . . . You don't have a lemon in your hand, but you have just changed a physiological function by using your imagination.

Imagery can help the learner focus and prepare for optimal learning. As we discussed in Chapter 4 the students at the New Age School begin each day with exercises that promote both relaxation and coherence. Many of these exercises involve imagery. These techniques can also be used to present new information in content areas.

Spelling—Ask the students to gently close their eyes, then ask them to see in their mind's eye something to write on: a chalkboard, a piece of paper, sand, etc. Ask them to write (or print if younger children are involved) each word as you spell it. Ask them to visualize each word clearly. Ask them to gently open their eyes and look at each word as you have written it and compare it with their own image. Later have them see their imagined list of words again. Remind them to check their list image when they are spelling each word as you check for retention.

Math—To teach concepts such as diameter, radius, and circumference ask students to close their eyes and visualize a large round swimming pool. Ask them to swim around the edge of the pool; they are now swimming around the circumference of the pool. Ask them to swim from the side to the middle of the pool; they are now swimming the radius of the pool. Ask them to swim back to the edge and then swim directly from one side of the pool to the other; they are now swimming the diameter of the pool. Ask the students to gently open their eyes and draw each way they just swam. Write the words on the board and ask them to use them in describing the route they swam.

Composition—Galyean (1983a) reports that very original and creative compositions can be elicited from students by using their own internal images. For example, ask the students to write about "Things I Like at School" and "Things That Bother Me at School." Begin the lesson by asking the students to close their eyes and imagine themselves as photographers taking pictures of things they like and don't like around the school. After they have had sufficient time to "see" several photos for each topic ask them to draw and write about their topics using the pictures they just "took" with their mind camera. Galyean finds that this intuitive beginning helps students to succeed in their writing.

If you want to read more about imagery, fantasy journeys, and visualization, refer to Bagley and Hess (1982), Galyean (1983a), Hendricks and Roberts (1977), Hills and Rozman (1978), Samples (1976, 1977), and Vaughan (1979).

Alternative Thinking and Futuristics

Good decision making and the development of intelligence are highly dependent on our ability to produce and evaluate alternatives. Probability guessing is an activity that brings the intuitive function into the learning process.

For example, when the Westward Expansion is the topic of study the teacher might ask the students to consider the following: What if France had not been willing to sell the Louisiana Territory? What if there had been twice as many Indians living on the plains? What if gold had not been discovered in California and Colorado? This kind of questioning can lead to some interesting discussions and motivate students to learn more. Student-generated scenarios forecasting future events are a natural result. The field of Futuristics is rich in the use of intuitive processing.

Once students feel safe in the environment provided and know that you value and encourage their intuitive ability you will learn a great deal from them about intuitive functioning. As with all other human abilities intuition becomes better with use.

In a sculpture lesson at the New Age School the students were asked to form their clay into a large ball. They were then instructed to put a flat end on their clay ball so that it could stand by itself on the table. The students were asked to place their hands on the sides of their clay ball and to gently close their eyes. The teacher then said, *Relax and focus on the feeling in your hands. . . . Be very aware of the feel of the clay. . . . Let all of your attention be on the clay and what it feels like. . . . Imagine the clay deep inside. . . . Know your clay all the way through. . . . Allow your mind's eye to see what figure is inside the clay . . . what form is resting in there waiting for you to free it. . . . Once you have a feeling or an image of what your clay holds inside, you may open your eyes and begin to remove the clay that surrounds the figure or shape waiting inside.* Later, in the discussion of how they felt about this activity and what they felt they had accomplished, the teacher mentioned that the great sculptor Michaelangelo had always worked with his clay and marble in this manner. It is truly amazing how creative and talented students become when this approach is used.

The following exercise has been used with students from preschool age to graduate level. All find it an amazing experience, assuring them that they have a great deal of intuitive ability. "Lady Bug" gives them an opportunity to notice how the intuitive process feels and allows them to stretch their ability further. When Chris Cenci first originated the exercise she used a stuffed toy lady bug with her preschool students as the object they were to "find." Older students have used cookies, flowers, or crackers with excellent results.

Exercise 8.2. Lady Bug

Purpose: to allow the students to experience a way of knowing other than the rational and to give them concrete experiences with some of the intuitive processes

Time involved: 20 to 30 minutes, perhaps longer if the students have a lot of interest in their experience and want to talk or write about it

Materials needed: a stuffed animal (e.g. lady bug); cookies, crackers or flowers (each person involved should be given two cookies or crackers if these are to be used as the object)

Organizational pattern: total class or small group activity

Teaching role: director and guide throughout the activity, facilitator of follow-up discussions

Procedure: When the students are seated in a circle or semi-circle pass around a stuffed toy. Ask the students to observe it carefully. Ask the students to look at the color of the object, to feel the texture, experience the smell, the feel (for cookies and crackers, the taste). If you are using cookies or crackers invite the students to eat one now. Now take the object and place it where the students cannot see it, preferably in a different room or outside. Once the object is out of sight ask the students to close their eyes and remember all they can about the lady bug: how it felt, how it looked, how it smelled (and tasted). Ask the students to become the lady bug. Then say, *The lady bug is no longer in this room. Can you imagine where it is? Is it in a place that is light or dark? Hot or cold? Is it over something or under something? What colors are around it? Is there anything else you are aware of around the lady bug that I have not thought to ask you?*

Ask the students to open their eyes and record all that they can about the whereabouts of the lady bug. Ask the questions again, this time tallying the answers on the board to see if today *we are mostly on target or off target.* Invite the students to follow you or the person who hid the lady bug and see just where it is. When they return ask them to refer to their papers. Discuss what details they visualized that had been validated by their observation. Do not collect the papers; they may or may not choose to show them to you. There are no right or wrong answers, only observations that are on or off target for the day. Remind them that as with any other skill intuitive ability can be improved with use.

Some amazing on target experiences with this exercise include students who have "seen" patterns on the sofa next to the cookies, the color and shape of the drying rack on which the cookies were placed, the crystal glasses on shelves alongside the cookies, and a chicken wire divider in a storage room close to where the cookies were hidden. What moved me most, however, was an experience during one of the discussions after the exercise.

A group of high school students had been participating and as we were discussing their experiences I asked if any of them had had similar experiences. Several of the students shared events they considered to be similar, times when they knew something before it happened, dreams that seemed to be precognitive, etc. A young student in a wheelchair raised her hand to speak and when the group turned their attention to her she said quietly, *I just want to thank you for sharing those experiences with me.* She sat perfectly still for a moment and with a catch in her voice continued, *I have had things like this happen to me all my life, but I thought I was weird, an alien or something, so I never told anyone. I just continued to feel that I was so different that I didn't fit in anywhere. Now all of you are saying that you have had these experiences too. I'm not so weird, and for the first time I feel like a part of things, I feel that I belong. Thank you.* It was obvious that she was about to cry. Everyone was very quiet.

We were all affected by the understanding and affection in the room. If allowing students to own part of themselves and letting them feel like they belong is the only thing that ever results from these kinds of exercises I consider them well worth the time and tremendously important.

Here is another mind-stretcher that students find fascinating. Some years ago research indicated that the cells in our body have the same capabilities but have been programmed to perform different functions (Hattersley, 1970). Theoretically, then, it should be possible for one area of the body to exhibit the same function as another area. The specific function I addressed was the act of seeing. If the brain actually does the seeing, can messages be sent to the brain giving visual information (color, shape, size, patterns, etc.) through the fingertips? The research indicated that it might be possible. I decided to find out. The following exercise is the result of that inquiry.

Exercise 8.3. Seeing with Your Fingers

Purpose: to give students an opportunity to discover unknown intuitive capabilities and to let them experience an intuitive stretch
Time involved: 30 to 40 minutes
Materials needed: magazines with full-page color pictures (one per student would be best)
Organizational pattern: groups of three seated on the floor or at tables
Teaching role: explain and demonstrate the process, facilitate discussion
Procedure: Ask the students to form groups of three. Give each group two or three magazines or a group of colored pictures taken from magazines. Tell them that they are going to try an experiment. Discuss the theoretical possibilities indicated by the cell research described previously. Demonstrate how one student at a time in each group will "view" a colored picture selected by the others in the group. During the selection and viewing processes the viewing students must have their eyes closed and are to place their fingertips at the top of the colored picture and slowly move their hands downward over the entire page. They may move their fingertips over the surface of the page or just above in any way and as many times as they choose.

The "viewing" students are instructed to say aloud whatever impressions they receive while repeatedly scanning the page with their fingertips. The most difficult part of the exercise is to keep the viewing students from censoring themselves; encourage them to say whatever comes to mind. The other students in the group are to be supportive, asking leading questions such as *What about the picture makes you think of horses?* or *Do you feel any sensation of color?* or *Are there any different areas on the page?* Under no circumstances should these non-viewers comment on whether the observations made by the "viewing" student are right or wrong. No judgemental comments (*That's very good!*) should be made.

After the viewing students have taken as much time as they wish to "see" the picture they may open their eyes and discuss the experience with the others. Continue this process until each member of the group has had an opportunity to view at least one picture.

Allow time for those who wish to share their experience with the total group to do so. The students may wish to speculate on what was actually happening to make the viewing possible.

I don't know if information is picked up from the picture or from other people who are looking at the picture, but in either case the results are always interesting. An art teacher recently told me that the most difficult thing he had to teach the students in his classes was how to see things in a different manner. His students always seemed to want to see from only one perspective, one familiar point of view. This exercise can certainly convince a student that there is more than one way to view things, and that we are capable in ways we don't even suspect.

Other ways to practice stretching the intuitive processes are:

making quick decisions on minor matters
making predictions about:
    who is calling on the phone
    the outcome of sporting events
    what someone will wear
    which line will move most quickly
covering the captions on newspaper photographs and quickly stating what is going on
describing the age, profession, hobbies, home, etc. of the person(s) in photographs carried by friends (Goldberg, 1983)

Many professional educators will need to change their attitudes and practices if intuition is to become a valued part of the curriculum. In a study of teacher attitudes toward students who exhibit characteristics of creativity all cultures sampled punished children who were considered intuitive thinkers, emotionally sensitive, and/or who were unwilling to accept matters as traditionally presented (Dettmer, 1981). Rockenstein (1985), in her development of a taxonomy for the Intuitive Domain, comments, "Teachers know very well how to train students to prepare and verify. But if incubation is prevented, and illumination is blocked, there may well be little of worth to verify" (p. 94).

Wescott (1968), Raudsepp (1980), Krippner (1983), and Goldberg (1983) view the following characteristics as indicative of intuitive thinkers. Most intuitive thinkers

1. accept and trust the intuitive process
2. are unconventional and willing to take risks
3. are confident, secure, and independent
4. think holistically
5. enjoy abstract thinking
6. focus on outcomes, the long term view
7. are frequently involved in art, drama, and/or music
8. read enthusiastically
9. tolerate ambiguity and change and are flexible
10. are playful, whimsical, and enjoy humor and informality

If ever a society needed the wisdom and inspiration of intuitive people, it is ours. A growing awareness of the contribution of intuitive and integrative processes in our lives is now taking place. More and more eminent figures can be heard openly alluding to the part such experiences play in their growth and in their achievements. Pete Rose, during an interview just after he had broken Ty Cobb's batting record, admitted that he was very excited but that *it was only when I looked up and saw my dad and Ty Cobb standing just above me smiling that it got me and I started crying*. When in a televised interview Barbara Striesand was asked why she demands perfection in all things she explained that she just sees things differently, as though they are complete, perfectly finished; she will not settle for less. The business world is not the only area interested in developing the intuitive potential, and it will be up to teachers to find ways to expand and enhance this valuable resource. Integrative Education can help in this search.

PART III
Developing Curriculum

9

The Integrative
Curriculum:
Strategies and Lessons

In this chapter all of the information from previous chapters will combine to form the basis of effective curricular strategies. As a result many of our basic beliefs about teaching and learning need to be changed or replaced. New practices developed from these new beliefs are in order.

1. Because intelligence is dynamic we must develop an environment that can respond appropriately to each learner. This environment must allow:

   access to content at many levels of difficulty, e.g. advanced and off-grade-norm material;

   the opportunity to pursue content with a variety of pacing, e.g. faster, more in depth pacing that allows for more intense levels of study;

   access to content at a variety of processing levels, e.g. Bloom's Taxonomy.

2. Because the brain processes and accesses more function when tension is reduced we must teach and use strategies for tension reduction in the classroom for the beginning of the day, before and during testing or high stress learning activities, and to energize.

3. Because use of the physical sensing function of the brain provides support for learning by increasing understanding and retention of concepts we must use movement and physical encoding strategies as part of the teaching process.

4. Because the brain uses emotions to trigger the production of biochemistry to enhance or inhibit the thinking functions we must plan and implement emotional support for learning by:

   using language that empowers the learner;

   including strategies which build community and interpersonal communication and understanding;

   using strategies to align student goals with school goals;

   teaching communication skills;

   including choice in the environment and in learning experiences;

   including strategies which build perceived control;

   including self-evaluation.

5. Because there are at least two ways to process thinking we must provide opportunities for learning that allow use of both linear, rational and spatial, gestalt processing.

6. Because the brain seeks novelty, complexity, variety, and challenge we must provide these in the classroom as the standard for each lesson.

7. Because intuition, future planning, and creativity are unique to human beings and may be their most powerful brain processes we must include use of these functions in planning and implementing the learning experience via

   visualization and imagery;

   "what if" experiences;

   strategies that allow intuitive awareness and stretching;

   strategies that encourage future thinking;

   strategies that encourage divergent thinking and production.

8. Because the brain's major function is to synthesize and integrate all previously mentioned brain functions we must provide opportunities for learners to learn through integration of all the brain's functions by:

   teaching with multi-sensory strategies;

   teaching multi-disciplinary content;

   integrating thinking, feeling, physical sensing, and intuitive processing in the learning experience.

9. Because we as teachers directly influence development of all learners' capacities, abilities, motivations, and views of reality what we do is tremendously important to each

individual learner, to the collective society and the way it will be structured, and to the future of the planet.

For these reasons I truly believe that you and I as teachers are creating the future.

Implementation of each of the seven Key Components presented in earlier chapters will be unique in each classroom. Integrative Education is a structure or framework for optimal learning; the Key Components are part of that structure. Once again, they are:

Key Component I—The Responsive Learning Environment
Key Component II—Relaxation and Tension Reduction
Key Component III—Movement and Physical Encoding
Key Component IV—Empowering Language and Behavior
Key Component V—Choice and Perceived Control
Key Component VI—Complex and Challenging Cognitive Activities
Key Component VII—Intuition and Integration

It is important that teachers use the Model flexibly and incorporate their personalities and their teaching styles. Just as no two teachers are alike no two groups of students are alike, and each class will create its own structure. Teacher and learner interaction will determine the unique use of this Model.

It is with this in mind that the following curricular ideas are offered as beginning points to be improved upon, modified, and adapted for the classroom and the needs of each student. You are invited to include in these lessons every tool or technique you know that works for you. The lessons were devised by many different teachers and have all been used successfully. Inherent in these lessons are many good ideas that can support and enrich your teaching.

As you begin to work with Integrative Education think about the possibility of establishing your own teaching and learning support system. Just as you will be "talking" with a number of teachers on these pages you should talk to teachers in your school or area who are also interested in optimizing learning. Pooling ideas, suggesting solutions for problems, and just sharing what worked—your joys in succeeding—are very productive experiences and make teaching and learning exciting.

ORGANIZERS FOR PLANNING INTEGRATIVE LESSONS

The *Teacher's Planning Sheet for Integrative Lessons* (Form 9.1.) presents a structure or format that can be used over and over to help plan for integrative learning regardless of the subject or content. The sheet serves as a reminder to include all human functions and also allows more effectiveness with less time involved. You can see at a glance what you want the students to learn, what brain functions you will be using in that learning, and the strategies you will use to include them. The lessons presented in this chapter will use this format.

The section that outlines the *Purpose* of the lesson or unit is divided into the four areas of the IEM. Not all lessons or units will be planned to meet goals in all four sections; however, by organizing the purposes in this way the amount of class time spent on each area of growth becomes apparent.

Form 9.1. Teacher's planning sheet for integrative lessons

Purpose:	
Cognitive	Intuitive
Physical/Sensing	Affective

Time involved:

Materials needed:

Organization preferred:

Teacher role:

Procedure:
1.

2.

3.

4.

5.

6.

7.

The *Time Involved* and *Materials Needed* sections allow for pre-planning to aid in the efficiency and effectiveness of the lesson or unit. The section *Organization Preferred* allows preparation for the preferred structure for the classroom and grouping of students. The *Teacher Role* suggests the level of instruction or facilitation the teacher may want to assume for the lesson or unit to be most successful.

The *Procedure* section gives step by step directions for implementation and includes strategies that will be used to create optimal learning. This section carries a symbol indicating which of the four functions is being used with each step and strategy, giving the teacher a quick indication of which functions are stressed and which are being underdeveloped. The symbol follows:

Finally, *Evaluation* of the lesson or unit will depend on the purposes stated; whatever procedure is designed for evaluation should collect data that directly assesses the level of attainment of these purposes.

The *Student's Integrative Education Planning Sheet* (Form 9.2.) is one way of presenting curriculum choices to help students become more responsible for their

Form 9.2. Integrative education planning sheet

*Non-negotiable

Content/Skills	Your Choice	Ways to Learn	Your Choice
* _____	* _____	*Cognitive _____	*Choose at least one from each _____
* _____	* _____	_____	_____
* _____	* _____	_____	_____
_____	Other:	*Affective _____	_____
_____	_____	_____	_____
_____	_____	_____	Other:
_____		*Physical _____	_____
		_____	
		_____	
		*Intuitive _____	
		_____	
		_____	

Products	Evaluation Criteria	Your Choice
* _____	_____	* _____
* _____	_____	* _____
_____	_____	_____
_____	_____	Other:
_____	_____	_____
_____	_____	_____

Form 9.2. *continued*

Time Line

Task				Dates						

Your Plan:

Content/Skills	Ways to Learn	Products	Evaluation
	Cog.		
	Aff.		
	Phys.		
	Int.		

own learning. Allowing students to participate in the learning process at the planning level makes them feel far more empowered.

In the upper left corner you will find *Non-negotiable.* That tells students that whatever is on a line with an asterisk is not a negotiable item and must become a part of their plan of study. Under the heading *Content/Skills* the teacher lists all of the content or skills involved in the lesson being taught, with non-negotiables listed first. The teacher may then list a number of other areas of content or skills that could be studied but that are not required. For example, if the lesson were Westward Expansion of the United States the non-negotiable content might be the geography of the Westward Expansion, the dates involved, and the major events leading to this movement. Other areas of content that might be interesting to study but which would not be required could include the economic climate of the times, the role of women, or the affect of the discovery of gold in California. Students use the box on the right of the teacher's listing of content or skills to list the content or skills choices they wish to put in their study plan.

Under *Ways to Learn* you will note four sub-categories: cognitive, affective, physical, and intuitive. Using the Westward Expansion example some of the activities that might appear under the cognitive sub-category could be "Read the text pp. 22 to 115," "Read and report on 4 sources other than your text," or "Collect a series of maps showing the Westward movement." The text reading would be preceded by an aster-isk, indicating required reading. The affective area might have suggestions such as, "Participate in a class simulation of the Westward Expansion," "Prepare a monologue revealing the feelings of a Plains Indian as the land of these people began to be invaded by the pioneers," or "Read the open-ended vignettes about life in the covered wagons and discuss with one or two classmates the possible resolutions to the problems posed." The physical category could include, "Develop a salt and flour map of the territories explored during the Westward movement," "Collect and display items for a museum on this historical period," or "Build a model of a covered wagon." The intuitive area might read, "Participate in a class fantasy trip back in time to the days of the movement West," "Write a short essay on what would have changed if there had been no mountains in the West," or "Can you imagine the outcome if there had been thousands more Indians in the West?" Again the students choose those ways to learn that they prefer, writing them in the spaces to the right of the teacher's list. Students are required to list one activity from each sub-category.

The section labeled *Products* lists suggested outcomes and the criteria the teacher will use to evaluate them. Using the same Westward Expansion example some products might be "An examination," "A filmstrip of life in the West," or "A study center on Women of the West," asterisks again communicating which products were non-negotiable. Students are free to add ideas agreeable to the teacher to any of the sections.

The *Time Line* allows both the student and the teacher to project the deadline dates for different areas of study.

At the bottom of the sheet is a shortened version of the student planning sections. After students have used this type of planning sheet for a while they know the kind of items the teacher will accept and can design their own study plan with only non-negotiables necessary from the teacher. The students can develop this shortened plan, allowing them to feel involved in the learning experience in a very meaningful way. Such experiences add to the responsible behavior teachers wish to build.

INTEGRATIVE EDUCATION IN THE CLASSROOM

Before presenting any of the integrative material to your students I would like to suggest that you teach them about how they learn and how their brains function. At the New Age School we give them as much information as possible about how what they do affects their learning and enables their brains to be more effective and efficient.

In Chapter 2 we briefly reviewed the contributions made by neurobiologists to our understanding of the learning process and related brain functions. As an aid to understanding the organization and structure of the brain I would like to borrow from Paul MacLean (1978) an analogy he used that has helped me in teaching these concepts to my students. It is useful, with a change in terminology, to both young children and to graduate students.

First, make a fist with each of your hands so that you can see the fingernails and then place your hands together with the fingernails touching. As you look down at your hands they now form a very respectable model of the human brain. Wiggle your little fingers and you have identified the area through which vision enters the brain.

Move your middle finger and you have located the motor area. The language area is just below the middle knuckle on the left hand. It is well supported by the specializations of the right hemisphere (right hand) through the corpus callosum (fingernails). There are more neural connections joining the right and left hemispheres of the brain than there are in any other part of the body. Clearly the interconnection or integration of the right and left hemisphere specializations is biologically intended. With this model "in hand" we can now explore with the students which brain functions have to do with learning.

Carefully separate the two hemispheres (hands); using the inside of the model of the brain (one hand) let us outline some of the basic brain functions. The arm/wrist area represents the most primitive and simplest system of the brain, the brain stem. In the lower brain stem and the innermost areas of the cerebrum we find the seat of autonomic (automatic) function. This system relieves us of consciously processing each breath and each beat of our hearts. Those working in the area of biofeedback have in recent years shown us that we can, if we choose, bring the awareness of these automatic functions to consciousness, allowing us to monitor or change a destructive or inefficient process (Taylor & Bongar, 1976; Taylor, Tom, & Ayers, 1981). Here we find the neural pathways for many higher brain centers. Here too are nuclei concerned with motor control and the communication link between the rest of the brain and the cerebellum located at the very base of the brain. Also located in this area is the reticular formation, the physical basis for consciousness that plays a major role in keeping us awake and alert.

By partially unclenching your fist and looking at the palm of the hand we can view the second system of the triune brain, the midbrain or limbic system. One can see the ventricles of the brain that hold the cerebrospinal fluid as well as the mounds and depressions of the limbic system itself. Here are the biochemical systems activated by the emotions of the learner and the interactions that enhance or inhibit memory. This area affects such diverse functions as anxiety, rage, sentimentality, and attention span. We depend on this area of the brain to combine internal and external experience to give us our feelings of personal identity and uniqueness. It is in this limbic area that affective feelings provide the connecting bridge between our inner and outer worlds, providing us with our construct of reality, our model of a possible world. This gateway to higher thought—to the cortical and neocortical functions—releases neurotransmitters to the cells of the cortex to either facilitate or inhibit their functioning. Novelty helps activate growth of this function (Restak, 1979). Feelings of pleasure and joy increase stimulation to this area (Sagan, 1977).

The exposed surface of your fingers and thumb held tightly together represent the convoluted mass known as the neocortex or the cerebrum. It is the largest area of the brain, comprising five-sixths of the total, and envelops the lower brain stem and the limbic system. Here sensory data are processed, decisions made, and action initiated. The neocortex is necessary for language and speech, its overriding functions involve the reception, storage, and retrieval of information.

The most recently evolved section of the neocortex, the prefrontal cortex (represented by the thumbs), provides for behaviors associated with planning, insight, empathy, introspection, and other bases for intuitive thought (MacLean, 1978). As mentioned earlier, it is engaged in firming up intention, deciding on action, and regulating our most complex behaviors (Restak, 1979).

Once the students understand how the brain functions and what they can do to optimize that functioning they are ready to be more responsible for their learning and to participate in brain-compatible strategies and lessons. This is an excellent starting point for optimizing learning.

INTEGRATIVE LESSONS FOR PRESCHOOLERS

At the New Age School the Early Age Program is designed as a decentralized structure that parallels the program offered the older students. The following are lessons designed to be used in centers with small groups of children ages three to five.

At the Science Center

Exercise 9.1. The Traveling Balloon (Taken from an exercise by Kaz Tanaka.)

Purpose:

Cognitive	Intuitive
To develop the concept of action/reaction	To enhance the skill of visualization
Physical/Sensing	**Affective**
To expand awareness of sensorium in learning	To develop feelings of personal competency

Time involved: Little children will enjoy this activity for long periods of time. As with all activities in a preschool curriculum the length of time must be flexible and responsive to the interests of the children.

Material needed: pictures of rockets and jet planes in flight, one round and one elongated balloon for each child, twenty to thirty feet of string for each child, masking tape, a straw for each child

Organization preferred: one child or small group with the teacher

Teacher role: demonstrator, facilitator

Procedure:

1. Blow up the round balloon and explain how every action has a reaction; demonstrate this by showing that as the air comes out of the back of the balloon the balloon moves forward.
2. Discuss rockets and jet planes and how this same principle allows them to fly. Demonstrate with pictures of rockets and planes.
3. Ask the children to close their eyes and see a rocket taking off. Give them a count down for their image to take off. After several imaginary flights have the children gently open their eyes.
4. Ask the children to become rockets; as you count them down they are to blast off into a flight pattern. Be sure to set the perimeters of their flight.
5. Discuss how it feels to be a jet or a rocket. Powerful? Free? Pushed?

6. Attach one end of a string to a wall with masking tape while the child holds the other end. Blow up one elongated balloon and attach a straw to the side with masking tape. Run the string through the straw, pointing the balloon toward the wall. Have the child hold the end of the blown-up balloon, which is now attached to the string running through the straw. Count down for blast off. At blast off the child releases the open end of the balloon and it jets toward the wall along the string.

7. Discuss what just happened from the perspective of action/reaction.

Evaluation: Ask the child what other things work with the concept of action/reaction.

Exercise 9.2. Touch Color (Chromatography) (Taken from a lesson by Chris Cenci.)

Purpose:

Cognitive	**Intuitive**
To develop the concept of color	To develop the skill of intuitive knowing by using and trusting personal impressions
Physical/Sensing	**Affective**
To discriminate colors, use of touch for intuitive knowing	To become aware of the affect of color on feelings

Time involved: approximately 45 minutes

Materials needed: plastic water glasses, round paper towel disks with strips cut out of each, set of disks with a color in the middle and no strip cut out, felt tip pens of various colors

Organization preferred: small group of children around table with teacher

Teacher role: demonstrator, facilitator, questioner

Procedure:

1. Demonstrate how color placed on a paper towel disk separates into different designs as water is absorbed into the disk. The color will separate into its color components as this absorption takes place. Fill a clear plastic glass 2/3 full of water. Place a disk of paper toweling cut as indicated below and slightly larger than the top rim of the plastic glass flat across the top of the glass. Allow the tab attached to the disk to fall into the water. As the tab absorbs the water the color will begin to separate into lighter and lighter elements. In the discussion of this demonstration introduce color words and discuss descriptors (blue—cool; red—hot, etc.).

2. Ask the children to experiment with various colors on paper towel disks. Encourage the children to make different mixtures of color with different felt tip pens, as well as different designs at different points on the disk's surface.

3. After each child has had an opportunity to create several disks with various designs say, *Some of the papers give you certain feelings. How do you feel when you see this color? This design?*

4. *Is there something in one of the designs specifically about you? Find it and outline it in black pen.*

5. Set up a chart rack. Put slits in the form of an *x* on a tagboard hanging from the rack, then have the children relax and reach through. Ask them to determine the color of the disk on the other side.

On a different day:

6. *Each of us has a special, lovely color that gives us a special feeling. Look around the room. If you see that color move to it.*

On a different day:

7. Put an item of one color in a bag. When the children are in their circle show them the bag and ask them to close their eyes and imagine something there. Ask them to open their eyes and pass the bag around the circle (use the touch and pass technique from Chapter 4). Then ask them what color is the item in the bag. You may give them several color words from which to choose. Discuss and then show. Be sure to acknowledge the idea of "on target" and "off target."

At the Math Center

Exercise 9.3. The Four Puppies

Purpose:

Cognitive	Intuitive
To develop the concept of four; skills of observation, recall, classification, and grouping	To enhance visualization skills
Physical/Sensing	**Affective**
To develop eye-hand coordination and physical encoding to optimize learning	To use feeling as support for recall

Time involved: 20 minutes

Materials needed: three sets of four simple objects (e.g. beans, cars, marbles), pictures with four items in each, a page for child's notebook with number 4 at the top and divided into four sections, a box full of stickers (any kind)

Organization preferred: one child or small group of children at table with teacher

Teacher role: demonstrator, facilitator

Procedure:

1. Ask the children to gently close their eyes and imagine that they see four puppies.

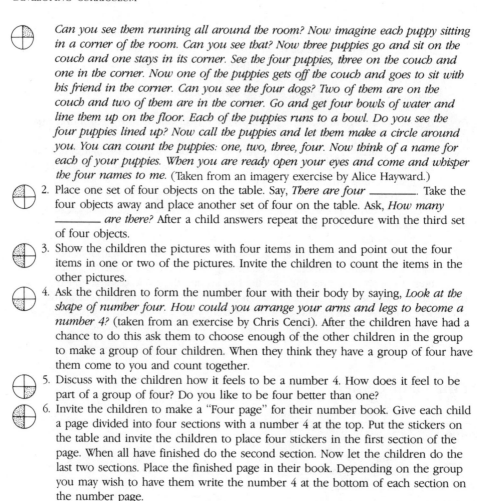

Can you see them running all around the room? Now imagine each puppy sitting in a corner of the room. Can you see that? Now three puppies go and sit on the couch and one stays in its corner. See the four puppies, three on the couch and one in the corner. Now one of the puppies gets off the couch and goes to sit with his friend in the corner. Can you see the four dogs? Two of them are on the couch and two of them are in the corner. Go and get four bowls of water and line them up on the floor. Each of the puppies runs to a bowl. Do you see the four puppies lined up? Now call the puppies and let them make a circle around you. You can count the puppies: one, two, three, four. Now think of a name for each of your puppies. When you are ready open your eyes and come and whisper the four names to me. (Taken from an imagery exercise by Alice Hayward.)

2. Place one set of four objects on the table. Say, *There are four* _____. Take the four objects away and place another set of four on the table. Ask, *How many _____ are there?* After a child answers repeat the procedure with the third set of four objects.

3. Show the children the pictures with four items in them and point out the four items in one or two of the pictures. Invite the children to count the items in the other pictures.

4. Ask the children to form the number four with their body by saying, *Look at the shape of number four. How could you arrange your arms and legs to become a number 4?* (taken from an exercise by Chris Cenci). After the children have had a chance to do this ask them to choose enough of the other children in the group to make a group of four children. When they think they have a group of four have them come to you and count together.

5. Discuss with the children how it feels to be a number 4. How does it feel to be part of a group of four? Do you like to be four better than one?

6. Invite the children to make a "Four page" for their number book. Give each child a page divided into four sections with a number 4 at the top. Put the stickers on the table and invite the children to place four stickers in the first section of the page. When all have finished do the second section. Now let the children do the last two sections. Place the finished page in their book. Depending on the group you may wish to have them write the number 4 at the bottom of each section on the number page.

At the Reading Center

Exercise 9.4. Treasure Box

Purpose:

Cognitive	**Intuitive**
To learn the letters and the sounds of the alphabet	To learn to use visualization to aid recall
Physical/Sensing	**Affective**
To use movement to enrich the learning activity	To include in the learning activity things the child likes and chooses

Time involved: 20 minutes or as long as the child is interested

Materials needed: shoe boxes with letters of the alphabet on the front (use two or three at a time), objects placed around the room or house that have the initial sound found on the front of the boxes

Organization preferred: individual activity or with small groups

Teacher role: facilitator

Procedure:

1. Ask the children to look for "treasures" (anything that has the same sound as can be seen on the front of the boxes). Show an example and place it in the box (e.g. apple for the "A" box).

2. Accompany the children on the "hunt" for a few minutes to make sure they have the idea. Invite them to guess whether or not an object begins with the appropriate letter if they are not sure.

3. After 10 minutes or when the children begin to lose interest ask them to share what they have found. Enthusiastically approve of all correct choices. Instead of saying that the spoon that was found for the "C" box is wrong, say, *What is this? What sound do you hear when I say spoon? Good. When we have an "S" box we will put this in it.*

4. After sharing all the objects in the boxes ask the children to close their eyes and think of all the objects they have seen. *Decide on one object you like best and become that object. See if the others can guess in which box you belong.*

Evaluation: As the game is played again see if the children can increase the number and accuracy of their choices and the placement of the objects.

Exercise 9.5. My Own Alphabet/Picture Cards

Purpose:

Cognitive	**Intuitive**
To learn the letters and the sounds of the alphabet	To learn to use hunches in learning

Physical/Sensing	**Affective**
To improve the school skills of cutting and pasting	To empower children by allowing them to make their own learning materials

Time involved: 10 to 15 minutes or as long as the children are interested

Materials needed: old magazines, scissors, paste, file cards with letters at the top (e.g. "A, a", "B, b", etc.)

Organization preferred: individual activity or small group

Teacher role: facilitator

Procedure:

1. Sit with the children and look through old magazines for small pictures of objects with a beginning sound like the letter at the top of the card. Invite them to guess when they are not sure.
2. Cut out the picture (or allow the child to do so under your supervision) and help the child paste it on the card.
3. Ask the children to say the names of the objects as they paste them onto the card.
4. Invite a child to choose from his or her cards a picture that she or he really likes. Have the child think of that picture, seeing it in his or her mind. The other children are invited to guess what picture the child is seeing. Save the cards for other games.

Evaluation: Check for accuracy of letter names and sounds when playing with the cards later.

Games to play with Alphabet/Picture Cards:

Scramble: mix up all the cards and ask the child to sort them into piles or by rows.

Matching Letters: use a large chart with the letters printed on one side. Ask the child to match the card to the letter on the chart. (Variation: place on the table two cards which have the same letter and one with a different letter. Ask the children which doesn't match.)

Alphabet Dominoes: use alphabet cards to play dominoes.

Take Away: place several alphabet/picture cards on a rack or table. Have the children close their eyes while you take away one card. Ask the children to open their eyes and identify which card is missing.

Guess My Card: have one child choose one card and be sure no one else can see it. Invite the other children to guess which card the child is holding. Use "on target" or "off target" to indicate the accuracy of the guess.

Exercise 9.6. Fishing

Purpose:

Cognitive	**Intuitive**
To learn the letters and sounds of the alphabet	To try to predict next events
Physical/Sensing	**Affective**
To develop eye-motor coordination	To practice sharing as an empowering skill

Time involved: 20 minutes or as long as the children are interested

Material needed: a small horseshoe magnet attached by string to a pencil or small rod, construction paper cutouts of fish with paper clips attached to each and printed with the letters of the alphabet, a shallow box

Organization preferred: small group around a table or in a circle on the floor

Teacher role: facilitator

Procedure:

1. Place the paper fish in the shallow box and place the box (pool) in the middle of the group of children. Have each child, in turn, use the pole with the magnet to "catch" the paper clipped fish.
2. Ask the child who caught the fish to make the sound of the letter printed on it. If successful the child may keep the fish; if not, the child throws it back.
3. After the children are familiar with the game and letters ask them to predict which and how many fish their next cast will bring in.

Exercise 9.7. Consonant Leis (Taken from a lesson by Chris Cenci.)

Purpose:

Cognitive	**Intuitive**
To learn the meaning, sounds, and functions of consonants	To learn to trust inner self as a resource
Physical/Sensing	**Affective**
To enhance eye-motor coordination; to improve school skills of cutting, listening, etc.	To improve interpersonal skills of sharing materials, to value other's work

Time involved: 20 minutes

Materials needed: string, one-inch pieces of plastic straws, felt tip pen, paper hole punch, several colors of construction paper cut in the following shape:

Organization preferred: small group of students working at a table with the teacher

Teacher role: demonstrator, facilitator

Procedure:

1. Discuss and give examples of consonant letters.
2. Instruct the children to close their eyes and find a letter from deep within themselves. When they have one they may open their eyes and discuss the letter. Point out whether the word is a consonant or a vowel. Now ask the children to again close their eyes and as you make the sound of their letter ask them to *Let the letter say a word to you.* When they have the word they again open their eyes and share the word.
3. On the construction paper shapes print the children's consonant letters on one side and their words on the other. For example,

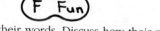

4. Ask the children to share their words. Discuss how their word makes them feel and why it is an important word to them.
5. Give the children their printed shapes to:
   a. fold in half:

   b. punch with the hole punch:

   c. string the printed shapes into a lei (use straw pieces to separate each printed shape):

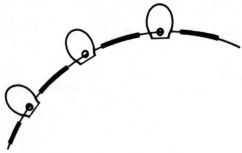

   d. tie off and put around their necks.

Evaluation: Review letters and words from each child's lei.

Exercise 9.8. Author's First Book

Purpose:

Cognitive	**Intuitive**
To show words as expressions of ideas	To show imagination as a help in creating stories
Physical/Sensing	**Affective**
To develop art ability as a form of expression, eye-motor coordination	To develop perceived control by helping child create own teaching tool

Time involved: 20 minutes

Materials needed: sheets of oversized paper lined at the bottom, felt tipped pens, crayons

Organization preferred: small group of children at table with teacher

Teacher role: facilitator

Procedure:

1. Show each child a "book" prepared with pages stapled together and a cover made of colored construction paper. Tell the children they are going to be authors and write their own books. Give each child a piece of paper and have the crayons and felt pens available on the table.

2. Ask the children to close their eyes and see someone they like very much (use the theme for the week and guide the child to imagine a story about that theme). Ask them to see the places and people in their mind's eye and then to gently open their eyes.

3. Invite the children to discuss their stories. How did they feel about where they went? The people they saw? What happened?

4. Invite the children to use the crayons and felt pens to draw one of the pictures about their story.

5. Have the children dictate one at a time what they want to say about their picture story as you write it in the lined space on the page. Read it back to make sure that is what they wanted to say and then help them to read the story they have just written.

Evaluation: The next day have the child read the story written the previous day.

During Physical Education

Exercise 9.9. Total Toe Touching

Purpose:

Cognitive	**Intuitive**
To understand the relationship between mind and body	To experience the ability to use visualization to change a body process
Physical/Sensing	**Affective**
To enhance physical ability through mind/body integration	To empower learners by developing an awareness of abilities within their systems

Time involved: three to five minutes
Materials needed: none
Organization preferred: total class with room to stand and bend over
Teacher role: demonstrator, guide
Procedure:

1. Ask students to bend forward and try to touch their toes.
2. Instruct them to notice how far down they can go, when they feel strain, and the tone of their muscles.
3. Now ask students to *Bend back bouncing four times, 1 . . . 2 . . . 3 . . . 4. Then gently bend forward to your toes again. Notice how much further you can go.*
4. *Now stand still and gently close your eyes. See yourself bend backwards even further. Bounce 1 . . . 2 . . . 3 . . . 4. Don't do it, just see yourself do it.*
5. *Now open your eyes and gently bend toward your toes. What happened? Did you go further?*
6. *How do you feel about your ability to do this? How could you use this knowledge? What other parts of your body do you think could improve by thinking before you use it?*

Some Ideas to Add to Your Curriculum Planning

When learning about time have children become clocks; their arms are the hands of the clock. Ask the children to show you 3:00, 6:00, 12:00, 4:30, etc.

When learning directions:
Ask the child to stand and move to the south wall, the east wall, etc.

Develop a treasure hunt. Tell or write directions such as *Go three steps east, then four steps south, etc.* For older children writing the directions in rhyme is fun.

Develop an archeological dig. Pace off in the direction given to find prehidden artifacts.

When learning about the phases of the moon, the seasons, etc., have children become the sun, the moon, the Earth, and have them move around each other appropriately. Have them discuss the process as they are moving. To make it even more interesting use props to identify each body.

When reading stories to small children identify their chairs as helicopters for helicopter stories, train seats for train stories, etc.

When learning the alphabet use dot to dot pictures labeled by letters instead of numbers. Asking the child to try to "see" what the finished picture will be before connecting the dots provides an intuitive stretch.

INTEGRATIVE LESSONS FOR ELEMENTARY STUDENTS

During Reading and Language Arts

Exercise 9.10. A Personal Word List

Purpose: (following the reading of a new story)

Cognitive	**Intuitive**
To improve spelling skills, word attack skills, vocabulary	To use inner authority for planning a lesson
Physical/Sensing	**Affective**
To improve handwriting skills	To empower by allowing students to contribute needs to the lesson

Time involved: 15 to 20 minutes
Materials: chalkboard
Organization preferred: total group
Teacher role: facilitator
Procedure:

1. Ask students to find any new or difficult to remember words from the new story that was just read.
2. Ask them to gently close their eyes and see three new or difficult words inside their head. *Now open your eyes and let's put them on the board.*
3. The teacher writes words on the board as children call them out.
4. The teacher then says, *Notice how you feel about each of these words. If some of them are new or difficult for you you can borrow them from the person who gave them to us. They can be added to the words on your list.*
5. Ask the children to choose one word from their lists; have one child at a time act out a word for the others to guess.

6. *Now make a list of all the words you would like to have as your words. This will be your own special list to learn to use.*

The teacher can use the word lists for spelling, phonics lessons, vocabulary building, etc.

Evaluation: Have the students use words in writing and reading exercises.

Exercise 9.11. The Story Carpet (Taken from a lesson by Chris Cenci.)

Purpose:

Cognitive	**Intuitive**
To improve listening skill and recognize reading as an enjoyable activity	To use guided fantasy to enrich learning
Physical/Sensing	**Affective**
To use the senses to enrich the learning activity	To improve motivation for reading by developing a deeper understanding of how a story character might feel

Time involved: approximately 20 minutes

Materials needed: storybook, carpeted floor (optional, can be done at desks), food that relates to the story (e.g. chocolate bars for *Willie Wonka and the Chocolate Factory*)

Organization preferred: total group

Teacher role: set up and direct the experience, storyteller

Procedure:

1. Ask the children to get comfortable in their chairs or to lie down on the carpet.
2. Read the story as realistically as possible by giving characters their own voices, using sound effects, etc.
3. Have the children gently close their eyes when the story is finished. Invite them to imagine their own story of what happened next to the characters in the story you read. You may wish to guide some of this fantasy trip.
4. Ask the children to open their eyes and look in their desks (or wherever you previously hid the food) for something that came from the story.
5. As everyone eats the food discuss the story. Invite the children to share their own stories, their feelings about the characters, and what happened to them.

Evaluation: Notice the excitement about storytime and reading in general.

Exercise 9.12. Haiku (Developed by Holly Sutton.)

Purpose:

Cognitive	Intuitive
To learn a poetry form from the Eastern world, and to create a poem in this form	To use images and visualization to heighten creative production

Physical/Sensing	Affective
To use music and a simulated ritual of the culture to deepen the understanding of a poetic expression	To develop an appreciation of the attitudes, beliefs, and aesthetic values of another culture

Time involved: 45 to 50 minutes

Materials needed: books for a display on Japanese culture and Haiku poetry, area with carpet or mats, materials for a tea ceremony, Koto music, posters depicting the culture of Japan, charts with the characteristics of Haiku and samples of this form of poetry, flowers arranged in the Japanese tradition, colored paper, colored pencils, markers, and paints

Organization preferred: small group and teacher seated on the floor on tatami mats or floor pillows around a low table

Teacher role: demonstrator, facilitator

Procedure:

1. Invite a small group of students to join you in an area of the room set up to simulate a Japanese tea house. Koto music is playing softly, a small flower arrangement and a tea service are on a low table surrounded by mats or floor pillows.

2. Ask the students to close their eyes and listen to the music. Describe in a guided fantasy the setting of the teahouse in a Japanese garden.

3. Ask the students to gently open their eyes and demonstrate a Japanese tea ceremony. As you are pouring tea and the children are drinking it discuss with them what they know of Japanese customs and culture.

4. From posters and charts explain characteristics of Haiku. Have students read several of the poems aloud. Discuss the characteristics.

5. Invite students to write their own Haiku poems. Give them pieces of colored paper to use for their poems and colored pens and crayons for poster pictures they will make to accompany the poems.

6. When the students have finished a few poems invite them to read them aloud while the rest of the group closes their eyes and shares the inner vision.

Evaluation: The enthusiasm for a form of poetry will be noticed.

During Science

Exercise 9.13. Inner and Outer Space

Purpose:

Cognitive	**Intuitive**
To develop a knowledge of the human body and its functions	To use predictive ability in changing conditions
Physical/Sensing	**Affective**
To develop school skills of cutting, etc., and to enhance knowledge of the body by creating a model	To be aware of the feelings about one's body

Time involved: 20 to 30 minutes
Materials needed: butcher paper in a large roll, scissors, colored markers, crayons, paste
Organization preferred: small group or individual activity
Teacher role: demonstrator, facilitator
Procedure:

1. Invite children to cut a piece of butcher paper large enough for them to lie on. Ask them to estimate the size.
2. Ask the children to lie down on their piece of butcher paper. Trace around their body or allow a partner to do so. Encourage them to lie in any action position they feel good about.
3. Ask the children to cut out their figure and then trace and cut another piece of paper exactly like the first. Attach the two figures at the top of the head.
4. Have the children look into a mirror to help them draw their likeness on one of the papers. They may wish to draw in clothing with their crayons.
5. Now ask the children to close their eyes and imagine the inside of their bodies. Take a fantasy journey through the body, describing the location, shape, and function of each part of the body and its organs.
6. Invite the students to take colored paper or to color paper and cut out organs such as the heart, the lungs, the stomach, etc. Ask them to place them inside the body by lifting up the outside paper image and attaching the organs to the second paper figure.
7. Ask the students, *What makes your chest move? Where does the air you breathe go? Can you feel your heart? What does it do? Why is it important? Where does the food go? What does the brain do? etc.*
8. Hang finished life-size figures around the classroom.

Evaluation: Knowledge of the body can now be tested or shown by filling in paper drawing of human body.

In the "Inner and Outer Space" exercise, children trace outlines of their bodies and learn about the unique human structure.

During Social Science—Geography

Exercise 9.14. California (Your State's Name) Some of this material was taken from a lesson by Beverly Galyean.

Purpose:

Cognitive	Intuitive
To learn the major regions and cities of California (or your own state)	To learn to notice the tone or characteristic ambience of a region or city

Physical/Sensing	Affective
To use movement to become more knowledgeable about geography	To use personal characteristics and values to better understand different geographic regions and improve recall

Time involved: 30 to 40 minutes
Materials needed: a large floor map of a state, "Values Guide Statements" (Galyean, 1976)
Organization preferred: total group, small groups, individual
Teacher role: facilitator

Procedure:

1. Ask students to read the section of the text that discusses cities and regions of California.
2. Write the names of California cities on slips of paper and put them in a bag, then ask the students to draw several slips from the bag (the number depends on the time allowed for this activity). When it is their turn, the children move one at a time to the floor map and walk from their home city to the city on their slip of paper (e.g. if they live in Los Angeles and they have drawn Fresno they must find both on the map and walk from L.A. to Fresno).
3. When each arrives at the destination, ask the class to share all they can remember about the city and the region in which the student now stands.
4. After most of the cities and regions have been described ask the students to fill out the "Values Guide Statements" (Galyean, 1976) (see Form 9.3).
5. After the students have filled out their individual guides have them form small groups to discuss their results.
6. As part of the small group discussion ask the students to predict what will happen to "their" city and region in the next 10 years.
7. Discuss in a total group.

Evaluation: The improved understanding and recall will be apparent on any test or evaluation procedure.

Form 9.3. Values guide statements

I am a person who is
likes
wants
hopes for
believes in
loves
dreams about
____(City)____ is most like me because _____.
____(Region)____ is most like me because _____.
Example: I am a person who is free and easy
who likes water
who wants lots of space
who hopes for lots of natural environment
who believes in love and peace
who loves people
who dreams about a home on the beach
____Eureka____ is most like me because it is open, small, has people who know each other well, and is by the beach.

During Math

Exercise 9.15. Measuring, Estimating, Graphing (From a lesson designed by Heide Kalmar.)

Purpose:

Cognitive	Intuitive
To improve the skills of making comparisons, relationships, counting, estimating, measuring, and data collection	To develop skills of estimating, predicting, and synthesizing data

Physical/Sensing	Affective
To develop school skills of measuring and using a ruler	To empower the learner by allowing involvement in the choice of what to measure and by building confidence in estimating

Time involved: 20 to 30 minutes

Materials needed: 10 to 20 "feet" (cardboard cutouts of feet exactly 12" long); rulers; paste; small containers which hold one, two, three, and four cups; containers holding four to six ounces; rice; cornmeal; gravel; water; paper; crayons; 10"x24" piece of cardboard; 1"x10" strips of construction paper in two colors; clothespins with names of children printed on them; tape to protect edges of board.

Organization preferred: small group of children and teacher around a table

Teacher role: demonstrator, facilitator

Procedure:

Measurement

1. Ask children to choose objects or areas they would like to measure. Show the children a "foot" and ask them to estimate how many feet they think will be in their chosen object or area.
2. Give the children each a "foot" and allow them to measure their chosen object or area.
3. Ask the children to draw their object or area and write the number of "feet" they found it to be.
4. Encourage the children to measure with other things like hands, books, pencils, etc., e.g. *How many books high is the door?*
5. Ask, *How many things did you find that were _____ feet long? How close to your guess was the measurement? Which things are longer? Shorter? The same?*

Estimating

1. Ask the children to predict how many cups can be filled from each container. Have the children write their predictions on a piece of paper in front of the containers.
2. Have the children experiment and check their estimates.
3. Discuss how close the prediction came to the actual measurement. *What did you find? Which container filled the most cups? Is that what you thought would happen? Which containers are largest? Smallest? The same?*
4. *How did you feel when you had more cups than you predicted you would? When you had less? When you came very close?*

Graphing

1. Ask the children to decide what they would like to find out about the people in the class, e.g. their favorite fruit, animals, colors, etc. Explain that they will survey the class to get that information.

2. Have the children decide on two possible choices that the person surveyed could make, e.g. *Is your favorite color red or blue?* Have them draw or color a picture to represent each category and clip each picture to opposite sides of the cardboard chart.

3. Have the children predict which color will get the most votes.

4. With a clothespin representing each person in the room have the children conduct their survey and place the clothespins on the appropriate sides of the chart.

5. Ask the children to summarize their data. *What did you find out? How many children did you ask? What color was chosen most? What does that mean? Which color do you like best? How do you feel about the class choice?*

Evaluation: Ask another question about preferences and have the children suggest how they could find out. Allow them to try their suggestion.

During Art or School Skills

Exercise 9.16. Color Experiences (From a lesson by Richela Chapman.)

Purpose:

Cognitive	Intuitive
To discriminate tones and shades of color	To be in touch with their ability to see inner color, and to use relaxation to enhance ability
Physical/Sensing	**Affective**
To become aware of the ability to see many shades and tones of color	To notice how color affects feelings

Time involved: 30 minutes to an hour (option: teaching exercise into two sessions)

Materials needed: a wide variety of colors of crayons, black tempera paint, one inch paint brushes, drawing paper, small paper clips

Organization preferred: small group of children with teacher at a table

Teacher role: demonstrator, facilitator

Procedure:

1. Say to the children, *Quiet time is very important to me and I would like to share it with you. We will sit on the floor crosslegged with our backs straight, our eyes closed, in our own special place.* The teacher demonstrates. *We must not intrude into anyone else's quiet time by touching, giggling, talking or moving about. It is very important to respect your friend's desire to be quiet and peaceful.*

2. Have the children sit as directed and suggest that they begin by taking three deep

breaths and letting the air out slowly and quietly. Giving them plenty of time to follow your directions, say, *Now tense your shoulders. Pull them way up to your ears. Harder. Harder. Now let them go and relax. Let your shoulders be very relaxed and peaceful. Gently close your eyes. Now see in your mind a beautiful picture. Maybe it will be your favorite place to go or your favorite person or animal.* After a few minutes invite the children to gently open their eyes and return to the room.

3. Allow the children to share their pictures and the experience they had with their quiet time.

4. Now that the children are relaxed tell them that they are going on a color walk. *A color walk is a very special walk where we will see as many kinds of colors as we can. You will be surprised just how many colors we can see.* Take the children on a short walk around the school and call their attention to all the colors you can. Invite them to share any colors they see. As you describe the colors introduce the concepts of light/dark, cool/warm, etc., as they apply to color.

5. Discuss the experience once you have returned to the room. Ask the children to describe how they felt about their color walk. As they talk about the colors invite them to share how each color makes them feel: *How does red make you feel? Is that the same or different than blue makes you feel?*

6. Distribute a selection of light- and bright-colored crayons and a piece of drawing paper to each child. Direct the children to cover the paper with the colors so that each color appears at least twice on different parts of the page. The areas of color may be squares with each square covering one to two inches of paper.

7. When the paper is covered with colors ask the children to cover the entire surface with black paint.

8. After the paint has dried have the children close their eyes and think about their color walk. Ask them to see with their minds the colors and shapes they saw on their walk. Ask them to open their eyes.

9. Give each child a paper clip and invite them to use the curved end to scrape away the black paint to show a picture or a design of something they saw, e.g. butterflies, flowers, leaves, trees, etc.

Evaluation: Child's enjoyment and understanding of color

Exercise 9.17. Saturn Man (From a lesson by Richela Chapman.)

Purpose:

Cognitive	**Intuitive**
To develop a concept of space, planets, and space travel for learning	To develop the use of visualization and guided imagery as a support
Physical/Sensing	**Affective**
To learn to use the school skills of cutting, pasting, drawing, and to develop fine motor skills	To enhance use of feelings to understand concepts, and to explore personal feelings of difference, belonging, and alienation

Time involved: 30 minutes
Materials needed: paper plates, yarn, colored pens, fabric scraps, construction paper
Organization preferred: small group of children and teacher at a table or on the floor
Teacher role: demonstrator, facilitator
Procedure:

1. Ask the children to gently close their eyes. Take them on a space journey. *Allow yourself to become aware of your breathing. Notice how your breathing becomes slow, deep, as though your whole body is breathing. Now let yourself become a part of all the air in this room and outside of the room. Feel yourself beginning to float out of your chair. As you look down you can see the school, the city, the hills and lakes around the city* (use descriptors of your geographic area). *You are slowly rising higher, higher. You can see the whole country below you. The entire planet Earth is now below you and still you rise. Now you are moving through the solar system. Look at all of the planets, the sun, the asteroids, and still you rise.* Continue the space journey by describing the solar system, the galaxy, etc. Then return, pausing over Saturn to "see" the people living there. *Invite one of these people from Saturn to return to our planet with you. As you slowly begin to move back toward the Earth look closely at your new friend. What does your friend look like? What is your friend wearing?* Guide the children back from their journey and into their seats. Invite them to open their eyes.

2. Discuss the journey and the friends from Saturn. Ask, *If you really were to find people from Saturn here on our planet how would you treat them? How would you feel? If you were to be alone on a different planet how would you feel? Are there ever times you feel a little like that now?* Allow the children to discuss their feelings of being alone, being different, the need to belong, etc.

3. Ask the children to create a puppet of their friend from Saturn using the paper plates, yarn, etc.

4. Using the puppets discuss life in space. Both the children and the teacher can ask the puppets questions.

Evaluation: As the children answer for the puppet note what they know about space, the planets, etc.

Exercise 9.18. Chagall and Klee (From a lesson by Rhoda Coleman.)

Purpose:

Cognitive	Intuitive
To become familiar with the lives and work of two famous artists, and to understand how artists use color, shapes, and lines to give expression to feelings	To improve ability to use imagination and dreams

Physical/Sensing	Affective
To learn alternative techniques of painting	To become aware of the different feelings of colors, shapes, and textures, and to develop self expression through art

Time involved: 30 to 45 minutes
Materials needed: recording of "Petrouchka" by Stravinsky, the book *Through the Magic Mirror* by Anthony Browne, prints and/or slides of paintings by Chagall and Klee, paper, watercolors, black marking pen, construction paper, magazine pictures, scissors
Organization preferred: small groups of children with teacher
Teacher role: storyteller, demonstrator, facilitator
Procedure:

1. Create an environment that includes paintings and objects appropriate to the time and nationality of artists Chagall and Klee.
2. As you discuss the lesson ask these questions: *Why do Chagall's paintings seem like dreams? What does it mean to say that Klee wanted to make visible what is invisible by his painting? In what way were symbols important to both artists? How are the works of the two artists alike? Different?* Tell the children to be thinking about these questions (which are written on a chart they can see) as they learn about these artists.
3. Invite the children to listen to the recording of Stravinsky's "Petrouchka". While the music plays tell the children about Chagall's life in Russia. Discuss how Chagall's childhood, his imagination, and his dreams influenced his paintings. Show some of his paintings and discuss these influences.
4. Discuss Klee's life and show some of the influences on his paintings.
5. Compare the art elements and techniques of both artists.
6. Allow the students to choose a favorite picture done by each artist and discuss how the pictures make them feel and what they like about them.
7. Ask the children to create a painting in the style of each artist. They may choose from:
   Shape drawings—cut out shapes and glue onto paper in the manner of Klee.
   Magic squares—use watercolors in the manner of Klee to make squares of color and a black marking pen to show the use of lines.
   "Twittering Machine"—have the students look at the painting by Klee. Let them invent and draw their own machine based on something in nature.
   Collage dreams—use magazines in the style of Chagall to express dreams or imagination.
   "Petrouchka"—have the students listen again to the recording and draw in the style of Chagall what comes to their minds.
8. In small groups pretend you are living in Germany in the 1940s. The Nazi government has told you to destroy the paintings of Klee and Chagall. Discuss how you feel and what you would do (this can also be a writing assignment).

Evaluation: Look again at the questions on the chart. Discuss.

An Idea to Add to Your Curriculum Planning

When learning "silent e" give all the students a card with a letter. Have one student become a "silent e." The other students group themselves to make words without the silent e at the end (e.g. mat, bar, tap, etc.). As the "silent e" joins the group have the children show what happens to the sound of the vowel in the word. This can be fun if the "silent e" is rather dramatic in carrying out the task.

Make a collage from magazines to express dreams or imagination like the artist Chagall.

INTEGRATIVE LESSONS FOR SECONDARY STUDENTS

In Science

Exercise 9.19. Mitosis: Cell Division (From a lesson by Tobias Manzanares.)

Purpose:

Cognitive	**Intuitive**
To develop an understanding of the process by which the body replaces worn or damaged cells, and to introduce terminology used in the study of mitosis	To use visualization as a support for the learning process, and to develop the ability to predict outcomes based on known facts

Physical/Sensing	**Affective**
To use movement and physical encoding to support learning	To deepen the understanding of information by investigating the feelings such information elicits

Time involved: one 50 minute class period

Materials needed: handout of a drawing of mitosis (see Figure 9.1), classroom space representing a fertilized egg cell

Organization preferred: total class with room to move around

Teacher role: information giver, facilitator

Procedure:

1. Ask students to examine the diagram representing the mitotic process and note that

   many cells in the human body are damaged or die of old age each second and must be replaced;

   a human beginning as a fertilized egg begins to divide by a process in which the chromosomes (units of heredity) duplicate themselves just prior to cell division; the cell replicates itself going from a 2 cell stage to stages where there are 4, 8, 16, 32, 64, 128 cells and so on.

2. Ask the students to close their eyes and see the cells inside their own body magnified like the cells in the diagram. Use the correct terminology to describe the parts of the cell. Ask the students to gently open their eyes.

3. Ask for four students to become two pairs of centrioles. After they are identified they may remain seated until needed.

4. Ask for volunteers to become the chromosomes of the cell (use about half of the class). Have them stand close together in an open area of the room. Suggest that they imagine a cell wall or nuclear membrane surrounding them that draws them tighter and tighter. They are now entering the phase referred to as interphase.

5. Direct the students within the cell to find a student in the room to become their matching chromosome. Ask the two matching chromosomes to join by touching elbows as though there were glue on the elbow. This area of joining is called the centromere. The pairs are referred to as chromatids.

6. Ask the centrioles to take positions at either side of the room in pairs. They will send out spindle fibers which will project across the cell center from one pair of centrioles to the other. Now instruct the students to line up in pairs across the room with one matching chromosome attracted to one centriole and the other chromosome attracted to the other centriole. This begins the metaphase.

7. As the anaphase begins the chromatid divides at the centromere and each part moves to the attracting centriole. The centrioles are to physically mime the "reeling in" of the spindle fibers. There are now 46 chromosomes separately ready to form two new cells or daughter cells.

8. During telophase the cytoplasm begins to cleave and pinches the dividing cell into two new cells.

9. As the cell wall forms around each group of chromosomes remind the students of the gathering together and tightening of the cell as they again approach interphase. The cycle is ready to begin again.

10. Ask the students to take their seats and review the process of mitosis.

Evaluation: The ability to recall and the depth of understanding of the process will be reflected on any test or traditional evaluation instrument.

Figure 9.1 *Cell division/mitosis*

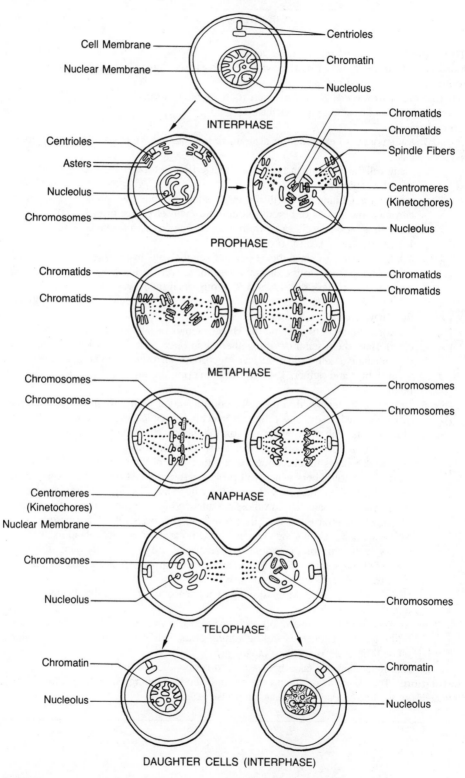

Cell Membrane

Nuclear Membrane

Centrioles

Chromatin

Nucleolus

INTERPHASE

Centrioles

Asters

Nucleolus

Chromosomes

PROPHASE

Chromatids

Chromatids

Spindle Fibers

Centromeres (Kinetochores)

Nucleolus

Chromatids

Chromatids

Chromatids

Chromatids

METAPHASE

Chromosomes

Chromosomes

Centromeres (Kinetochores)

ANAPHASE

Chromosomes

Chromosomes

Nuclear Membrane

Chromosomes

Nucleolus

Chromosomes

TELOPHASE

Chromatin

Nucleolus

Chromatin

Nucleolus

DAUGHTER CELLS (INTERPHASE)

208

Exercise 9.20. The Heart and the Human Circulatory System (From a lesson by Tobias Manzanares.)

Purpose:

Cognitive	Intuitive
To develop an understanding of the human circulatory system and the movement of blood through that system, and to learn the vocabulary relevant to the cardiovascular system	To increase visualization abilities to support learning

Physical/sensing	Affective
To use movement and physical encoding as a support for learning	To deepen the understanding of a basic body process by involving feelings, and to increase the ability to predict future events from known facts

Time involved: one 50 minute class period

Materials needed: 30 red and 30 blue cards or pieces of construction paper, movable classroom furniture

Organization preferred: total class with teacher in open space in classroom

Teacher role: information giver, facilitator

Procedure:

1. Ask the students to draw the diagram of the circulatory system (see Figure 9.2).
2. Ask the students to visualize the room as being a human body with the desks arranged in the center of the room to represent the four-chambered heart. Ask for volunteers to represent the brain, the lungs, and the digestive tract. Direct them to their appropriate places in the room (body).
3. Distribute one red and one blue card to each of the remaining students. They are now red blood cells. When they reach the lungs and become oxygenated they are to hold up the red card until they reach an organ using oxygen, where they will lower their red card and raise their blue card representing deoxygenated blood. The blue card will be held overhead until they reach the lungs to be recharged with oxygen.
4. With the red card in their right hand and the blue card in their left have students begin a walkthrough of the cycle using the following sequence: right atrium, right ventricle, pulmonary artery, lungs, pulmonary veins, left atrium, left ventricle, aorta, upper body (brain) or lower body (digestive tract), superior vena cava or inferior vena cava, right atrium. This completes the cycle and begins the next trip.
5. Ask for a student volunteer to retrace the ten sequential steps (assist the student as necessary).
6. Instruct the remaining students to fall in line behind the student leader to begin the first cycle. As the student red blood cells pass remind the students representing the lungs to raise their right hands (red cards); as the students pass those representing the brain or intestine remind them to lower the red cards and raise the blue cards. Instruct the student red blood cells to name out loud each of the ten structures as they pass these locations in the room.
7. Stop the cycle. ***HEART ATTACK!!***

Figure 9.2 *The Heart and Circulatory System*

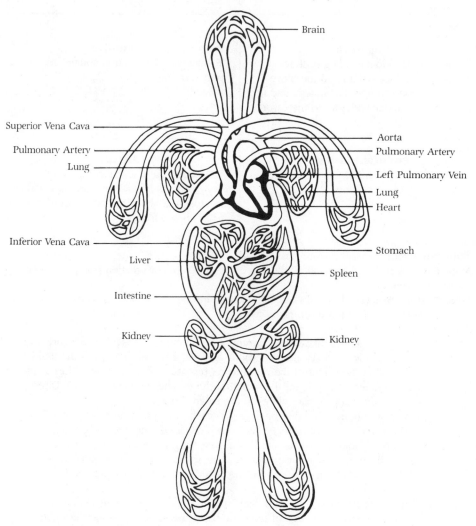

From *Growing up gifted* (p. 308) by B. Clark, 1983, Columbus, OH: Charles E. Merrill. Reprinted by permission.

 8. At this point the brain can control the pace of circulation and the group can play with the various ideas affecting the speed of circulation (running, sleeping, yawning, meditating, watching a scary movie, etc.). Ask for volunteers to replace the students representing the brain, lungs, and intestines so those students can go through the process.

 9. Stop the process again and ask how long the students think it will take to go through one complete cycle. Record the guesses on the board and time one cycle. Ask the class to see if they can improve the time while still verbally indicating the name of the structure they are passing. On your mark—get set—go!

 10. After the class has returned the room to its usual order discuss the entire procedure and how it feels to learn in this way.

Evaluation: The improved retention and understanding of the information will surface as improved scores on traditional testing and other forms of evaluation.

In Social Science

Exercise 9.21. An Anthropological Expedition (From a lesson by Tobias Manzanares.)

Purpose:

Cognitive	Intuitive
To acquaint students with the lifestyle and communication system of an ancient people	To improve the ability to use fantasy journeys and visualization to deepen an understanding of history

Physical/Sensing	Affective
To learn to use drawing to improve recall and the understanding of information	To learn to deepen the understanding of information by the use of empathy and role identification

Time involved: one 50 minute class period

Materials needed: recording of music typical of ancient peoples being studied, paper, colored pens, textbook, pictures of the geographic area being studied, other resources appropriate to the period

Organization preferred: total class with teacher

Teacher role: information giver, facilitator

Procedure:

1. Ask the students to get as comfortable as possible in their chairs. *Quietly breathe in through your nose, out through your mouth. Each time you exhale, allow your muscles to relax a little more: your neck, your arms, your back, your legs. In a few moments I'm going to turn out some of the lights. As I slowly count back from 10 allow your eyes to restfully close. Some students feel self-conscious about this and it's perfectly normal. Just allow the feeling and by the time I reach zero allow your eyes to close. When your eyes are closed make everything you see blue. Now imagine that you're looking up at the sky from a high mountain plateau* (begin playing the music). *Twelve thousand years ago this plateau was occupied by a group of very peaceful people. Just over a small glacial moraine is the shore of an ancient lake, its basin now dry. Grasses fill the shallow depression and rustle in the breeze. Not far away huge granite slabs rise sharply from the surface. Pathways zig-zag about the thick granite walls. After months an extraordinary find: five feet of thick granite rotates silently, effortlessly, revealing a small room.*

   The room contains several various-sized carved wood tubes, some with several 1 cm. holes along their lengths; flat, rectangular stone plates, some painted, all with symbols drawn generously about. Stop for a moment and take a mental photograph of the one most appealing to your senses. A dust covered mandolin-like instrument, strings loose, fine implements. Perhaps surgical tools from an ancient time?

Thought-provoking discussions around the evening's campfire enliven the starlit night. Ever-so-faintly on the evening breeze the sound of a flute calls from just over the moraine. The sound gently pulls you in the direction of the small rise. Just over the hill you see another encampment. Figures are silhouetted against the campfire glow; on the breeze is the fresh smell of water, a large body of water. Crisp! Clean! Moonlight sparkles off the lake, mixes with this unexpected campfire quite near the shore. You feel cool sand beneath your feet.

Those around this new campfire notice you as you approach but this has little effect on the group. Someone shifts slightly to make a space for you near the warmth of the fire. One indian strokes a stringed instrument, two others bring handcarved flutes up to their lips. Others begin to slowly move as the music rises through the trees and into the night sky. Their faces are kind, beautiful expressions filled with health; their eyes speak though not a word is spoken. Their skin is bronze and reflects the fire's glow; lines lend deep, gentle character to the ageless faces. Natural movements, quiet laughter, gentle smiles let you know the wonderful beauty of these people. Watch the celebration. Then a gift is brought for you by two, one very old, one very young. Notice the magic in their eyes, the authenticity of the gift. A very special treasure is in your hands, a cherished gift for the archaeologist, the human being. Yours forever, and again through those beautiful eyes the words are clear.

Their evening draws to an end as the fire turns to embers. They quietly rise and knowingly move toward the shoreline and the far end of the lake. Before the group disappears the two turn to look back at you. A feeling swells within. You know.

As you return over the moraine you glance back, and in your hands is a gift. In a few moments you may open your eyes. Notice how your body feels. Shortly I'll ask you to record 5 or 10 words that drift back from that high mountain plateau.

As you open your eyes choose someone to talk with about your gift. Ask them to share theirs with you.

2. After the students have shared their journey with another student ask them to describe their gift on a page in their journal. Allow them to draw it if that is easier.

3. Ask the students to recall the mental photograph they took while on the journey. As you again play the music from the journey invite them to draw the images, symbols, and designs they saw on the rectangular stone plates. *What tale does the tablet tell?*

4. Ask the students to write a poem based on the 5 to 10 words they originally recorded.

5. Collect the data from the entire class; share and discuss.

6. Ask the students to turn in their texts to the section on these ancient people and compare the text information with the group data. *Where are the similarities? Where do the data diverge?*

Evaluation: The improved recall and understanding of the data will be shown through traditional testing or any other evaluation technique.

In English and Literature Classes

Exercise 9.22. Senior English Unit: Violence in Society (From a lesson developed by GeorgeAnn Collins.)

Purpose:

Cognitive	Intuitive
To study literary genres that explore the causes, manifestations, and consequences of violence for society and the individual	To use relaxation and visualization to move backward and forward in time to develop a deeper understanding of problems faced by people historically and those that may be faced in the future
Physical/Sensing	**Affective**
To use art production, audio taping, and dramatic enactment to deepen the understanding and improve the retention of information	To use role play to deepen understanding of problems and develop possible solutions, and to explore attitudes and values of self and others regarding violence and the causes of violence

Time involved: several 50 minute class periods—a unit of study

Materials needed: access to suggested books and other readings; resources for research of issues; slides, tapes and films depicting themes of violence; notebooks

Organization preferred: total class, small groups, and individual spaces

Teacher role: information giver, facilitator

Procedure:

1. Present a lecture on terminology, expectations, and evaluation of the unit. Discuss with the students and clarify.
2. Discuss with the students the use of the student's *Integrative Education Planning Sheet* (see Form 9.2.). The following non-negotiables (*) and choices may be made available.

Content

*Greek Mythology—Homer: *The Illiad*

*Novels—
(Choose 1)
Remarque: *All Quiet on the Western Front*
Hemingway: *Farewell to Arms*
Crane: *The Red Badge of Courage*
(Choose 1)
Ibuse: *Black Rain*
O'Brien: *The Nuclear Age (Comic Mode)*
Morris: *The Seeds of Hiroshima*
Science Fiction—
(Choose 1)
Hoban: *Ridley Walker*
Rand: *Anthem*
Miller: *A Canticle for Leibowitz*

*Short Stories—
(Choose 2)
Hemingway: *Short Stories*
Bradbury: *Embroidery, Twice Twenty-two*
Angell: *Some Pigs in Sailor Suits, the Stone Arbor and Other Stories*

*Essays
  (Choose 1)
  James Baldwin
  Martin Luther King
*Plays
  Shakespeare: *Hamlet*
  Arthur Miller: *The Crucible*
*Poetry
  (Choose 3)
  Tennyson: "The Charge of the Light Brigade"
  e.e. cummings: "next to god America"
  Levertov: "Life in the Forest"
  Porter: "Your Attention Please"
  Mah: "The Horses"
Autobiographical
  Pizar: *Of Blood and Tears*
Additional References
  Capra: *The Turning Point*
  Ornstein: *The Nature of Human Consciousness*
  Fuller: *The Critical Path*

Ways to Learn

Cognitive:

*Compare and contrast the effectiveness of various genres in portrayal of theme.
Debate the pros and cons of technological advancement.
Investigate individually or with a small group
"Violence: Subject and Treatment."
  Use newspaper stories, magazine articles (for crime statistics), gun control editorials, advertisements.
  Use musical lyrics and art to investigate themes of violence.
Prepare questionnaires to be sent to members of the community, parents, and other students.
Research the traditions of violence in the American Frontier.
Propose a societal solution to decrease contemporary violence.
Develop a universal set of laws that would eliminate violence.
Write a letter to the author expressing your attitudes and feelings about the literature.

Affective:
  *Valuing exercises focusing on content areas.
  *Simulations of violence-producing situations.
  *Group discussions of affective responses to slides, tapes, and films dealing with the theme of violence. Write reactions: "I see . . . I feel . . ."
  Give responses to questions such as *Which attitude is better? What are the alternatives?*
  Express your feelings about violence through editorials, letters to editors, films, slides or taped presentations.
  Present quotations as points of view as in Tennyson's "Charge of the Light Brigade" and e.e. cummings's "next to god America."

Physical/Sensing
  *Dramatize scenes and situations that have promoted or that can currently provoke violence; discuss.

Develop a collage depicting attitudes toward violence.

Tape sounds of violence from media and community; discuss.

Intuitive

*Participate in fantasy trips to past and future periods or situations that involve violence.

*Participate in guided imagery exercises that allow you to speak with the author or characters in literature about the issue of violence.

> Example: The class is seated in a circle. A chair is placed in the middle. A student chooses an author or character and pretends to become that person, sits in the chair, and answers questions from the group.

Products

*Examination—Criteria: knowledge of elements of plot development, technique, imagery, methods of characterization.

*Composition (poem, essay, editorial, short story, or musical lyrics)—Criteria: quality and relationship to an aspect of the theme.

*Choose from:

  debate

  research project

  dramatization

  film making

  artwork or illustration

  speech

Criteria: quality and relationship to an aspect of the theme.

The lessons and units suggested here are only examples of ways in which Integrative Education can be developed in a classroom. These exercises are presented only as suggestions; change, adapt, and modify them to fit your classroom situation and students. Once you begin using the planning sheet to structure your lessons you will see which areas of brain function you use as support for learning. As you include more areas of function students will find more support for learning. They will become more successful and powerful learners.

10

Looking Ahead

To summarize the purpose of the Integrative Education Model and a belief I have as to its need, I would like you to come with me high into the hills in a remote area of the Western United States.

A small boy is climbing among the craggy rocks behind his father's ranch. Suddenly he comes upon a young eagle with a broken wing lying among the rocks. The child approaches the beautiful bird and while talking soothingly to him picks him up and gently cradles the eagle in his arms. He climbs back down and runs home to care for the injured bird.

Days and weeks pass and the eagle gains strength under the care of the child until one day the eagle can be taken outside to be fed. The boy puts his new friend into the chicken house and builds a special roost for him, feeding him with the other birds on the ranch. Months go by and the child and the bird become fast friends. They spend hours together; the boy loves the beauty and the majesty of the eagle while the eagle responds to the gentleness and sensitivity of the boy.

One day a wise teacher stops by the ranch and sees the boy with the eagle in the chicken yard. *Isn't that an eagle?* inquires the teacher. *Why is he in the chicken yard?*

I found him hurt and alone in the rocks and I cared for him and he became my friend so he lives with us now, the boy answers.

My son, an eagle belongs among the highest mountains, soaring high in the sky. He is the most majestic of creatures. He does not belong here on the ground among the chickens, says the teacher. *You must encourage him to be all that he can be. If you really love him you must set him free.*

The boy does not want to hear the teacher and runs into the house to close his ears, but he cannot close his heart. He knows the teacher is right. Several days later the boy takes the eagle up into the hills and says to his friend, *You are an eagle. You belong to the sky.* He lifts the bird up over his head and encourages him to fly away.

The eagle looks confused. He does not spread his wings but remains in the boy's outstretched hands. The boy is glad and takes his friend again to the ranch chicken yard. He continues to feed him and love him as the days pass.

After a few weeks the boy thinks again about the words of the wise teacher and again he decides to free the eagle. This time he climbs high among the cliffs and lifts the eagle as far up as his arms can stretch. *You are a beautiful eagle. You belong to the sky,* the boy cries. *Go and join those who soar. I will always love you, but you must be who you are and I cannot go there. Go now, you are free!* With that the child stretches even higher and opens his hand to free the magnificent bird.

The eagle is very still for a moment. Then he stretches his wings and the air catches beneath him. He begins to rise toward the sky. Slowly the eagle begins to soar, climbing high into the sky until the child can hardly see him. The eagle circles once around where the boy stands watching and then, calling once more to his friend, flies into the sun and disappears.

The boy never again sees the eagle though sometimes he imagines he hears him call. And though the eagle may sometimes look down again at the child and at the chicken yard on the ranch where he once lived, he has never come back. His vision is of a different world than that of the child. And no matter how much the child loves him he cannot share that world. The wise teacher is right; the eagle has to be who he is meant to be.

Sometimes children are like this. No matter how much we love them they must be given a chance to be as much as they can be, not limited by who we think they should be. Sometimes I wonder if as parents teaching in the home and teachers in the schools we have forgotten what our real goal is. I wonder if we may be asking the wrong questions. We say we want our children to know the basics: to read, to write, and to cipher. These are our goals. But are they? It seems that something is missing. Our goal isn't limited to knowledge. It must not be just to teach what we already know. Our goal is to discover, and to help our children discover who they are and how much they can be.

Wise teachers through the ages have shared their visions of how this might be accomplished, how we might nurture excellence. The ancients of our own country spoke of many paths; not just the path of the mind, but also the path of the heart, the path of the body, and the path of the spirit. Across the world in Galilee a wise teacher lived a message of love and taught that it was not enough to pursue the wisdom of the mind; it was also necessary to include the wisdom of the body, of the heart, and of the soul.

Another teacher whose roots come from the Eastern traditions, Kahlil Gibran, tells us

> Your children are not your children.
> They are the sons and daughters of Life's longing for itself.
> They come through you but not from you,
> And though they are with you yet they belong not to you.

We must not limit children to our limits; they have a vision of their own.

You may give them your love but not your thoughts.
For they have their own thoughts.
You may house their bodies but not their souls,
For their souls dwell in the house of tomorrow, which you cannot visit, not
   even in your dreams.
You may strive to be like them, but seek not to make them like you.
For life goes not backward nor tarries with yesterday.
You are the bows from which your children as living arrows are sent forth.
   (Gibran, 1923, pp. 17, 18)

To teachers he wrote

No one can reveal to you aught but that which already lies half asleep in the
   dawning of your knowledge.
The teacher who walks in the shadow of the temple, among his followers,
   gives not of his wisdom, but rather of his faith and his lovingness.
If he is indeed wise he does not bid you enter the house of his wisdom, but
   rather leads you to the threshold of your own mind. (Gibran, 1923, p. 56)

A wise teacher from early psychology, Carl Jung, believed that truly balanced humans must acknowledge all four of the functions of which they were capable: thinking, feeling, physical/sensing, and intuiting. Even before the biological validation of brain researchers, our wise teachers of today, Jung intuitively knew.

And so it seems that through the ages and more powerfully today the goal is to use all the human functions so that we can become the most we can be. That is the intent of the Integrative Education Model, a goal that provides its structure and its purpose.

What difference does it make if our goal is to teach skills or to allow a person to discover just how much he or she can be? If your goal in the classroom is only the development of skills then you can feel satisfied when students come up to grade level, pass tests, and complete all their assignments. But we know that some students can be two to eight years beyond those tests and assignments. We know that some invent and discover, think new thoughts, and have new ideas. What of these students?

If your goal at home is to teach what you already know and to insist upon your rules and to allow only those things that you believe then you can feel satisfied when your child follows the rules, completes the homework, brings home the outstanding grades. But we know there are children who can lead us into areas of our mind and into thoughts that we have never yet experienced and did not know even existed. There are children who can help us understand rules of connectedness and unity and belonging that we have not yet known, and children who can lead us to a unity of humankind that we have yet to consider. What of these children?

I believe that our goal as parents and as teachers is one far more important than the development of skills, although skills may be very much a part of that goal. Our goal is more realistic than just grade level expectations, although that too may be a part of the larger goal.

We have chosen to be teachers of children in the home and in the school. That's a very special and wonderous thing. If we can agree that the old goals are not enough, that they are not adequate to the more important and realistic goals of helping children to discover the uniqueness that they brought with them, then perhaps we need to ask how their special gift might best be used. But even then what can we do?

I am convinced that once we ask the right question and include the child in this search that many good ideas will begin to find us. I wanted to share in this book some of the good ideas that have found me as I have taught in the home and in the school.

We must first attend to the **environment:** the surrounding in which the child is housed and the opportunities for that child's growth. Integrative Education suggests that there be:

a responsive environment;
cooperation between parents, teachers, and students;
choice among alternatives and variety in the environment;
attention to individual needs;
a safe environment;
easy access to ideas;
the use of errors as clues for learning; mistakes must be considered learning tools.

Integrative Education then nurtures the child's **intelligence** by encouraging the use of all four human brain functions:

The Physical Sensing
    by teaching and using relaxation and tension reduction as part of the learning experience;
    by using movement and physical encoding to support learning.
The Feelings or Emotions
    by using language and behaviors that empower learners and add to their self worth and dignity;
    by teaching and encouraging the students to use empowering language and behavior with themselves and with others;
    by providing choice and building decision-making skills so that students might truly become responsible and effective learners;
    by allowing learners to perceive that they have control over their own learning and that they share with the teacher the responsibility for their learning.
The Cognitive
    by including in the learning experience both specializations of the cortex: the linear, rational of the left, and the spatial, gestalt of the right;
    by including variety, novelty, challenge, pleasure, and complexity in the learning experience.
The Intuitive
    by including imagery, visualization, and fantasy trips to support learning experiences;
    by including "what if" inquiry and futuristics as part of the learning experience;
    by encouraging and modeling creative, insightful, and intuitive thinking.

We seek wholeness for children: integration, unity, and balance. The Integrative Education Model was designed to encourage you to share yourself, your enthusiasms, your vulnerability, and to let you openly show affection and love. Your growth and your attempts to be all that you can be are what sets the tone for their learning.

As with the eagle, however, we must not limit our children to our limits. We must provide them with access to their unique visions and allow them to share those visions with us. We can begin by providing our knowledge, our tools, and our encouragement. But it is our love and joy in being with them that can best help them to learn without fear and without concern that they will not be accepted. The full use of their fine mind/brains will present us with the unity for which we have all searched. Humankind will be enriched.

Optimal learning leads to excellence. Excellence is more than high ability, more than high levels of performance; excellence allows dreams, visions, and idealism, and it values love. True excellence is the expression of the uniqueness of each of us; it is the expression of the soul. As teachers it is our quest to nurture true excellence.

As we end this discussion may I encourage you to believe that

change is possible
the potential of all of us is unlimited
each of us has a unique contribution to make
educators can be more effective and efficient
you are in the position to make it happen

While Integrative Education is one way of developing a more brain-compatible curriculum, learners will benefit only as you value these new possibilities. Integrative Education can happen only if these new ideas become a part of your professional judgement and experience. You must believe true excellence in our schools is important. You must value intelligence and each child's right to excel and achieve without limits. It must be all right, even marvelous to be different.

If you are an administrator you can empower teachers. If you are a teacher, at home or at school, you can empower learners. You can improve education now. If you believe you can, you can make it happen. You are truly the critical beginning.

REFERENCES

Albrecht, K. (1979). *Stress and the manager.* Englewood Cliffs, NJ: Prentice-Hall.

Allen, G., Giat, L., & Cherney, R. (1974). Locus of control, test anxiety and student performance in a personalized instruction course. *Journal of Educational Psychology, 66,* 968–973.

Allen, R. W. (1968). Grouping through learning centers. *Childhood Education, 45,* 200–203.

Ames, C. (1984). Competitive, cooperative, and individualistic goal structures: A cognitive-motivational analysis. In R. Ames & C. Ames (Eds.), *Student motivation* (pp. 177–207). New York: Academic Press.

Anderson, S. M., & Prawat, R. S. (1983). Responsibility in the classroom: A synthesis of research on teaching self-control. *Educational Leadership, 40* (7), 62–66.

Andrews, G., & Debus, R. (1978). Persistence and the causal perception of failure: Modifying cognitive attributions. *Journal of Educational Psychology, 70,* 154–166.

Arlin, M., & Whitley, T. (1978). Perceptions of self-managed learning opportunities and academic locus of control: A causal interpretation. *Journal of Educational Psychology, 70,* 988–992.

Aspy, D. (1969, February). *Self theory in the classroom.* Paper presented at the annual meeting of the American Educational Research Association, Los Angeles.

Aspy, D., & Bahler, J. (1975). The effect of teacher's inferred self concept upon student achievement. *The Journal of Educational Research, 68,* 386–389.

Assagioli, R. (1973). *The act of will.* New York: Viking.

Backman, M. (1972). Patterns of mental abilities: Ethnic, socioeconomic, and sex differences. *American Educational Research Journal, 9,* 1–12.

Bagley, M. T., & Hess, K. K. (1982). *200 ways of using imagery in the classroom.* Woodcliff Lake, NJ: New Dimensions of the 80s.

Barnett, M., & Kaiser, D. (1978). The relationship between intellectual-achievement responsibility attributions and performance. *Child Study Journal, 8,* 209–215.

Bar-Tal, D., Kfir, D., Bar-Zohar, Y., & Chen, M. (1980). The relationship between locus of control and academic achievement, anxiety, and level of aspiration. *British Journal of Educational Psychology, 50,* 53–60.

Beach, D. (1977). *Reaching teenagers: Learning centers for the secondary classroom.* Santa Monica, CA: Goodyear.

Benson, S. S. (1978). *The school enrichment-parent education program.* Unpublished masters thesis, California State University, Los Angeles, CA.

Benson, S. S. (1979). The responsibility training program. In B. Clark, *Growing up gifted* (pp. 291–303). Columbus, OH: Charles E. Merrill.

Bentov, I. (1977). *Stalking the wild pendulum.* New York: E. P. Dutton.

Bidwell, C. (1973). The social psychology of teaching. In R. Travers (Ed.), *Second handbook of research on teaching.* Chicago: Rand McNally.

Blakemore, C. (1974). Developmental factors in the formation of feature extracting neurons. In F. O. Schmidt & F. G. Warden (Eds.), *The neurosciences: Third study program* (pp. 31–41). Cambridge, MA: M.I.T. Press.

Bloom, B. (Ed.). (1956). *Taxonomy of educational objectives. Handbook I: Cognitive domain.* New York: David McKay.

Bloom, B. (1964). *Stability and change in human characteristics.* New York: John Wiley & Sons.

Bloom, B. (1982). The role of gifts and markers in the development of talent. *Exceptional Children, 48* (6), 510–522.

Bogen, J. E. (1977). Some educational aspects of hemispheric specialization. In M. C. Wittrock (Ed.), *The human brain* (pp. 133–152). Englewood Cliffs, NJ: Prentice-Hall.

Bohm, D. (1980). *Wholeness and the implicate order.* Boston: Routledge & Kegan.

Boocock, S., & Schild, E. (1968). *Simulation games in learning.* Beverly Hills, CA: Sage.

Bordan, R., & Schuster, D. (1976). The effects of suggestion, synchronized breathing and orchestrated music on the acquisition and retention of Spanish words. *SALT Journal, 1* (1), 27–40.

Bowers, W. (1964). *Student dishonesty and its control in college.* New York: Bureau of Applied Behavioral Science.

Brier, C., & Tyminski, W. (1970). PSI applications: Parts I and II. *Journal of Parapsychology, 34,* 1–36.

Brookover, W. (1969). *Self and school achievement.* Paper presented at the annual meeting of the American Educational Research Association, Los Angeles.

Brown, B. (1974). *New mind, new body. Biofeedback: New directions for the mind.* New York: Harper & Row.

Bruner, J. (1960). *The process of education.* Cambridge, MA: Harvard University Press.

Bryden, M. (1970). Laterality effects in dichotic listening: Relations with handedness and reading ability in children. *Neuropsychologia, 8,* 443–450.

Buell, S., & Coleman, P. (1981). Quantitative evidence for selective dendritic growth in normal human aging but not in senile dementia. *Brain Research, 214* (1), 23–41.

Buzan, T. (1983). *Use both sides of your brain.* New York: E. P. Dutton.

Calsyn, R. (1973). *The causal relationship between self-esteem, a locus of control and achievement: A cross-lagged panel analysis.* Unpublished doctoral dissertation, Northwestern University, Evanston, IL.

Canfield, J., & Wells, H. (1976). *100 ways to enhance self-concept in the classroom.* Englewood Cliffs, NJ: Prentice-Hall.

Capra, F. (1975). *The Tao of physics.* Berkeley, CA: Shambhala.

Capra, F. (1982). *The turning point: Science, society, and the rising culture.* New York: Simon and Schuster.

Chansky, N. (1962, March). The x-ray of the school mark. *The Educational Forum,* 347–352.

Chansky, N. (1964). A note of the grade point average in research. *Educational and Psychological Measurement, 24,* 95–99.

Christianson, B. (1969). Learning centers that work. *Instructor, 79,* 135.

Clark, B. (1983). *Growing up gifted* (2nd ed.). Columbus, OH: Charles E. Merrill.

Clark, F. (1977). Building intuition. In G. Hendricks & T. Roberts, *The second centering book.* Englewood Cliffs, NJ: Prentice-Hall.

Clarke-Stewart, K. (1973). Interactions between mothers and their young children: Characteristics and consequences. *Monographs of Society for Research in Child Development, 38,* (No. 153).

Clemes, H., & Bean, R. (1980). *How to teach responsibility to children.* San Jose, CA: Enrich.

Covington, M. V. (1984). The motivation for self-worth. In R. Ames & C. Ames (Eds.) *Student motivation* (pp. 77–113). New York: Academic Press.

Covington, M. V., & Beary, R. G. (1976). *Self-worth and school learning.* New York: Holt, Reinhart & Winston.

Davies, A. (1965). The perceptual maze test in a normal population. *Perceptual and Motor Skills, 20,* 287–293.

Dean, D., Mihalasky, J., Ostrander, S., & Schroeder, L. (1974). *Executive ESP.* Englewood Cliffs, NJ: Prentice-Hall.

deCharms, R. (1976). *Enhancing motivation: Change in the classroom.* New York: Halsted.

deCharms, R. (1984). Motivation enhancement in education. In R. Ames & C. Ames (Eds.), *Student motivation* (pp. 275–310). New York: Academic Press.

Deci, E. (1975). *Intrinsic motivation.* New York: Plenum Press.

Dettmer, P. (1981). Improving teacher attitudes toward characteristics of the creatively gifted. *Gifted Child Quarterly, 25* (1), 11–16.

Dexter, E. (1935). The effect of fatigue or boredom on teacher's marks. *Journal of Educational Research, 28,* 664–667.

Diamond, M. (1976, February). *Developments in brain research.* Paper presented at the annual Conference of the California Association for the Gifted, San Diego, CA.

Diamond M. (1980, May). Education and the brain. Lecture presented at the conference *The human brain: New frontiers in learning.* Los Angeles, CA.

Doyle, W. (1978). Classroom tasks and student abilities. In P. P. Peterson & H. Walbert (Eds.), *Conceptions of teaching.* Berkeley, CA: McCutchan.

Drews, E. M. (1972). *Learning together: How to foster creativity, self-fulfillment and social awareness in today's students and teachers.* Englewood Cliffs, NJ: Prentice-Hall.

Dubos, R. (1969). Biological individuality. *The Columbia Forum, 12* (1), 5–9.

Dunn, B. (1969). *The effectiveness of teaching early reading skills to two-to-four-year-old children by television.* Unpublished doctoral dissertation, University of California, Los Angeles.

Dweck, C., & Goetz, T. (1978). Attributions and learned helplessness. In J. Harvey, W. Ickes, & R. Kidd (Eds.), *New directions in attribution research* (Vol. 2). Hillsdale, NJ: Erlbaum.

Edwards, P. (1956). The use of essays in selection at 11 plus: Essay markings experiment: Shorter and longer essays. *British Journal of Educational Psychology, 26,* 128–136.

Einstein, A., & Infeld, L. (1961). *The evolution of physics.* New York: Simon and Schuster.

Ellis, A. (1977). *Handbook of rational emotive therapy.* New York: Springer.

Epstein, H. (1978). Growth spurts during brain development: Implications for educational policy and practice. In J. Chall & A. Mirsky (Eds.), *Education and the brain* (The seventy–seventh yearbook of the National Society for the Study of Education, Part II, pp. 343–370). Chicago: University of Chicago Press.

Fala, M. (1968). *Dunce cages, hickory sticks and public evaluations: The structure of academic authoritarianism.* Madison, WI: The Teaching Assistant Association, University of Wisconsin.

Farber, A. & Mazlish, E. (1980). *How to talk so kids will listen and listen so kids will talk.* New York: Avon.

Feldhusen, J., & Klausmeier, H. (1965). Anxiety, intelligence and achievement in children of low, average and high intelligence. *Child Development, 33,* 403–407.

Ferguson, M. (1980). *The aquarian conspiracy.* Los Angeles: J. P. Tarcher.

Ferguson, M. (1982a). New theory: Feelings code, organize thinking. *Brain/Mind Bulletin,* 7 (6), 1, 2.

Ferguson, M. (1982b). The new reality: Interacting approximations. *Brain/Mind Bulletin,* 7 (10), 1, 2.

Feuerstein, R. (1978). *Learning potential assessment device.* Baltimore, MD: University Park Press.

Galin, D. (1976). Educating both halves of the brain. *Childhood Education, 53* (1), 17–20.

Galyean, B. (1976). *Language from within.* Santa Barbara, CA: Confluent Education Development and Research Center.

Galyean, B. (1977–80). *The confluent teaching of foreign languages* (ESEA Title IV-C Project, Year-end Reports). Los Angeles. Los Angeles City Unified Schools.

Galyean, B. (1978–81). *A confluent language program for K–3, NES LES students* (ESEA Title IV-C Project, Year-end Reports). Los Angeles: Los Angeles Unified Schools.

Galyean, B. (1979). *The effects of guided imagery activities on various behaviors of one class of low achieving students.* Research paper. Los Angeles: Ken-Zel.

Galyean, B. (1983a). *Mind sight.* Long Beach, CA: Center for Integrative Learning.

Galyean, B. (1983b). Guided imagery in the curriculum. *Educational Leadership, 40* (6), 54–58.

Gazzaniga, M., & LeDoux, J. (1978). *The integrated mind.* New York: Plenum Press.

Gibb, J. (1961). Defensive communication. *Research Reprint Series Number 12 of National Training Laboratories.* Washington, DC.

Gibran, K. (1923). *The prophet.* New York: Alfred A Knopf.

Goldberg, P. (1983). *The intuitive edge.* Los Angeles: J. P. Tarcher.

Goodman, D. (1978). Learning from lobotomy. *Human Behavior, 1,* 44–49.

Gordon, D. (1977). Children's beliefs in internal-external control and self-esteem as related to academic achievement. *Journal of Personality Assessment, 41,* 383–386.

Gordon, W. (1961). *Synectics: The development of creative capacity.* New York: Harper and Row.

Gordon, W., & Poze, T. (1980). SES Synectics and gifted education today. *Gifted Child Quarterly, 24* (4), 147–151.

Greene, D. (1974). *Immediate and subsequent effects of differential reward systems on intrinsic motivation in public school classrooms.* Unpublished doctoral dissertation, Stanford University, CA.

Guilford, J. P. (1967). *The nature of human intelligence.* New York: McGraw-Hill.

Haggard, E. (1957). Socialization, personality and academic achievement in gifted children. *School Review, 65,* 388–414.

228

REFERENCES

Hart, L. (1978). The new "brain" concept of learning. *Phi Delta Kappan, 59* (6), 393–396.

Hart, L. (1981). Brain, language, and new concepts of learning. *Educational Leadership, 39,* 443–445.

Hart, L. (1983). *Human brain and human learning.* New York: Longman.

Hassett, J., & Weisberg, A. (1972). *Open education: Alternative within our tradition.* Englewood Cliffs, NJ: Prentice-Hall.

Hattersley, R. (1970). Do you have eyes in your skin? *Popular Photography. 66* (3), 55–59, 107–108.

Hayward, A. (1985). *Early learners.* Los Angeles, CA: The Education Institute.

Heilman, K. (1978). Language and the brain: Relationship of localization of language function to the acquisition and loss of various aspects of language. In J. S. Chall & A. F. Mirsky (Eds.), *Education and the brain,* (The seventy–seventh yearbook of the National Society for the Study of Education, Part II, pp. 143–168). Chicago: University of Chicago Press.

Heline, C. (1969). *Color and music in the new age.* Oceanside, CA: New Age Press.

Hendricks, G., & Roberts, T. (1977). *The second centering book.* Englewood Cliffs, NJ: Prentice-Hall.

Hendricks, G., & Wills, R. (1975). *The centering book.* New York: Prentice-Hall.

Herrmann, N. (1981). The creative brain. *Training and Development Journal, 35* (10), 10–16.

Hills, C., & Rozman, D. (1978). *Exploring inner space.* Boulder Creek, CA: University of the Trees Press.

Hoyt, P. (1965). *The relationship between college grades and adult achievement* (ACT Research Report No. 7). Iowa City, IA: American College Testing Program.

Hunt, J. McV. (1961). *Intelligence and experience.* New York: Ronald Press.

Hunt, M. (1982). *The universe within.* New York: Simon & Schuster.

Huxley, A. (1962). *Island.* New York: Harper & Row.

Ilg, F. L., & Ames, L. B. (1972). *Child Behavior.* New York: Barnes and Noble.

Ismael, C. (1973). *The healing environment.* Millbrae, CA: Celestial Arts.

Jacobson, E. (1957). *You must relax.* New York: McGraw-Hill.

James, C. (1968). *Young lives at stake: The education of adolescents.* New York: Schocken Books.

Jeffrey, W. E. (1980). The developing brain and child development. In M. C. Wittrock (Ed.), *The brain and psychology* (pp. 345–370). New York: Academic Press.

Jellison, J., & Harvey, J. (1976). Give me liberty: Why we like hard positive choices. *Psychology Today, 9* (10), 47–49.

Johnson, S. (1983a). *The one minute father.* New York: William Morrow.

Johnson, S. (1983b). *The one minute mother.* New York: William Morrow.

Jung, C. (1933). *Psychological types.* New York: Harcourt.

Kahl, D., & Gas, B. (1974). *Learning centers in the open classroom.* Encino, CA: International Center for Educational Development.

Kaplan, S., Kaplan, J., Madsen, S., & Gould, B. (1975). *A young child experiences.* Pacific Palisades, CA: Goodyear.

Kaplan, S., Kaplan, J., Madsen, S., & Taylor, B. (1973). *Change for children.* Pacific Palisades, CA: Goodyear.

Kimura, D. (1967). Functional asymmetry of the brain in dichotic listening. *Cortex, 3,* 163–178.

Knowlton, J., & Hamerlyneck, L. (1967). Perception of deviant behavior: A study of cheating. *Journal of Educational Psychology, 58,* 379–385.

Krech, D. (1969). Psychoneurobiochemeducation. *Phi Delta Kappan, 1,* 370–375.

Krech, D. (1970). Don't use the kitchen sink approach to enrichment. *Today's Education, 59,* 30–32.

Krippner, S. (1983). A system approach to creativity based on Jungian typology. *Gifted Child Quarterly, 27* (2), 86–89.

LaBenne, W., & Greene, B. (1969). *Educational implications of self-concept theory.* Pacific Palisades, CA: Goodyear.

Lao, R. (1970). Internal-external control and competent and innovative behavior among Negro college students. *Journal of Personal Social Psychology, 14,* 263–270.

Lassen, N., Ingvar, D., & Skinhoj, E. (1978, October). Brain function and blood flow. *Scientific American, 239* (4), 62–71.

Lavin, D. (1965). *The prediction of academic performances.* New York: Russell Sage Foundation.

Leonard, G. (1974). *The ultimate athlete.* New York: Viking Press.

Leonard, G. (1978). *The silent pulse.* New York: E. P. Dutton.

Lepper, M., Greene, D., & Nisbett, R. (1973). Undermining children's intrinsic interest with extrinsic rewards. *Journal of Personality and Social Psychology, 28* (1), 129–137.

Levy, J. (1980). Cerebral asymmetry and the psychology of man. In M. Wittrock (Ed.), *The brain and psychology* (pp. 245–321). New York: Academic Press.

Lewis, M. (1972). State as an infant-environment interaction: An analysis of mother-infant behavior as a function of sex. *Merrill-Palmer Quarterly, 18,* 95–121.

Loye, D. (1983). *The sphinx and the rainbow.* Boulder, CO: Shambala.

Lozanov, G. (1977). A general theory of suggestion in the communications process and the activation of the total reserves of the learner's personality. *Suggestopaedia-Canada, 1,* 1–4.

Luria, A. R. (1973). *The working brain: An introduction to neuropsychology* (B. Haigh, Trans.). New York: Basic Books.

MacLean, P. (1978). A mind of three minds: Educating the triune brain. In J. Chall & A. Mirsky (Eds.), *Education and the brain* (The seventy–seventh yearbook of the National Society for the Study of Education, Part II, pp. 308–342). Chicago: University of Chicago Press.

Maehr, M. (1984). Meaning and motivation: Toward a theory of personal investment. In R. Ames & C. Ames (Eds.), *Student motivation* (pp. 115–144). New York: Academic Press.

Maehr, M., & Stallings, W. (1972). Freedom from external evaluation. *Child Development, 43,* 177–185.

Martin, R., & Pacheres, J. (1962, February). Good scholars not always the best. *Business Week,* 77–78.

Martindale, C. (1975). What makes creative people different? *Psychology Today, 9* (2), 44–50.

Maslow, A. (1968). *Toward a psychology of being* (2nd ed.). New York: Van Nostrand Reinhold.

Maslow, A. (1971). *The farther reaches of human nature.* New York: Viking.

Mason, E. (1972). *Collaborative learning.* New York: Schocken Books.

Matheny, K., & Edwards, C. (1974). Academic improvement through an experimental classroom management system. *Journal of School Psychology, 12,* 222–232.

Meeker, M. (1969). *The structure of intellect: Its use and interpretation.* Columbus, OH: Charles E. Merrill.

Meer, J. (1985). The light touch. *Psychology Today, 19* (9), 60–67.

Miller, G. P., & Oskam, B. O. (1984). *Teaching your child to make decisions.* New York: Harper & Row.

Moore, T. (1967). Language and intelligence: A longitudinal study of the first eight years. Part 1. Patterns of development in boys and girls. *Human Development, 10,* 88–106.

Morrison, A., & McIntyre, D. (1971). *Schools and socialization.* Baltimore, MD: Penguin.

Nichols, J. G. (1984). Conceptions of ability and achievement motivation. In R. Ames & C. Ames (Eds.), *Student motivation* (pp. 39–73). New York: Academic Press.

Ott, J. (1973). *Health and light: The effects of natural and artificial light on man and other living things.* Old Greenwich, NY: Devin-Adair.

Owens, R. E. (1984). *Language development.* Columbus: Charles E. Merrill.

Pallett, J. (1965). *Definition and predictions of success in the business world.* Unpublished doctoral dissertation, University of Iowa.

Pearce, J. C. (1977). *The magical child.* New York: E. P. Dutton.

Pelletier, K. (1977). *Mind as healer, mind as slayer.* New York: Delta.

Perrone, P., & Male, R. (1981). *The developmental education and guidance of talented learners.* Rockville, MD: Aspen.

Pflum, J., & Waterman, A. (1974). *Open education: For me?* Washington, DC: Acropolis Books.

Phares, E. (1975). *Locus of control in personality.* Morristown, NJ: General Learning Press.

Pizzamiglio, L., & Cecchini, M. (1971). Development of the hemispheric dominance in children from 5 to 10 years of age and their relations with the development of cognitive processes. *Brain Research, 31,* 363–364.

Porteus, S. (1965). *Porteus maze test: Fifty years' application.* Palo Alto, CA: Pacific Books.

Prescott, J. (1979). Alienation of affection. *Psychology Today, 13* (7), 124.

Pressey, S. (1925). Fundamental misconceptions involved in current marking systems. *School and Society, 21,* 736–738.

Pribram, K. (1977). Primary reality may be frequency realm. *Brain/Mind Bulletin, 2,* 1–3.

Pribram, K. (1978). Modes of central processing in human learning and remembering. In T. Teyler (Ed.), *Brain and learning.* Stamford, CT: Greylock.

Pribram, K., Spinelli, D., & Reitz, S. (1969). Effects of radical disconnection of occipital and temporal cortex on visual behavior of monkeys. *Brain, 92,* 301–312.

Prichard, A., & Taylor, J. (1980). *Accelerating learning: The use of suggestion in the classroom.* Novato, CA: Academic Therapy Publications.

Purkey, W. (1970). *Self-concept and school achievement.* Englewood Cliffs, NJ: Prentice-Hall.

Raths, L., Harmin, M., & Simon, S. (1966). *Values and teaching.* Columbus, OH: Charles E. Merrill.

Raudsepp, E. (1980). Intuition: A neglected decision making tool. *Machine Design, 52,* 91–94.

Reid, M. (1980). *Cerebral lateralization in children: An ontogenetic and organismic analysis.* Unpublished doctoral dissertation, University of Colorado, Denver.

Restak, K. (1979). *The brain: The last frontier.* New York: Doubleday.

Roberts, T., & Clark, F. (1976). Transpersonal psychology in education. In G. Hendricks & J. Fadiman (Eds.), *Transpersonal education.* Englewood Cliffs, NJ: Prentice-Hall.

Rockenstein, Z. (1985). *A taxonomy of educational objectives for the intuitive domain.* Unpublished doctoral dissertation, University of Georgia.

Rogers, C. (1942). *Carl Rogers on personal power.* New York: Delacorte Press.

Rogers, C. (1961). *On becoming a person.* Boston: Houghton Mifflin.

Rogers, C. (1969). *Freedom to learn.* Columbus, OH: Charles E. Merrill.

Rosenberg, B., & Sutton-Smith, B. (1969). Sibling age spacing effects upon cognition. *Developmental Psychology, 1,* 661–668.

Rosenthal, R., & Jacobsen, L. (1969). *Pygmalion in the classroom: Self-fulfilling prophecies and teacher expectations.* New York: Holt, Rinehart & Winston.

Rosenzweig, M. (1966). Environmental complexity, cerebral change and behavior. *American Psychologist, 21,* 321–332.

Rubble, D. W., & Boggiano, A. K. (1980). Optimizing motivation in an achievement context. In B. K. Keogh (Ed.), *Advances in special education: Vol. 1. Basic constructs and theoretical orientations* (Chap. 5). Greenwich, CT: J.A.I. Press.

Sagan, C. (1977). *The dragons of eden.* New York: Random House.

Saltzberger-Whittenberg, I., Henry, G., & Osborne, E. (1983). *The emotional experience of learning and teaching.* Boston: Routledge & Kegan.

Samples, B. (1975). Learning with the whole brain. *Human Behavior, 4,* 18–23.

Samples, B. (1976). *The metaphoric mind: A celebration of creative consciousness.* Reading, MA: Addison-Wesley.

Samples, B. (1977). Mind cycles and learning. *Phi Delta Kappan, 58,* 668–692.

Schultz, J., & Luthe, W. (1959). *Autogenic training: A psychophysiological approach to psychotherapy.* New York: Grune & Stratton.

Seidner, C. (1976). Teaching with simulations and games. In N. Gage (Ed.), *The psychology of teaching methods: The seventy-fifth yearbook of the National Society on the Study of Education,* (pp. 217–251).

Selye, H. (1956). *The stress of life.* New York: McGraw-Hill.

Selye, H. (1979). Foreward. In K. Albrecht, *Stress and the manager* (pp. v–vii). Englewood Cliffs, NJ: Prentice-Hall.

Simon, S. (1974). Please touch! How to combat skin hunger in our schools. *Scholastic Teacher, 105,* 22–25.

Simon, S., Howe, L., & Kirschenbaum, H. (1972). *Values clarification.* New York: Hart.

Singer, J. (1975). *The inner world of day dreaming.* New York: Harper & Row.

Singer, J. (1976). Fantasy: The foundation of serenity. *Psychology Today, 10* (2), 32–37.

Sisk, D. *Teaching gifted children.* Developed in conjunction with a Federal Grant from Title V, Section 505. Project Director, James Turner, SC (FL component).

Sisk, D. (1975). Communication skills for the gifted. *The Gifted Child Quarterly, 19,* 66–68.

Sparling, S. S. (1984). *Sharing responsibility with students.* Unpublished paper, California State University, Los Angeles.

Spivak, G., Platt, J. J., & Shure, M. B. (1976). *The problem solving approach to adjustment.* San Francisco: Jossey-Bass.

Starch, D. (1913). Reliability of grading work in mathematics. *School Review, 21,* 254–295.

Starch, D., & Elliott, E. (1912). Reliability of grading of high school work in English. *School Review, 20,* 442–457.

Stevens, J. (1971). *Awareness: Exploring, experimenting, experiencing.* Moab, UT: Real People Press.

Stevenson, H., Hale, G., Klein, R., & Miller, L. (1968). Interrelations and correlates in children's learning and problem solving. *Monographs of the Society for Research in Child Development, 33.*

Stipek, D. J. (1984). The development of achievement motivation. In R. Ames & C. Ames (Eds.), *Student motivation* (pp. 145–174). New York: Academic Press.

Stipek, D., & Weisz, J. (1981). Perceived personal control and academic achievement. *Review of Educational Research, 51* (1), 101–137.

Stollak, G. E. (1978). *Until we are six.* Huntington, NY: Robert E. Krieger.

Suchman, J. R. (1961). Inquiry training: Building skills for autonomous discovery. *Merrill Palmer Quarterly of Behavior and Development, 7,* 147–169.

Suchman, J. R. (1962). *The elementary school training program in scientific inquiry.* Urbana, IL: University of Illinois Press.

Taylor, J., & Walford, R. (1972). *Simulation in the classroom.* Baltimore, MD: Penguin Books.

Taylor, L., & Bongar, B. (1976). *Clinical applications in biofeedback therapy.* Los Angeles: Psychology Press.

Taylor, L., Tom, G., & Ayers, M. (1981). *Electromyometric biofeedback therapy.* Los Angeles: Biofeedback and Advanced Therapy Institute, Inc.

Temple University. (1968). *Report of the college of education ad hoc committee on grading systems.* Philadelphia.

Thomas, J. (1980). Agency and achievement: Self-management and self-regard. *Review of Educational Research, 50* (2), 213–240.

Tiegs, E. (1952). Educational diagnosis. *Educational Bulletin, Number 18.* Monterey, CA: California Testing Bureau.

Truesdell, B., & Newman, J. (1975). Can jr. highs make it with wide open spaces? *Learning, 4* (3), 74–77.

Van Duyne, J., & D'Alonzo, B. (1976). Amount of verbal information and ear differences in 5- and 6-year-old boys and girls. *Perceptual and Motor Skills, 43,* 31–39.

Van Horn, M., & Hanson, R. (1975). Leading creative participation. *The Futurist, 4,* 72–75.

Vaughn, F. (1979). *Awakening intuition.* New York: Doubleday.

Verny, T. (1981). *The secret life of the unborn child.* New York: Summit Books.

Voight, R. (1971). *Invitation to learning: The learning center handbook.* Washington, DC: Acropolis Books.

Wang, M., & Stiles, B. (1976). An investigation of children's concept of self-responsibility for their school learning. *American Educational Research Journal, 13,* 159–179.

Webster's new collegiate dictionary (1981). Springfield, MA: G. & C. Merriam.

Weiner, B. (1979). A theory of motivation for some classroom experiences. *Journal of Educational Psychology, 71,* 3–25.

Weiner, B. (1984). Principles for a theory of student motivation and their application within an attributional framework. In R. Ames & C. Ames (Eds.), *Student motivation* (pp. 15–38). New York: Academic Press.

Weiner, B., Anderson, A., & Prawat, R. (1983). *Affective experiences in a classroom.* Unpublished manuscript, University of California at Los Angeles, CA.

Weisz, J. R. (1980). Developmental change in perceived control: Recognizing noncontingency in the laboratory and perceiving it in the world. *Developmental Psychology, 16* (5), 385–390.

Wescott, M. (1968). *Toward a contemporary psychology of intuition.* New York: Holt, Rinehart & Winston.

White, B. (1975). *The first three years of life.* Englewood Cliffs, NJ: Prentice-Hall.

Wigner, E. P. (1970). *Symmetries and reflections* (Scientific essays). Cambridge, MA: M.I.T. Press.

Winters, K., & Felber, M. (1980). *The teacher's cope book.* Belmont, CA: Pitman Learning.

Witelson, S. (1976). Sex and the single hemisphere. *Science, 193,* 425–427.

Wittrock, M. C. (1980). Learning and the brain. In M. C. Wittrock (Ed.), *The brain and psychology* (pp. 371–403). New York: Academic Press.

Wright, J., & Mischel, W. (1982). Influence of affect on cognitive social learning person variables. *Journal of Personality and Social Psychology, 43,* 901–914.

Wright, P. (1965). *Enrollment for advanced degrees.* (E:5401–63, Circular No. 786). Washington, DC: Office of Education, U. S. Department of Health, Education and Welfare.

Zuckerman, D., & Horn, R. (1973). *The guide to simulations/games for education and training.* Lexington, MA: Information Resources.

Zukav, G. (1979). *The dancing Wu Li masters.* New York: William Morrow & Co.

INDEX